Preaching Matthew's Gospel

A Narrative Approach

Richard A. Jensen

CSS Publishing Company, Inc., Lima, Ohio

37.55

PREACHING MATTHEW'S GOSPEL

Scripture quotations are from the *New Revised Standard Version of the Bible*, copyright
1989 by the Division of Christian Education of the National Council of the Churches of
Christ in the USA. Used by permission.

Library of Congress Cataloging-in-Publication Data

Jensen, Richard A.
  Preaching Matthew's Gospel : a narrative approach / Richard A. Jensen.
      p.   cm.
    ISBN 0-7880-1221-5 (alk. paper)
    1. Bible. N.T. Matthew—Homiletical use. 2. Bible. N.T. Matthew—Criticism, Nar-
rative. I. Title.
BS2575.5.J46   1998
226.2'06—dc21   98-5618
                                                                            CIP

This book is available in the following formats, listed by ISBN:
      0-7880-1221-5   Book
      0-7880-1222-3   IBM 3 1/2
      0-7880-1223-1   MAC
      0-7880-1224-X   Sermon Prep

For Robert Smith:
friend, colleague, mentor
in Matthew as narrator.

Table Of Contents

Preface

A Postmodern World

There are many significant descriptors of our times. It has become common, for example, to refer to our time as a *postmodern world*. Stanley J. Grenz, in a work titled *A Primer on Postmodernism*, defines the postmodern mood as one that challenges the central assumptions of the Enlightenment. The modern world as given shape by the Enlightenment had an optimistic mood. It was optimistic about human potential and the future. The postmodern world, on the other hand, replaces this optimism with pessimism. Secondly, the modern world took it for granted that truth was certain and that it could be grasped with our rational minds. The postmodern world is much less certain about absolute truth and about the rational mind as the only means of grasping truth. Thirdly, the Enlightenment believed that knowledge was objective. It was "out there" somewhere for all of us to comprehend rationally. The postmodern mood challenges the objectivity of truth. It operates with a more community-based understanding of truth. Truth, therefore, has a more subjective nature. It is relative to the community in which the truth seeker participates.[1]

The postmodern mood offers many challenges to the knowledge and presentation of the Christian faith. It is difficult for the Christian church to accept the fact, for example, that truth is relative or that multiverse has replaced universe. Grenz calls *pluralism* the central hallmark of postmodern cultural expression. Pluralism! That's not what the church has stood for. The church has stood for truth in its *singularity*. Jesus Christ is the way, the truth, and the life! If the mood really has shifted in our world, then we are faced with the challenge of presenting a singular truth to persons who have a pluralistic, relativistic mind set.

11

Grenz addresses this matter in his Chapter 7: "The Gospel and the Postmodern Context." He outlines four contours for a contemporary presentation of the gospel:

1. "A postmodern articulation of the Christian gospel will be *post-individualistic.*" We bear testimony to our faith, that is, born out of communities. We speak out of our communal experience and we invite people into our communal world. "Members of the next generation are often unimpressed by our verbal presentations of the gospel. What they want to see is a people who live out the gospel in wholesome, authentic, and healing relationships."[2]

2. Grenz's second suggestion for preaching the gospel in our time is that our preaching must transcend the use of reason as our fundamental way of communicating the faith. Preaching in the modern western world has been captive to reason for centuries. We have traditionally understood the sermon as a rational explanation of the ideas of the Christian faith. Our sermons have generally had three ideas. The three-point sermon is legendary among us. Grenz challenges us to ask if such rational, explanation-oriented preaching communicates with postmodern people. He really calls upon us to consider a *post-rational* presentation of the gospel message.

I find Grenz's point here to be quite astonishing. Grenz is an Evangelical Christian. He defines the heart and soul of Evangelical teaching and preaching to be a demonstration of the rational truth of Christianity in such a way that it is finally persuasive and leads to conversion. It is Grenz's claim that this "evangelical" approach to proclamation will not work very well in our world. One of the reasons it will not work is because it leaves little room for *mystery*: "...our understanding of the faith must not remain fixed on the *propositionalist* approach that views Christian truth as nothing more than correct doctrine or doctrinal truth." Rather, we need to be more in tune with mystery. We need to become *storytellers.* In our stories

persons are encountered by the person of God. That's what Christianity is all about. Christianity is fundamentally about God's Word-made-flesh encounter with the human race. This divine-human encounter is the first order experience of

Christian reality. We encounter the Word-made-flesh. Prop-
ositions, ideas and doctrines are second order reflections on
this first order reality. Preaching, he infers, is about encounter.
It ought to be primarily a first order event.[3]

3. Grenz claims further that "...a postmodern articulation of the gospel will also be *post-dualistic.*" We need to preach a holistic gospel—a gospel for the whole person.[4]

4. Finally, Grenz claims that "...a postmodern articulation of the gospel will be *post-noeticentric.* That is to say, our gospel must affirm that the goal of our existence encompasses more than just the accumulation of knowledge." In this point Grenz calls for us to hold together head and heart, Orthodoxy and Pietism. Personal renewal and social activism must blossom from each believing person.[5]

For homiletical purposes I am most intrigued by Grenz's call for us to become better storytellers of the faith. We are to tell more stories that *evoke* Christian reality. That's his call. We have been conditioned for centuries in the church to present ideas that *explain* Christian reality. Evoke or explain? This is not an either/or situation. Our preaching ought to do both. More and more I believe that this is the basic choice that faces us each week as preachers. As we study the text and move towards a sermon we have a choice. Shall we tell stories that evoke the gospel reality or shall we make points that explain this reality? Clearly, some texts and contexts call for evocation. Other texts and/or contexts call for explanation. Evoke or explain? We must make this decision each week about our preaching.

Evoke or explain? This book, this narrative approach to Matthew's Gospel, will help you in the evocation process. I try herein to set each of Matthew's stories in a wider context of Matthean stories. That is the thrust of this "narrative commentary." I expect you to study the standard commentaries each week as well. They will give you all the help you need in explaining texts. My concern is with Matthew as narrative. My concern is with evocation of faith. I have intentionally, therefore, sought to avoid giving much help in terms of explaining texts. Other commentaries can guide you in the task of explanation of texts for didactic teaching.

Generation X

Kevin Graham Ford has written a wonderful book about proclaiming the gospel to postmodern adolescents. This generation has many names. "Generation X" is one popular designation. Ford's is the best book by far that I have read on the nature of this generation and on communicating the gospel to this new world of young people. I recommend it highly.

Ford devotes three chapters to the question, "How To Reach Us?" The first of these chapters, Chapter 9, is titled "A Faith That Works." The thrust of this chapter is that Generation X is filled with people that feel unwanted and unneeded. Ford believes that the Christian story offers them a place for involvement, a place where their lives can be used in service of a purpose that is larger than themselves. It is for this reality that this generation cries out, according to Ford. They want a *faith that works.* They want to be put to work. They want to lend their lives to meaningful activity. They want a faith that works in the public world for justice and peace. This helps to explain their grand outpouring of grief over the deaths of Mother Teresa and Princess Diana. These were women whose faith worked!

Ford's next chapter (Chapter 10) on the question "How To Reach Us?" is titled "Process Evangelism." The question of the '90s, according to Ford, is "Which God is God?" Generation Xers will respond best to our presentation of God as revealed in Jesus Christ "...over a longer period of time—a gradual result of a process of relationships." Here is another Evangelical Christian putting forth an evangelism process that has little to do with the presentation of the rational truth of the Christian faith towards the goal of conversion. Conversion, if it comes, will be gradual. It will come as a result of personal relationships over time.

Chapter 11 of Ford's insightful work is titled "How To Reach Us, Part 3: Narrative Evangelism." Here I will quote extensively:

> *The concept of story or narrative gives us a new way of looking at evangelism and a new paradigm for reaching my generation.... This approach to evangelism is ideally suited*

for reaching the soul of Generation X because it is a "new-old" approach. It is a new approach when compared with other twentieth-century strategies because it has not been actively attempted until recently. It is an old approach because it is the same approach used by Jesus himself and by the early evangelists.

...the only evangelism that speaks the language of the culture is a story-oriented evangelism. Narrative evangelism speaks the language of a media-saturated, story-hungry generation. It gives people a point of connection in their everyday lives, enabling them to see how God has interacted with human history and how he [sic] can interact with their own individual lives.

Stories are intensely important to Generation X.... We want the feelings, the action, the story.... It should come as no surprise, then, that the vehicle of story is a powerful and effective vehicle for reaching Generation X. In fact the story of Jesus Christ seems custom-designed to give Xers a story to identify with....[6]

Ford makes a powerful case as he challenges us to be storytellers of the faith once again. In his eyes this is an evangelism tactic that will work well in the postmodern world. Storytelling was and is the hallmark of oral communities. African American preaching in our land has been largely shaped by this oral heritage. We have much to learn in our time from the African American religious experience. James Cone suggests that when African American Christians look over the credentials of a potential pastor there is one question paramount in their mind: "Can the Reverend tell the story?" This appears to be a question that Generation X might ask as well. Our world cries out to hear the story of Jesus. Explanations can wait! First, tell the story.

In his book, *God Of The Oppressed*, James H. Cone elaborates on the storytelling tradition of African Americans.

What then is the form and content of black religious thought when viewed in the light of their social situation? Briefly, the form of black religious thought is expressed in the style of story and its content is liberation.... White theologians built logical systems; black folks told tales.

The relation between the form and content of black thought was dialectical. The story was both the medium through which the truth was communicated and also a constituent of truth itself. In the telling of a truthful story, the reality of liberation to which the story pointed was also revealed in the actual telling of the story itself. That was why an equal, and often greater, emphasis was placed on the storyteller.[7]

This word from Cone is particularly important for our understanding of the nature of preaching as storytelling. Such preaching has a distinct goal. When we preach sermons that *explain* Christian truth we demand *understanding* from our hearers. When we tell stories, however, we *evoke* Christian reality; we invite *participation*. The gospel happens in the very telling thereof. Forgiveness of sins is no longer a doctrine that we are to understand. Forgiveness is what we are to experience in, with, and under the telling of the story in which forgiveness is enacted. We *participate* in the reality of a story if it captures our imagination. A story in which forgiveness of sins happens can bring us to tears or bring us to joy. In any case, we feel the reality of forgiveness in our bones. We participate in the forgiveness of sins.

Cone also speaks to the participatory reality of storytelling:

It is difficult to express this liberating truth [freedom of the oppressed as told in stories] in rational discourse alone; it must be told in story. And when this truth is told as it was meant to be, the oppressed are transformed, taken into another world and given a glimpse of the promised land. And when they leave the church, they often say to one another what the disciples said after having experienced the Risen Lord: "Did not our hearts burn within us while he talked to us on the road, while he opened to us the scripture?" (Luke 24:32)[8]

16

Thinking In Story

This discussion of James Cone leads me to a discussion of the changing nature of our communications culture. Let me say at the outset that I relate very closely to Cone's vision for preaching in general and preaching as storytelling in particular. Through our storytelling the oppressed are transformed. Through our storytelling sinners are forgiven. Through our storytelling new life comes to birth within us. In listening to the gospel as story we are born anew by the power of the word that we hear. We have participated in the word of the gospel and we have been changed.

In my book on preaching, *Thinking in Story: Preaching in a Post-literate Age*, I begin with a description of the three communication cultures that have affected the human race. The first era of communication was an oral world. We have just heard James Cone give a contemporary description of the oral world. In an oral world communication was and is mouth-to-ear. The storyteller, or "Rhapsode," is the primary teacher, communicator. His/her teaching is done primarily by stitching stories together. These stories could be characterized by a use of much repetition, beginning with the particular, a tone of conflict, right brain communication, and communication through metaphors of participation.

A further word about metaphors of participation. John Dominic Crossan has made the distinction between metaphors of *participation* and metaphors of *illustration*. Metaphors of illustration are told to illustrate a point and then meant to be forgotten. Forget the story. Remember the point. A metaphor of participation, on the other hand, creates meaning. Meaning happens through the metaphor, through the story. Jesus' parables work like this. They create meaning. It is unfortunate that in much of our preaching we take the meaning out of the story and arrange points for a sermon on a parable or story of Jesus. The world of homiletics today is calling us to return to storytelling as a metaphor of participation. We are invited to tell stories that create meaning!

In order to communicate through stories the Rhapsode of old learned to "think in stories." I am grateful to Thomas Boomershine for his enlightening word in this matter. It is clear that most of our

Bible was written by persons who "thought" in stories. That is most certainly true of the Synoptic Gospels. Matthew, Mark, and Luke create meaning by telling stories. Their stories are not illustrations of points. Our preaching today can take a cue from our Gospel story tellers. We, too, can tell the biblical stories to make things happen, to make gospel happen.

Storytelling as the primary form of proclamation most probably died out in the Christian community when the early Christian church entered the literate world of ancient Greece. A literate world calls forth from humans a different form of communication. The literate world is the second form of communication in human history. It began with the Greek invention of the phonetic alphabet, got its biggest boost from the invention of the printing press, and began to die out the day electricity was invented. The literate world appeals to the eye, not the ear. The literate world presents information to the eye (just as you are experiencing it now on this page) in a linear form, logical construction, orderly manner, and so on.

When preaching came under the tutelage of the literate world it changed immensely. Preaching began to be characterized by linearity (three points), propositional content, an analytical nature, left-brain communication, and metaphors of illustration. Christian proclamation moved from "thinking in story" to "thinking in ideas." The goal of preaching moved from participation to understanding. Homiletical textbooks from the time of Gutenberg until very recently have been texts that taught us to preach by "thinking in ideas."

We live today, however, in the third phase of communication culture: the electronic age. The simplest way of describing the shift from one communication era to another is by asking what human sense or senses are engaged in the communication. Marshall McLuhan always said that *how* we learn something, the senses engaged, is as important for our total understanding as *what* we learn. The world of oral communication engaged the ear. The world of literate communication engaged the eye. The world of electronic communication can engage many of our senses simultaneously. Watching television, for example, is an ear and eye experience and much more.

Electronic forms of communication have created a post-literate world. People, and especially young people, spend far more time wired in to electronic forms of communication that they do in reading the old-fashioned way. We worry much in this world about our children's ability to read. Anyone who works in education today knows the seriousness of this issue! The only point I wish to make at this time is that electronic forms of communication which bombard our senses include the ear again as a receiver of information. Oral culture primarily engaged the ear. Literate culture, the world of "silent print," primarily engaged the eye. Post-literate culture brings the ear back into the equation (radio, television, record players, CDs, and so forth). Many communication scholars, therefore, have called our age "secondarily oral." The ear makes a comeback.

The basic thesis of my work, *Thinking in Story*, is that preaching to people whose ears are hard at work again in the communication process can receive much assistance by a look back at oral cultures. How did they communicate in the world of the ear, the oral world? They communicated primarily by telling stories. I believe that a recovery of storytelling is *one* of the ways we can communicate effectively with post-literate people. Storytelling, I believe, works for oral people. Storytelling also works for post-literate people, for postmodern people, and for Generation X. Let's take up Matthew's Gospel and get on with the telling of his great story.[9]

Matthew's Gospel

Biblical scholars have not come to firm agreement about the context in which the Gospels of Mark or Luke were written. Students of Matthew's Gospel, however, have come to some fairly unanimous conclusions on the precise setting and context of the Gospel. This has made an important difference in the interpretation of Matthew. Scholars are willing to interpret aspects of Matthew's Gospel in light of the conditions in Matthew's supposed community.

Robert Smith states this scholarly consensus clearly in his commentary on Matthew:

...the dominant view today, situates Matthew and his com-
munity in the '80s and '90s of the first century, locked in
controversy with the Jewish Pharisaic leadership of Jamnia.
The war of liberation fought by the Jews against the vastly
superior power of Rome had ended disastrously in A.D. 70....
The very life of Judaism was in jeopardy. The Essene
communities, like the one at Qumran, had been destroyed....
The future of Judaism lay with the Pharisees.... A Pharisee
named Johanan ben Zakkai gathered around himself at the
town of Jamnia a council of Pharisaic sages and began the
task of rebuilding Judaism...two vigorous Jewish communi-
ties lived side by side: the Pharisaic synagogue community
and the Christian congregation.... Both had deep convic-
tions regarding Scripture and the will of God, the identity of
the people of God, the meaning of the destruction of Jerusa-
lem, and the direction to take into the future.... Many believe
that Matthew's Gospel must be interpreted as a product of
the dialog or polemical exchange between leaders of the two
communities, as church and synagogue competed for the
loyalties of the same people, offering divergent interpreta-
tions of the life of Jesus and events of the recent past.[10]

This consensus view of Matthew summarized by Smith has its roots in the work of W. D. Davies. Davies saw the Gospel of Matthew as a work of confrontation between Christian and Jewish communities in the late first century. The issue for Davies was a matter of *identity*. After the destruction of Jerusalem both Jewish and Christian communities had to struggle with the issue of their identity. What does it mean to be a Jew without Jerusalem? What does it mean to be a Christian in contradistinction to Judaism? The Jewish council at Jamnia alluded to above was a reality. Jews had worked together to forge a new identity.

Davies was convinced that Matthew's gospel, especially the
sermon on the mount, was "a Christian response to Jamnia."
...Matthew's church, a majority of whose members were
Jewish Christians, was concerned about its own identity
now that it was cut off from its Jewish roots and being
absorbed into the Gentile world. Matthew, therefore,

attempted to define Christian identity over against the reform of Jamnia.[11]

Warren Carter (*Matthew: Storyteller, Interpreter, Evangelist*) also sees the matter of identity as the fundamental issue for Matthew and his community. He believes that Matthew's community, living probably in Antioch in Syria, found itself as a community living on the edge of history. They were a minority community living in a large and very diverse urban area. They were a minority in this city filled, some suggest, with pagans. They were also in the minority in relationship to the Jewish religious community of Antioch. The identity of these "little ones" could easily be swallowed up. So Matthew must urge the Christian community to "live against the grain," as Carter puts it. Living "against the grain" of one's culture might also describe the need of the Christian community in North America at the turn of the millennium. Matthew, therefore, might be a very relevant Gospel for our time.

Scholarly consensus on Matthew himself asserts that Matthew was a Jewish Christian who knew Greek well. He lived with his community in Antioch in Syria. Jack Dean Kingsbury believes that Matthew's community was urban and prosperous. Of Matthew himself Kingsbury writes: "Perhaps, therefore, the first evangelist can best be described as a Greek-speaking Jewish Christian of the second generation after Jesus who possessed a universal missionary outlook and had most probably enjoyed rabbinical training."[12]

Donald Senior concludes his review of the items we have discussed thus far in this way:

> *The evangelist wrote for a group of Christians who were undergoing a transformation from a predominantly Jewish Christian church to an increasingly Gentile church, from a church whose roots and cultural origin were Palestinian to a church plunged into the midst of the Roman empire. The destruction of Jerusalem by the Romans signaled the end of the form of Judaism known to Jesus and to the earliest apostolic church. Both Judaism and Jewish Christianity had to strike a new course. This search for identity and for continuity within discontinuity seems to have been one of the*

21

primary purposes of Matthew's Gospel.... Virtually all recent studies on Matthew's gospel would agree that this evangelist and his community have strong roots in Judaism and that Matthew's gospel was concerned with such Jewish issues as fidelity to the law and the destiny of God's people. And all would agree that the community's faith in Jesus as the messiah, as God's authoritative teacher and redeemer, is the fundamental reason for the tension with the rest of the Jewish community...the primary purpose of his gospel is to encourage his readers to understand reality, past, present and future, in the light of Jesus.[13]

Given that which we have reviewed so far concerning the nature and purpose of Matthew's Gospel, we realize that *conflict* will dominate the pages of this story. Kingsbury writes that conflict is central to the plot of Matthew. He goes so far as to say that the conflict in Matthew's Gospel is cosmic in scope. Insofar as Matthew's Gospel is dominated by conflict it will certainly have a *polemical* nature. The polemic, as we have seen, is between a fledgling Christian community searching for its identity and rabbinic Judaism as defined by the Jewish Council of Jamnia. This fact can lead us, however, to an unfortunate tendency to read and preach Matthew's Gospel in its *over-against* character. Anti-Semitism lurks ever so close to the surface when we read and preach Matthean texts as polemical words intended to clarify communities and put down opponents. We need to be very careful in our preaching at this juncture. It will not do to interpret text after text in Matthew as showing the superiority of Christianity to erring Jews! An easy straw man can be set up in our minds as we wend our way through Matthew. Christianity is *not* what these people (these straw men) do. *NO!* Christianity is defined as follows.... We must be very careful not to let ourselves get caught in this kind of polemical interpretation of Matthew on a steady basis. It is best to approach texts of scripture with gracious hearts and love for all the persons therein.

Robert Smith goes a completely different way in his interpretation of Matthew at the point of the polemics. He does not like the Judaism-bashing that can come with the standard interpretation of

Matthew. He reads Matthew's polemic as a word spoken not against outsiders to the faith but as spoken to *Christian insiders.*

> *I think of Matthew as a Christian sage disturbed primarily by developments inside the Christian community. He recalls harsh words of Jesus against Pharisees and other leaders, not because he is locked in combat with the Pharisaic leaders of Jamnia, but because he is probing the mind of Jesus regarding issues of authority and leadership. At the same time he addressed issues of discipleship and followership.... In his own day Matthew sees Christian leaders displaying the very sorts of behavior and attitudes criticized by Jesus.... He trusted his first readers to catch the point of his retelling of Jesus' story and to make the appropriate applications to their lives.*[14]

We will call upon Smith's exegesis in this mode as we look at the pericope texts from Matthew. Let it suffice to say here that the opponents within the Christian community as identified by Smith are the "false prophets" (e.g. Matthew 7:15-23). These false leaders see themselves as being "filled" with the Spirit. As Spirit-filled people they see themselves as the true heirs of Jesus. God favors them. Their charismatic gifts make that clear. The Christian community is, therefore, divided. Matthew speaks to this division.

Smith is such a lone voice in this matter that some may have a hard time taking his hypothesis seriously. We need to note, however, that there are some immediate advantages to his reading of Matthew. The polemic that we spoke of above is now an internal matter within the Christian community. Matthew's opponents are not some outsiders who can easily be criticized and dismissed. The opponents, rather, are other Christians. Maybe some of the ways of these Christians are like our ways! Matthew's polemic may well be addressed to you and to me as we walk a faith journey that strays from the path of righteousness. It is quite another matter to grapple with the polemic nature of Matthew's Gospel when we are put on guard that this polemic may be addressed to us!

It is a well-known fact that Matthew speaks very little about the Holy Spirit in his work. We note, for example, that in the climax of the Gospel Jesus does not refer to the Holy Spirit when he sends the disciples to preach and teach to the nations. "Remember," Jesus tells them in the Gospel's final words, "I will be with you always, to the end of the age" (Matthew 28:20). Matthew could have spoken here of the work of the Holy Spirit. He does not. His gospel message is an *Emmanuel* message. "God is with us." See also Matthew 1:23. Did Matthew carefully avoid talking about the Holy Spirit in these instances because there were so many misinterpretations of the work of the Spirit among false prophets? Smith thinks this may well be possible. Matthew may have reined in the work of the Spirit. He always binds the work of the Spirit to the work of the Father (Matthew 3:16; 10:20) or to the Son (12:18, 28). Smith points out that "The Spirit has no fresh mission separate or distinct from that of Father and Son, contrary to what some inspired leader in the community may have believed."[15]

Smith makes other assertions about Matthew's Gospel that are worth noting. In our discussion of Matthew 16:13-20 in Chapter 21 we have occasion to quote Smith's opinion that Matthew understands his Gospel to be *the successor to Peter.* Matthew's Gospel, that is, contains all that Christ commanded us: 28:19.

> *Matthew reissued the words of Jesus because of confusion in the church resulting from the energetic and enthusiastic labors of prophets and teachers and leaders. It is Matthew's contention that anyone claiming to speak for the exalted Jesus should be tested by the norm of Jesus' own words, as enshrined in Matthew's Gospel.*[16]

Finally, a word about the structure of Matthew's Gospel. Interpreters of Matthew lay out the schema of the Gospel in a variety of ways. Jack Dean Kingsbury's outline is a simple one that is accepted by many scholars. His outline is as follows:

I.   Matthew 1:1—4:16 The Presentation of Jesus
II. Matthew 4:17—16:20 The Ministry of Jesus to Israel and
       Israel's Repudiation of Jesus
       4:17: "From that time Jesus began..."
       A. 4:17—11:1 Jesus' Ministry to Israel

B. 11:2—16:20 Israel Repudiates Jesus
III. Matthew 16:21—28:20 Journey of Jesus to Jerusalem
Jesus' Passion, Death, Resurrection
16:21: "From that time Jesus began..."[17]

Kingsbury's book *Matthew As Story* is a work of literary criticism on Matthew. He is, therefore, content to let Matthew designate his own outline. Note in the outline above that the first verse in II. and III. are identical. See Matthew 4:17; 16:20. Jesus *began* something new in each case.

Older outlines of Matthew use the five discourses in Matthew as their guide to the Gospel.

I.   Discourse One: Sermon on the Mount: 5:1—7:28.
II. Discourse Two: Missionary Discourse: 10:1—11:1.
III. Discourse Three: Parabolic Discourse: 13:1-53.
IV. Discourse Four: Discourse on the Church: 18:1—19:1
V.   Discourse Five: Discourse on the End of Times: 24:1—26:1.

These discourses are easy to discover in Matthew's text. Matthew 7:28 reads as follows: "Now when Jesus had finished saying these things...." The last verses indicated in each segment of the outline above each carry the message that now Jesus has *finished*. See 11:1; 13:53; 19:1; 26:1. A variety of interpreters see this five-fold structure as a kind of parallel with the five books of Moses. In this way of thinking Jesus might be conceived of as the *new Moses* who teaches the true path of God for a new age even as Moses taught God's way in an earlier era of God's revealing work.

Matthew As Storyteller

Donald Senior reminds us that, above and beyond all the details of possible outlines, *Matthew is a storyteller!*

> *This might mean that Matthew's "plan" was, in fact, much less systematic and much richer in variety than most scholars have thought. A storyteller does not work in the same way as a mathematician. The storyteller does not usually begin with a rigid comprehensive plan.... After all, as recent*

25

exegesis has emphasized, the gospels are stories and the evangelists are storytellers.... So his structure may be described as a retelling of the story of Mark.... The structure of the gospel is more like the flowing lines of a symphony than the fixed girders supporting a building. [18]

Warren Carter agrees with Senior: "Matthew is an ancient biography or story which functions as a vehicle for proclamation about Jesus."[19]

Jack Dean Kingsbury approaches his study of Matthew from the point of view of literary criticism. He, too, is interested in the story of Matthew.

Literary-critically, the Gospel of Matthew is a unified narrative, or "artistic whole." The story it relates is governed, as will be seen, by a single, overarching "evaluative point of view." Moreover, the action, thought, and interactions of the characters are all organized by means of a coherent plot. This plot has a beginning, middle and artful ending. [20]

Kingsbury's work on Matthew will be of major help to us as we seek to understand the ways in which the stories in Matthew's Gospel are part of a larger story. I spoke in my earlier works on Mark and Luke of *narrative analogy, allusion,* and *intertextuality.* Narrative analogy is a term used to describe the ways in which a storyteller connects his stories to other stories in order that we hear their full meaning. Allusion is a term used in much the same manner. One story in Matthew may allude to one, two, three or more other stories in the First Gospel. These allusions are important. Matthew interprets his stories by alluding to other stories. The preacher will need to tell several of these stories at times in order that hearers might be fully grasped by the particular text assigned for preaching. Intertextuality likewise refers to the ways in which texts *inter-* connect with other texts.

When we as preachers take these literary clues seriously it will become increasingly less possible for us to preach a sermon confining ourselves only to the six or eight or more verses assigned for a Sunday pericope. Exegesis for preaching has traditionally been a microscopic endeavor. We put the verses assigned under a microscope as we seek for ideas for our sermon. Literary critics call upon us also to learn how to do a more *panoramic* form of exegesis for preaching. The meaning of a given text is not necessarily in its dissected details. The reality of a text may, rather, emerge for us only as we see a given text in its interrelatedness to other Matthean texts. Preaching will do well at times to tell Matthean stories in addition to the assigned text in order to discover the more fully orbed reality that lies before us. If Matthew is a storyteller, we might well be storytellers, too. If Matthew yokes his stories with other stories to present them in their fullest possibility, then our preaching can do likewise. Literary readings of Matthew call upon us to be storytellers of Matthew's stories in order to call people into meaningful participation in the story of Jesus as presented in the First Gospel.

In order to try to keep to the flow of Matthew's story our chapters will come in their Matthean order, not their order in a pericope system. My comments on each chapter are basically comments on the narrative itself and its connection with other Matthew narratives near and far. In this process we shall comment on all of the material in Matthew's Gospel and not just on those texts appointed for a pericope system. There are many stories omitted from the Matthean lectionary that cry out to be told. We can tell many of them in conjunction with the appointed texts. The goal of my comments is to suggest, where possible, other Matthean narratives that can be stitched together with the textual narrative into a narrative sermon. This method does not work for every text. Nor would one want to preach such biblically based story-sermons every week. Sometimes, however, this is a helpful way of shaping the homiletical task in a world that no longer knows the biblical stories.

Just as you consult a number of commentaries each week, so I have consulted a host of commentaries in preparation for this work. Week by week I consulted the standard Matthew commentaries. I received the most help in making narrative sense out of Matthew from Jack Dean Kingsbury's *Matthew As Story*, and Robert H. Smith's *Matthew*. Smith's commentary, written with laity in mind, was by far the most helpful material I encountered. You will notice the truth of this as Smith is quoted in these chapters far more than any other work. This explains the dedication of this book to my good friend and biblical scholar *par excellence*.

I need to make it clear that exegetically I am dependent upon those who are blazing the narrative trail with a Gospel like Matthew. My contribution is to take the many narrative suggestions that are discussed in Matthean commentaries and suggest ways in which Matthew's stories can be stitched together for preaching.

Speaking for God

I am increasingly drawn to the phrase "speaking for God" as a way of describing what preaching is to accomplish. As pastors we speak for God on many occasions. We speak for God in our baptizing as we announce a new reality. "In the name of the Triune One I name you child of God." We speak for God at the table as we name bread and wine with the words "this is my body," "this is my blood." In the exercise of the Office of the Keys (Matthew 16:18-19; 18:19-20) sinners come to us to unburden themselves of their sins. We speak a word to them and their sins are forgiven. We say, "I forgive you all your sins in the name of the Triune God." Or we can speak a word of judgment and sins are retained. We speak for God in first person, present tense language. "By the power invested in me *I* announce to you that your sins *are* forgiven." We don't explain forgiveness to sinners. We announce forgiveness. We speak for God!

I understand preaching to be the public exercise of the Office of the Keys. Here, too, we speak for God. Our gospel preaching will be far more powerful if we can learn in our preaching to go beyond explanations of forgiveness (or other metaphors of salvation) and simply announce (first person, present tense, speaking for God) forgiveness.

At the close of many of the chapters below I will suggest to you a pattern for such "speaking for God" as a conclusion to the Matthew stories you have told. Matthew stories lead to speaking for God. It's that simple. Here is what Jesus is saying to us today through these stories! Then say it on behalf of Jesus. Please accept my suggestions at the end of chapters as just that: suggestions. You know your own context. You know what words need to be said. In any case, your words should be shaped by the metaphors for the nature of the human condition and the metaphors for the nature of Christ's salvation that arise from the particular stories you have told.

I learned this approach to gospel proclamation from giants like Martin Luther, Karl Barth, Rudolf Bultmann, and Gustav Wingren. I urge you with every fiber of my being to learn to "speak for God." The people in your pews do not come week by week to hear you *explain* Christian reality to them. They want you to make Christian reality *happen* to them. They want to hear you *speak for God*. They want to hear the word that forgives, the word that heals, the word that gives hope, the word that provides comfort.

The gospel of God's love for sinners is by far the most important message we have to proclaim to the world. Just about anything else we might say our hearers can hear elsewhere. It is only in the gathering of two or three where Christ is present in the midst of them, however, where we can hear God speak good news to us about our life here and hereafter. Preaching exists primarily in the church to make this good news happen. I am convinced that the best way we can make it happen is to learn to "speak for God" in our preaching just as we "speak for God" when we baptize, preside, and absolve.

* *

With this book on Matthew I come to the end of a series of books for narrative preaching on the Synoptic Gospels. On the one hand, this saddens me deeply. Giving birth to this material has been for me an incredible labor of love and I will miss it! It has been a lot of work but not hard work. It has been work that has given me life as I have come to know Matthew's, Mark's, and Luke's stories of Jesus in new and powerful ways. One of the things that has happened to me in the labor is that these stories have really begun to take root in my life. They have impressed themselves upon me. They travel with me now in my imagination as stories that guide and shape my Christian life. Thank you, Matthew. Thank you, Mark. Thank you, Luke. Thank you, Jesus!

1. Stanley J. Grenz, *A Primer On Postmodernism* (Grand Rapids: William B. Eerdmans, 1996), pp. 1-10.

2. *Ibid.*, pp. 167-169.

3. *Ibid.*, pp. 169-171.

4. *Ibid.*, pp. 171-172.

5. *Ibid.*, pp. 172-174.

6. Kevin Graham Ford, *Jesus For A New Generation* (Downers Grove: InterVarsity Press, 1995), pp. 220, 221, 228.

7. James H. Cone, *God Of The Oppressed* (San Francisco: Harper, 1975), pp. 54, 57.

8. *Ibid.*, p. 61.

9. The above material is a condensation of chapters in Richard A. Jensen, *Thinking in Story: Preaching in a Postliterate Age* (Lima, Ohio: CSS, 1993). *Preaching Mark's Gospel* (CSS, 1996) and *Preaching Luke's Gospel* (CSS, 1997) also contain in their Prefaces a version of this information.

10. Robert H. Smith, *Matthew: Augsburg Commentary on the New Testament* (Minneapolis: Augsburg, 1989), pp. 19-20.

11. Donald Senior, *What are they saying about Matthew?* (New York: Paulist Press, 1996), p. 9.

12. Jack Dean Kingsbury, *Matthew As Story* (Minneapolis: Fortress Press, 1988), p. 160.

13. Senior, *op. cit., pp.* 19-20.

14. Smith, *op. cit.*, pp. 20-21.

15. *Ibid.*, p. 340.

16. *Ibid.*, p. 108.

17. Kingsbury, *op. cit.*, p. 40.

18. Senior, *op. cit.*, pp. 35-36.

19. Warren Carter, *Matthew: Storyteller, Interpreter, Evangelist* (Peabody, MA: Hendrickson Publishers, 1996), p. 49.

20. Kingsbury, *op. cit.*, pp. 1-2.

Matthew 1:18-25

Our Matthew text for this week comes from the first chapter of Matthew. Matthew's telling of the Jesus' story is certainly unique. Matthew tells of the early years of our Savior stressing that his name is Jesus and Emmanuel; that wise sages from the East attend his birth; that Joseph and Mary escape to Egypt because of Herod's wrath. No other Gospel includes these realities.

Matthew is also the only Gospel writer to *begin* his story with a genealogy. This genealogy is of vital importance to Matthew's narrative. Genealogies are rarely included in the pericope system. Too boring! In truth, however, genealogies were not boring in their original context. Genealogies were one of the chief ways that oral people understood issues of identity. We can be sure that people read and heard this first chapter of Matthew with excited anticipation. Matthew opens his Gospel in this exciting way!

We must take a brief look at these verses of genealogy here. So many of the foundations of Matthew's Gospel are laid in these verses which are omitted from our lectionary. They need to be included in some of our year's preaching on Matthew. In fact, it would be well in some years to preach on Matthew 1 and 2 throughout the Advent Season.

Matthew's book of genealogy begins with Abraham. God had promised to bless all the families of the earth through Abraham (Genesis 12:1-3). In this very first name, the name Abraham, Matthew sends a clue to his Gospel. This story will include all the families of the earth. Gentiles and Jews. Sinners and saints. The first name, Abraham, hints at *mission.*

And then come the *women.* Genealogies of old did not include women. What are these women of old doing in a list like this? And such women! Tamar (Genesis 38), Rahab (Joshua 2, 6), Ruth (Book of Ruth) and Bathsheba (2 Samuel 11-12). Most of them are

Gentiles! Three of these women have been in involved in scandalous behavior: incest, prostitution, and adultery. Four women. Four Sundays in Advent. This would make a great Advent *mission* series. Yes, mission. God's grace clearly includes persons such as these. God's grace clearly includes sinners like you and me. Matthew sees these women as playing a crucial role in God's movement from promise to fulfillment.

In telling these stories we need to connect them to the end of Matthew's Gospel. Matthew's first word and last word are *mission* words. The last word is: "Go therefore and make disciples of all nations..." (28:19).

We can also connect the stories of these women to the fifth woman in Matthew 1: Mary.

> ...*these women may be related not so much to* Abraham *at the beginning of the story as to* Mary *at its climax.* Mary *of whom Jesus was born (v. 16) is a fifth woman in the genealogy. God's sovereign and surprising use of these four ancient women foreshadowed the astonishing use of Mary (v. 20) in the fulness of time. All those women are signs that God has intervened and will do so yet again. History is wide open to God's fresh initiatives.*[1]

The genealogy also lays out Matthew's view of history. "So all the generations from Abraham to David are fourteen generations; and from David to the deportation to Babylon, fourteen generations; and from the deportation to Babylon to the Messiah, fourteen generations" (1:17). History has a plan. God is in charge of that plan. All of history comes to fruition and fulfillment in the birth of a baby boy. The name of the baby is Jesus. The destiny of history is bound up in this child. That's a message we need to proclaim with power and clarity today as people look under every nook and corner and consult every so-called spiritual person they can find to discover some meaning to life. We know the meaning of history and his name is Jesus!

We come then to the text assigned for this Fourth Sunday in Advent: Matthew 1:18-25. The story is centered in Joseph, a righteous or just man. Righteousness is a key theme in Matthew's

Gospel. Right at the beginning, in the first two chapters, he tells us the story of what a righteous person looks like. It looks like Joseph. Matthew weaves the story of Joseph and the story of Herod together in a series of five stories. These stories portray a righteous man who believes in Jesus and an unrighteous man who does not. We'll look at these interlocking stories on the First Sunday after Christmas.

Matthew spends very little time on the drama of the birth of Jesus. We simply hear that Joseph, the righteous one, and Mary were betrothed. When they came together they discovered that she was pregnant. The Holy Spirit is credited with paternity! As we indicated in the Preface, Matthew says very little about the Holy Spirit in his Gospel. He may have been faced with a community of Christians who had, as Luther once put it, "swallowed the Holy Spirit feathers and all."

The tradition of Jesus' origin in the Godhead was so strong, however, that Matthew cannot omit the work of the Holy Spirit in this instance. In Genesis 1:2 we hear that the Creator Spirit was moving over the face of primeval waters in order to give life to the creation and to humankind. Jesus is the child of this creative spirit. That's his *identity*. Matthew 1 is preoccupied with this matter of Jesus' identity. Jesus is Son of Abraham, Son of David, Child of the Spirit and of the Spirit's chosen instruments: Joseph and Mary.

As Matthew tells the story, however, the *naming* of Jesus is more important than his birth. His name is to be called Jesus. The Hebrew equivalent of Jesus is Joshua and it means something like: "Yahweh is salvation." Jesus is to be our Savior. He is to save us from our sins. This motif of forgiveness of sins occurs many times in Matthew's Gospel: 9:10-13; 11:16-19; 26:26-29.

We note that the naming of Jesus is said to be a sign of the fulfillment of prophecy: 1:22. Fulfillment of prophecy is a very important part of the way that Matthew tells his story. It is true throughout his entire Gospel but most particularly so in the first chapters that he notes for us that a given deed fulfilled what the prophets had said: 2:5-6, 15, 17-18, 23; 3:3; 4:14-16, and so forth. Matthew reports faithfully on fulfillment of Scripture as a key to the identity of the One who stands stage center in his story: Jesus. Let there be no mistake about it. Jesus fulfills God's plan of the ages.

The implied message is that he fulfills the plan of the ages for us as well. God is a God who constantly intervenes in human affairs in order to move history towards its goal.

The first prophecy fulfilled has to do with Jesus' name: Emmanuel. Commentators note that Matthew is much more interested in the name of Jesus than he is in the story of his birth. Emmanuel. God is with us! This is the heart of the message of Matthew's Gospel. We saw above that the mission theme in Matthew is enunciated clearly in both the first and last chapters of Matthew. The Emmanuel theme is likewise enunciated in the alpha and omega of Matthew's story. The very last words of Matthew's Gospel are: "And remember, *I am with you* always, to the end of the age" (28:20). "I am with you" is the equivalent of Emmanuel. God with us. That is the fundamental message of Matthew's story.

The key passages 1:23 and 28:20, which stand in a reciprocal relationship to each other, highlight this (fundamental) message. At 1:23, Matthew quotes Isaiah in saying of Jesus: in "Emmanuel... God [is] with us." And at 28:20 the risen Jesus himself declares to the disciples: "I am with you always...." Strategically located at the beginning and the end of Matthew's story, these two passages "enclose" it. In combination, they reveal the message of Matthew's story: *In the person of Jesus Messiah, his Son, God has drawn near to abide to the end of time with his people, the church, thus inaugurating the eschatological age of salvation.*[2]

There is one other specific reference to the Emmanuel-reality in Matthew's Gospel. In Matthew 18 we read instructions for the life of the Christian community. One of these instructions has to do with what one is to do, "If another member of the church sins against you..." (18:15). Finally such disputes are to be brought to the community. "For where two or three are gathered in my name, *I am there among them*" (18:20). Jesus is God's presence among us not only as past fulfillment of prophecy or future promise of presence. Our Emmanuel God is with us *now* when the community of God's people gathers together. Matthew is concerned with the nature of the church! When the church gathers today in the name of Jesus Christ they experience Emmanuel!

Homiletical Directions

In the text above we brought forward the possibility of preaching on Matthew 1 or Matthew 1 and 2 throughout an Advent season. Matthew's genealogy contains a marvelous surprise. There are four "Advent Women" here—Tamar, Rahab, Ruth and Bathsheba—whose stories cry out to be told! When else will they ever get told? We suggest either one "Advent Woman" a Sunday for the four weeks of Advent or abbreviated versions of their stories compacted into one story for the Fourth Sunday in Advent. Matthew's Gospel is all about God as a God who keeps promises with Israel. Promises have been made to Abraham (Genesis 12:1-3) and David (2 Samuel 7:8-16). Promises have been kept. Matthew 1 clearly announces that Jesus is the fulfillment of age-old promises. Jesus is the climax of many fulfillments along the way. The women of Matthew 1 are the instruments of such promise keeping. "I am a God who keeps my promises" is the word of God that reverberates through Matthew 1. That's a wonderful word for us to hear today.

These "Advent Women" stories can also be told under the theme of *mission*. Gentiles and sinners are part of God's saving activity. The Great Commission with which Matthew concludes is no surprise. We see it coming right here in Matthew 1.

There is, of course, a fifth woman in Matthew 1. Her name is Mary. She can be the focus of a Christmas sermon. If you don't use the "Advent Women" during the Advent season then use them in the Christmas season as the prelude to Mary's story. God works in incredible ways to bring promise to fulfillment. Mary is the last in a long line of God's miraculous workings toward fulfillment! The stories of these women bear this out. Christmas is about such a fulfillment.

If we stay within the boundaries of this week's appointed Gospel a logical sermon theme would deal with Jesus as the *name of the one who forgives sin*. Tell this week's text as story with this reality as the focus. Jesus comes as the one who forgives. Other stories from Matthew can be told to carry forth this theme. Tell the stories of Matthew 9:10-13 and 11:16-19 and 26:26-29 as stories linked with the forgiveness of sins that is present for us in Jesus' name. The closing proclamation for a sermon on these stories will enable Jesus to speak his word of forgiveness to us today. Our proclamation might go like this: "My name is Jesus. I come to be born among you as a Savior. I come to be born among you as One who forgives sinners. I come not to call the righteous, but sinners. I came to be a friend to tax collectors. I came to give my body and blood that your sins might be forgiven. Listen, sinners. Today I say to you: 'Your sins are forgiven.' " Amen.

A third alternative for narrative preaching would be to focus on *Emmanuel.* Tell the textual story with the focus on the reality of God's presence among us. Tell the story of the Great Commission where Jesus ends by saying, "I am with you always, to the end of the age." Tell the story of Matthew's understanding that wherever two or three gather in Jesus' name he is present, he is Emmanuel, for us (18:15-20).

Our closing proclamation for this series of Emmanuel stories might go something like this: "I am Emmanuel come among you in the birth of a child. I am Emmanuel come among you whenever two or three of you gather in my name. I am Emmanuel come among you to empower your ministry and mission to the end of the age. I am Emmanuel come among you to fill you with my very presence." Amen.

---

1. Robert H. Smith, *Matthew: Augsburg Commentary on the New Testament* (Minneapolis: Augsburg, 1989), p. 33.

2. Jack Dean Kingsbury, *Matthew As Story* (Philadelphia: Fortress Press, 1988), pp. 41-42.

Matthew 2:1-12

The focus in Matthew 1 was on names. Name after name after name culminating in *THE Name: Jesus!* In Matthew 2 there is a focus on places. The first place mentioned is Bethlehem. Matthew begins his birth story by simply telling us that Jesus was born in Bethlehem. In the course of the story the Magi come from the east looking for the city in which the "child of the star" was to be found. Herod didn't know. The chief priests and scribes looked it up. Bethlehem! They tell Herod that Bethlehem is the place of the birth by quoting from the prophet Micah: "And you, Bethlehem in the land of Judah, are by no means least among the rulers of Judah; for from you shall come a ruler who is to shepherd my people Israel" (Micah 2:6).

Bethlehem, of course, was the birthplace of David! See 1 Samuel 16:1-13 (v. 1); 17:12-15. Matthew makes a big deal out of the place of this "by no means least" city. ("O Little Town of Bethlehem!") He makes a big deal of it because he is now telling us that by *place* Jesus is the Son of David. In chapter 1 he had told us by *names* that Jesus was David's Son. Jesus is Son of David. The entire genealogical list in Matthew 1 may be simply to make this point. Matthew calls his Gospel "An account of the genealogy of Jesus the Messiah, the Son of David..." (1:1).

Son of David means Messiah. Messiah means heir of the promise made to David in 2 Samuel 7:1-16. This is probably the most important promissory passage in the entire Old Testament. Nathan tells David that God will bring it to pass that David's sons will always rule in Israel. The kingdom shall be eternal. The present day heirs of Israel still cling to this passage as the clue to their destiny. For Matthew, and for Christians in general, the birth of Jesus-Messiah is the fulfillment of this age-old prophecy.

The Magi come from *the East* to Jerusalem. The Magi are Gentiles! If they are all men they match up alongside the four women in the Matthew 1 genealogy. All these Gentiles! The message of Matthew is pretty clear. Messiah, Emmanuel, comes for all people. (See the comments in Chapter 1 on *mission* in Matthew.)

The Magi are astrologers or philosophers or sages from the East. They are the best of the intellectual community in their cultural world. The stars were a part of what they were all about. And the star led them to Jerusalem and on to Bethlehem. *The very best in this Gentile culture led them to the Christ-child!* Their coming to the birth of Jesus was for them a very *public* event. They saw it in the stars. It's as if God had put a huge sign up over the Bethlehem stable that read: OPEN TO THE PUBLIC.

Today's world is full of people selling many brands of spirituality and religiosity. Those we call cults, and there are many of them, live by the philosophy that the public would not understand its inner secrets until they've undergone a long period of initiation or apprenticeship. Cult members, therefore, never tell you in public what the heart of the matter is for them. The heart of the matter is private information. It is secret. The religion of the gnostics in all ages is also always about a hidden mystery. Most of the cults in America are gnostic in their world view!

How different this is from the Christian faith! Our sign says: OPEN TO THE PUBLIC. What we believe is out there for everyone to see and hear. We'll tell you in our first conversation that Christianity is about a God who loves sinners. That's the heart of the matter for us. It's public information. We want everyone to know it!

The Magi come to King Herod. "Where is the child who has been born king of the Jews?" the Magi ask the King. How did the Magi know to ask the question this way? Did they see in the stars that a king had been born? At any rate, Matthew accepts their point of view on this matter. He tells us that the Magi *worshiped* this newborn King.

Herod is another matter. He is quite a piece of work! In contrast to the Magi, Herod the Great and all Jerusalem react with fear to the news that the Messiah, the King of the Jews, has been born.... Moreover, Herod proves himself to be prototypical of others with whom Jesus will become embroiled in conflict in the course of his ministry, namely, Pilate and the religious leaders.... According to Herod's evaluative point of view, Jesus is an insurrectionist. Similarly, Pilate also deals with Jesus on the presumption that the Messiah, the King of the Jews, is one who lays political claim to the throne of Israel (27:11-14)[1]

Jack Dean Kingsbury makes much of the prototypical nature of the role of Herod in Matthew's story.

The manner in which Herod reacts to the perceived threat the infant Jesus poses anticipates the manner in which the religious leaders will later respond to the adult Jesus. Both Herod and they reveal themselves to be "spiritually blind" (2:3; 27:63); "fearful" (2:3; 21:46); "conspiratorial" (2:7; 12:14); "guileful" and "mendacious"; "murderous" (2:13; 12:14); "wrathful" (2:16; cf. 21:15); and "apprehensive of the future" (2:16; 27:62-64). In Matthew's story, Herod is the precursor of the religious leaders, and his opposition to Jesus foreshadows theirs.[2]

Once they get their Bethlehem information the Magi are on their way to present their gifts and to worship the One born king of the Jews. King Herod does not join in this worship pilgrimage. Neither do the religious leaders. We're perhaps so familiar with this story that the shock simply passes over us. Jewish political and religious leaders remain fixed—in their positions, in their places. The Magi, the Gentiles, go to worship the newborn king. This is an incredible, turn-the-world-upside-down, Epiphany story.

Once the Magi arrive at the house we hear that they fell down and worshiped Jesus. Joseph and Mary are now of little significance. The focus is on King Jesus. The focus is on this God-in-hiding in a newborn babe. Luther said it long ago: The God of the Bible is a God who is revealed in hiding!

In his work of pastoral theology on Matthew, Mark Alan Powell devotes a chapter to worship. One of the forms of worship that he identifies in Matthew's Gospel is "epiphanic worship." This is worship in the presence of the divine. He points out that there are five occasions in Matthew's Gospel where Jesus is worshiped beginning with this passage concerning the Magi in 2:2, 11. The other instances are 14:33; 21:15; 28:9; 28:17. The focus in each of these worship passages is Jesus himself as the One he is revealed to be.

Powell also deals with a form of worship in Matthew which he labels "supplicatory" worship. "Four times in this narrative individuals come to Jesus, worship him, and then present him with a need or request that they hope he will address." These passages are 8:2; 9:18; 15:25; 20:20. At the end of his discussion Powell notes that there are, therefore, nine instances of supplicatory or epiphanic worship in Matthew's Gospel. Jesus is always the heart of these worship passages. Powell points out that all nine of these instances of worship of Jesus are unique to Matthew's Gospel: "...the worship of Jesus is a much more pronounced theme in Matthew than in the other Synoptic Gospels."[3]

The Magi came to worship and to bring gifts of gold, frankincense, and myrrh. The Old Testament reference for the bearing of such gifts is in the Old Testament lesson appointed for this week: Isaiah 60:1-6. Gerhard von Rad (*Old Testament Theology*, Vol. II) talks about two themes that occur repeatedly in the prophets of the later Persian period: Trito-Isaiah; Haggai, Zechariah, Malachi and Jonah. Both themes center on the city to which the exiles have recently returned: Jerusalem. One theme speaks of an eschatological day when all the nations will come upon Jerusalem in attack. This attack, however, will be foiled. (See 2 Samuel 5:6-7 on the pre-Israelite notion of the invulnerability of Zion. The Zion Psalms— 46, 48, 76—pick up this tone of invincibility.) This theme lives among us today in the form of Luther's hymn penned to Psalm 46: "A Mighty Fortress is Our God."

The second eschatological theme of the late Persian period is of a day when the nations will make a peaceful pilgrimage to Jerusalem. Whereas the first theme deals with war and the judgment on the nations, the second theme speaks of a time of peace and salvation for the nations. This theme is found in Isaiah 49:14-21,

Haggai 2:1-9, Zechariah 14:8-19, and in this week's text from Isaiah 60. What a stretch it must have been for returned exiles to imagine such glory for the future of their holy city! All the nations will come. They will bring their wealth. They will worship Yahweh. These stories can certainly be put together for preaching on the day of Epiphany. The story of the Magi come to Jerusalem with gifts and obeisance is the story of *light to the Gentiles.* This is what Epiphany is all about!

We haven't mentioned the one other prophet of the late Persian period: Jonah. The story of Jonah is also a story of light to the Gentiles.

Homiletical Directions

There are a myriad of possibilities for narrative connections with this week's Gospel text. Though it is not a strong Epiphany theme, the "Son of David" theme offers narrative possibilities. We might begin with some Bethlehem stories that link David to this place. Secondly, we would need to tell the story of the promise made to David by God through Nathan as told in 2 Samuel 7. David from Bethlehem is the Anointed (Messiah) of God to whom the great promise of an everlasting monarchy is proffered. This is the fundamental promissory text in the entire Old Testament. We're dealing with vital stuff here. Thirdly, the genealogy from Matthew 1 can be presented as Matthew's way of tying Jesus to David. In Chapter 1 we indicated that this genealogy would have generated great excitement in the ancient oral world where identity was a gift of genealogy. Discover a creative and exciting way to tell this genealogy. Finally, we come to today's text where the Magi come to *Bethlehem* guided by the star and helped along by Herod's counselors.

The Jesus that is revealed through this series of stories is Jesus as Son of David. A closing proclamation might begin with Jesus saying: "I am the Son of David. David and I are both Bethlehem boys. God promised to David and fulfills in me the promise of an everlasting kingdom. I bring this kingdom to the world. I bring this kingdom to you. My kingdom is the fulfillment of all worldly dreams of kingdoms. Walk with me and we will walk forever in God's promised and eternal kingdom." Amen.

A second narrative possibility would be to deal with the Magi. Tell their story, starting in Persia, with some real imagination. Some of the above comments can be included in your telling of the story. Let's think in terms of telling only this story on this Epiphany day. The key to the conclusion of the story and the key to any proclamation based upon it is the notion that God's kingdom is wide open to the Gentiles. The best of their culture leads them to Bethlehem. (This has many interesting implications for our work of evangelism and mission today.) It's written in the stars. Forget the astrologers ancient *and* modern! Here is the star that counts, and this star leads to a boy in diapers. See the stars. See the child. It's all OPEN TO THE PUBLIC. Make use of the above material contrasting this Christian posture of public disclosure to cultic and gnostic forms of secrecy. It's a great Epiphany story! The whole world is invited!

A third narrative possibility would be to tell the story of Herod and Pilate as the political rulers who are the bookends of Jesus' ministry. First, tell the story of Herod. Second, tell the story of Pilate. See the text above for guiding verses. Turn then to the story of Jesus and his declaration that he is King. The Magi come to worship him who was born king of the Jews (2:2). Jesus lives out his kingship between two great political powers. It seems that you just can't keep the Bible out of politics.

A closing proclamation to these political stories might go something like this: "I am God's true and only king. You can't trust Herod. You can't trust Pilate. You can't trust any earthly ruler in matters that are ultimate. You can trust me. I rule as your servant. I am a servant king who will walk with you through life. I am a servant king who will walk with you through death. I am a servant king who will walk with you into the dawn of an everlasting kingdom." Amen.

A final narrative possibility for this Magi text is to take a quick walk through the prophets of the later Persian period who looked for that eschatological day when the peoples of all the nations will come to Jerusalem to pay homage and give obeisance to Yahweh. (See texts in the above material.) Matthew knows these old texts. He sculpts the Magi as the fulfillment of prophecies that portray God's day of fulfillment as the day when the Gentiles, in the persons of the Magi, come to Jerusalem and to Bethlehem to pay homage and do obeisance to the child who is truly a light to the nations; a light to the Gentiles.

A closing proclamation might hear Jesus say: "I am the light of the world. I am the light to the Gentiles. I am the light to all the world's nations. All peoples shall come to me. The Magi are the sign. The Magi are the invitation. Today I invite you to come and worship. I invite you to come to me with your gifts. I invite you to let your light be kindled by my light that together we might be truly a light to the nations." Amen.

----

1. Jack Dean Kingsbury, *Matthew As Story* (Philadelphia: Fortress Press, 1988), p. 48.

2. *Ibid.*, pp. 48-49.

3. Mark Alan Powell, *God With Us* (Minneapolis: Fortress Press, 1995), pp. 33, 42, 57.

Matthew 2:13-23

The Matthean text assigned for the First Sunday after Christmas is very difficult to dislodge from its larger context in Matthew. Richard Edwards, for example, refers to the whole of Matthew 1:17—2:23 as the "Infancy Gospel." In this "Infancy Gospel" Matthew has

> *established major elements of the framework of the story. Its*
> *primary purpose was to verify the reliability of the narrator*
> *who reports to the reader that these events are in full accord*
> *with God's intentions. With a minimum of dialogue and with*
> *a liberal use of OT quotations, pinpointing the correlation*
> *between the OT and these narrated events, the reader is now*
> *ready to view Jesus from the "proper" perspective. There*
> *can be no doubt about the authority of the narrator, nor can*
> *there be any doubt about the Messianic nature of Jesus.*[1]

One can seriously consider, therefore, treating this so-called "Infancy Gospel" as a whole for preaching. Robert Smith proposes another way of reading the unity in 1:17—2:23. We'll come to that at the end of these remarks.

Matthew 2 continues to be dominated by *places*: Egypt, Bethlehem, Galilee, Nazareth. It is also time to pay some attention to the role that *dreams* play in the telling of Matthew's story. In today's story it is a dream that sends Joseph with his family to Egypt (2:13); a dream that is the signal for their return (2:19); and a dream that guides them to Galilee (2:22). It was a dream that saved Joseph's marriage (1:20) and a dream that guided the Magi to return to their distant land without reporting in to King Herod (2:11). The only other reference to a dream in Matthew is the dream of the wife of Pilate that Jesus was a righteous man (27:19). As readers we are constantly alerted that there is more to this story than appears on the surface. In the ancient world dreams were a recognized manner for the divine to communicate with humans. Very clearly, God is in charge of this story. The dreams tell us so.

Because of Herod's wrath and warned in a dream, Joseph takes his little family off to Egypt. The family is no longer safe. The Prince of *Peace* has been born and *war* has broken out! On Herod's orders baby boys are being killed in and around Bethlehem. So Jesus is bundled off to Egypt. Ancient readers would have immediately sensed the narrative analogies at work here. All of Israel was once in Egypt. Moses led the people out of Egypt. The story of Moses comes into our mind's eye here as a story with many links to the Jesus story. "The echoes of the story of Moses and the exodus ally Jesus with God's liberating will, placing him in continuity with God's previous actions of liberation on behalf of God's people and in association with such significant figures as Moses."[2]

We remember that the majority of scholars hold that Matthew's purpose was to identify the Christian community as the true heir of God's promises to Israel. This early identification of Jesus with Moses and the Israelite ancestors who had sojourned in Egypt would thus be Matthew's way of telling us of the meaning of Jesus by yoking the Jesus story to the story of the ancestors and Moses. That's how narrative analogy works!

Matthew sees the trek to Egypt as the fulfillment of prophecy. "Out of Egypt have I called my son." Matthew quotes this word from the prophet Hosea (11:1). Scholars see this as the first mention in Matthew's Gospel that Jesus is the Son of God. This reality is certainly implied in Matthew 1:18 where we hear that Mary is pregnant by the Holy Spirit. (The Son of God theme is dealt with in Chapter 5 of this work.)

We note that this part of Matthew's story is marked in almost every paragraph by a quotation from one of the prophets. See 2:15, 17, 23. There seems to be no independent evidence that Jesus went down to Egypt's land. It is mentioned in no other Gospel. Matthew anchors the Egyptian diversion, therefore, in the word of God.

The reference to prophecy in 2:17 is to Jeremiah 31:15. Rachel is weeping for her children. The media images of women weeping for their lost children all over the world today ought to flood our minds at this reference to a mother's tears. The tears of all of these women, past and present, is a bitter reminder to us that we live in a fallen world. Where does hope lie? Open your Bible to the Jeremiah text and keep reading! "Thus says the Lord: Keep your voice from weeping and your eyes from tears; for there is reward for your work, says the Lord: they shall come back from the land of the enemy; there is hope for your future, says the Lord: your children shall come back to their own country" (Jeremiah 31:16-17).

Rachel's tears are not the end of the story. God is in control here. This entire story in Matthew 1-2 looks on the outside as if it is driven only by human madness. On the inside, however, it is clear that this story is fully in God's hands. Rachel and her tears of sorrow are not the only reality in the story. Mary and her tears of joy are also part of the larger narrative. And Mary's son, Jesus, is set against the woeful wickedness of this world as the One who will ultimately wipe the tears from Rachel's eyes.

Reference has been made to Robert Smith's interesting reading of this narrative. Sometimes the chapter and verse headings simply put blinders on our eyes so that we miss the larger shape of the story.

Matthew has neatly plotted the material in 1:19—2:23 so that five successive scenes feature alternately Joseph and then Herod.... Joseph and Herod respond in exactly opposite fashion to divine revelation and to the child Jesus. The advent of Jesus is God's direct and potent eruption into human history, and that intervention provokes two totally different reactions, as the thoughts and deeds of Herod and Joseph vividly reveal.[3]

Homiletical Directions

A number of possibilities for biblical storytelling preaching present themselves to us in this text for the First Sunday after Christmas. One could tell the parallel stories of Israel's ancestors and Moses in Egypt and Jesus' sojourn into Egypt. To this day the people of Israel celebrate the deliverance from Egypt as their central event. God liberated them from bondage. For Christians, Jesus is the central event. Jesus, too, has come out of Egypt, like Moses, to bring liberation to God's people.

A second preaching possibility is to deal with the "Infancy Gospel" as a whole. Tell this story once from the perspective of all things gone awry. Herod will be the center of this story. This *outer* story is a story under the power of sin and rebellion.

Tell the story a second time from its *inner* side. The focus this time is on the way God moves this story forward for God's own purposes. The dreams are a big part of this inner story. The second telling of the story should be told from the perspective of God's child born in the midst of a world gone mad. It is precisely this child who will wipe the tears from Rachel's eyes and from our eyes as well. There is hope for us who live in a sinful world in this narrative that presents God as the inner mover of history's story. We mustn't let the tears in our eyes blind us to the hope of history whose birth we have just celebrated.

A third preaching possibility is to follow Robert Smith's suggestion and tell the interweaving stories of Joseph and Herod. The Joseph stories are told in 1:18-25; 2:13-15; and 2:19-23. The Herod stories are in 2:1-11 and 2:16-18. One of the very first things we learn about Joseph is that he is a righteous man. See 1:19. Righteousness may be the key theme in this Gospel. (See the discussion of righteousness in Matthew in Chapter 5.) We might just note here that Jesus' first words in this Gospel are spoken on the occasion of his baptism by John the Baptist. Jesus said: "Let it be so now [that is, that you baptize me]; for it is proper for us in this way to fulfill all righteousness" (Matthew 3:16). Righteousness is at the heart of Jesus' mission to the world. Jesus came to make sinners righteous: 9:13.

Jesus came to make us righteous. What would that look like? Well, look at Joseph the "righteous one." Matthew "...loves stories which connect divine epiphany and human obedience. The story of Joseph is the first picture of discipleship that Matthew offers in his Gospel."[4] The righteousness of Joseph consists of his dreams and his obedience. This is clear in the first story centered in Joseph: 1:18-25. When he awoke from his dreaming he did as the angel of the Lord commanded him. In the second Joseph story (2:13-15) he once again hears, obeys, and acts. In 2:19-23 he dreams for the third time. God is revealing divine plans to Joseph! Joseph once again hears the word of God, obeys this word, and acts upon it. Such is Matthew's picture of a righteous one.

Matthew also gives us a portrait of an unrighteous man. Herod is his model of unfaith and unrighteousness. In 2:1-11 Herod is troubled immediately at the prospect of one being born "King of the Jews." See the list of Herod's negative characteristics in Chapter 2. We quoted there from Jack Kingsbury who lists as Herod's qualities: spiritual blindness, fearfulness, conspiratorial scheming, guile, mendacity, wrath, and anxiety about the future. Tell the two Herod stories focusing in on these characteristics. They are the hallmarks of an unrighteous man.

This sermon would follow the structure of the "Infancy Gospel." Tell the story first of Joseph, then Herod, then Joseph, then Herod, then Joseph just in the order that Matthew puts them. Tell the story in such a way that your hearers see clearly that there are these two responses to the Christ child. The question that the interwoven stories ultimately raise is the question of our response. We have just celebrated the birth of the Christ child in our time. How shall we respond? Do we follow the model of Joseph or the model of Herod?

Let the sermon close on an open-ended note. Whose model will you follow? It comes down to Joseph or Herod. This sermon can simply end with a challenge to believe. In his catechism Luther writes: "I believe that I cannot by my own reason or strength believe in the Lord Jesus Christ or come to him. But the Holy Spirit calls me through the gospel." Following Luther's lead, do not leave people to their own inner resources to choose to follow Jesus. If we had such inner resources we wouldn't need a Savior at all! Our inner resources are sinful resources! So, invoke the Spirit, invite God's participation with us in our decision making. Close with a hymn that calls upon God to empower our decisions of faith.

---

1. Richard A. Edwards, *Matthew's Story of Jesus* (Philadelphia: Fortress Press, 1985), p. 15.

2. Warren Carter, *Matthew: Storyteller, Interpreter, Evangelist* (Peabody, MA: Hendrickson Publishers, Inc., 1996), p. 16.

3. Robert H. Smith, *Matthew: Augsburg Commentary on the New Testament* (Minneapolis: Augsburg Press, 1989), pp. 35, 38-39.

4. *Ibid.*, p. 38.

Matthew 3:1-12

Enter John the Baptist. Matthew doesn't introduce this desert prophet until now. John's message is simple and straight to the point. "Repent!" he cries. "Repent, for the kingdom of heaven has come near." Jesus will begin his ministry with the very same words. See 4:17. When Jesus sends out the twelve for their ministry among the Gentiles he describes their ministry in similar words: "As you go, proclaim the good news, 'The kingdom of heaven has come near' " (10:7). In Matthew's telling of the story this call to repentance and the advent of the kingdom of heaven are central realities.

We might note here that the phrase "kingdom of heaven" is unique to Matthew. It occurs 33 times in Matthew and nowhere else in the entire New Testament. *Kingdom of heaven* means the same as "kingdom of God" (four times in Matthew, at 12:28; 19:24; 21:31, 43). It is a pious phrase designated to avoid speaking the awesome and holy name of "God" (cf. 6:9). Note also "thy kingdom" (6:10, 13; 20:21), "the kingdom of their [my] Father" (13:43; 26:29), and the simple "kingdom" (6:33; 25:34).

> *Among New Testament writers Matthew alone has "the gospel [or word] of the kingdom...and the phrase "sons [=citizens] of the kingdom" (8:12; 13:38; cf. 17:25). All these phrases (kingdom of heaven, kingdom of God, kingdom of their (or my) Father, or simply the kingdom) are very nearly interchangeable.... [This] is not to assert that it has its source in heaven or in God, but that it comes as gift from above, and that it is something wholly different from earthly kingdoms and sovereignties. ...more than any other New Testament writer, Matthew stresses the vital connection between the kingdom and righteousness (cf. 6:10, 33).*[1]

Matthew understands John to be the one who carries out the role spoken of by Isaiah the prophet. John will prepare the way. He will make the way straight for the coming of the Messiah. This ministry is based on Isaiah 40:1-11. John's appearance and diet are also attested in such a way that the crowds know that this man is a prophet. He dresses just like Elijah: 1 Kings 1:8. He fulfills the prophecy of Zechariah: Zechariah 13:4. (See also Malachi 4:5-6.) He calls Israel again to the wilderness, the place of their spiritual origin.

In every way, John is the *forerunner* of Jesus! His ministry and message foreshadows the ministry of Jesus. Both John and Jesus are the agents of God sent by God (10:40; 11:10). Both belong to the time of fulfillment (1:23; 3:3). Both have the same message to proclaim (3:2; 4:17). Both enter into conflict with Israel: in the case of the crowds, a favorable reception ultimately gives way to repudiation; in the case of the leaders, the opposition is implacable from the outset (3:7-10; 9:3). Both John and Jesus are "delivered up" to their enemies (4:12; 10:4). And both are made to die violently and shamefully (14:3-12; 27:37). To know of John is to know in advance of Jesus.[2]

Matthew paints this picture of John as forerunner based on 20/20 hindsight. John the Baptist didn't necessarily know this script! There is much evidence that John's visions of a Messiah were much different than that which Jesus presented. In Matthew 11:2-6 an imprisoned John sends his disciples to Jesus in order to ask him: "Are you the one who is to come, or are we to wait for another?" This is the question of the ages in Israel. Every generation of Israel addressed this question to each new king. Every generation of Israel looked forward to the day when the one to whom this question was addressed might answer: Yes!

Jesus' answer was, Yes! "Go and tell John what you hear and see: the blind receive their sight, the lame walk, the lepers are cleansed, the deaf hear and the poor have good news brought to them. And blessed is anyone who takes no offense at me" (11:4-6). Clearly John did not know that this was the kind of ministry that he was forerunning! People in every age have been *offended* when they discover the reality of Jesus' ministry.

Matthew 11 is important in terms of the relationship of John and Jesus. Jesus gives a speech identifying the ministry of John. John is the greatest one who ever lived before the time of the coming of the kingdom. But John is the least in the kingdom of heaven. John belongs to the age of the law and the prophets. Jesus belongs to the age of the gospel and the kingdom. See 11:7-19. John's ministry is a ministry carried out at the very turning of the eons! It is a ministry featuring a call to repentance; a call to make ourselves ready and fit for the new reality that is to come.

Again, the focus of John's message is his call to *repentance*. Even religious leaders need to repent! Pharisees and Sadducees need to repent. John calls upon them to live lives that bear the fruits of repentance. He was clearly not convinced that they practiced what they preached. They relied too easily on their tradition. They were the children of Abraham after all! How could John be so impertinent as to ask them to repent?

Robert Smith usually interprets remarks such as these addressed to Jewish religious leaders to be a kind of code for an attack on the Christian religious leaders of Matthew's day. (See Preface.)

> *Members of Matthew's community may have been finding their security before God in the ceremony of baptism and in spiritual endowments. They may have somehow disconnected baptism from any thought of the deadly power of sin, from the solemn call to repentance, and from the summons to the new life of righteousness.... Matthew's report concerning John the Baptist amounts to a plea to his own community to rethink and reorder their lives.*[3]

Whether or not Smith is correct in his interpretation it is much more important that the focus of any repentance-preaching we do on the basis of this text be directed at problems within the Christian community rather than at the Sadducees and Pharisees of old. We can too easily and self-righteously judge the religious leaders of old all the time missing the reality that John would call *us* to repentance. So would Jesus!

We indicated above that John did not totally grasp the nature of Jesus' ministry. John did, however, realize that the baptism that would come in Jesus' name would be quite different from his own baptizing: "...one who is more powerful than I is coming after me.... He will baptize you with the Holy Spirit and fire" (3:11).

This message of John is vital to our preaching of repentance today. John calls for repentance that bears fruit. Fruit, however, does not grow on demand. Fruit grows only on healthy trees. This is a constant theme in Matthew: 7:16-20; 12:33; 13:8; 21:19, 34, 41, 43. Israel was not bearing the fruits of repentance. It may well be that Matthew's community wasn't, either. So what's the solution to such a problem? You can't command the fruits of repentance. Fruit grows from a good tree. It would appear that John the Baptist knew this and that is why he is pleased to announce that one mightier "than I" is coming. Bearing fruit is not the real problem. Healthy trees is the problem. Only one mightier than John can nurture healthy trees (healthy lives) that bear much fruit. Fruit-bearing is the work of the Spirit, not a work demanded through any kind of repentance.

Homiletical Directions

This text from Matthew has many narrative connections with material in both the Old and New Testament. Our biblical storytelling on this day could strike out in many directions.

A first suggestion for preaching is for a didactic sermon based on this text. The "kingdom of heaven" is so important to Matthew's Gospel that it might be wise here at the beginning of Matthew's year to teach our people what Matthew means by this phrase. The Smith quotation in the text above supplies you with the relevant biblical references for such a time of teaching. In this Advent season we will want to tie such a sermon to the coming of the kingdom of heaven in the person of Jesus Christ. Remember as well Smith's accent that for Matthew the kingdom and righteousness are nearly inseparable themes. Fortunately, the One whose birth we are preparing to celebrate not only brings the kingdom but also comes as *our righteousness!* As Luther once put it, our righteousness in Jesus Christ is always alien to us. It always comes to us from the outside. It comes to us as the gift of a baby wrapped in diapers.

A second and more narrative preaching possibility presents itself in the parallelism of the ministry of John and the ministry of Jesus. The Kingsbury quote in the material above provides us with all the relevant passages we need for this narrative sermon. Tell the story of John the *forerunner* as the precursor of Jesus' ministry. We have two choices here. We can either tell John's story first, following the Kingsbury outline, and then tell Jesus' story second as its parallel, or we can tell John's story, Part One, followed by Jesus' story, Part One, and so on. Either way, we have before us a story of conflict, repudiation, opposition, delivering up, and violent and shameful deaths.

God is revealed in our world through the ministry of John and Jesus. We are confronted here with a God who is revealed to us in hiding! The lives and destinies of John and Jesus don't look much like God's way in the world. They do, however, look a lot like our way in the world. That is just the point. God identifies with us all the way from cradle (Jesus' cradle and ours) to grave.

"I am a God whose presence in this world is hidden in the life of John the Baptist. I am a God whose presence in this world is hidden in the life of Jesus Christ. I am a God whose presence in this world is hidden in the trials and struggles of your life. On the last day all the world will see that which is hidden now revealed as my way with the world; as my way with you." Amen.

A third preaching possibility deals with the overriding theme of repentance. Repentance, of course, is a strong Advent theme. The first story to tell is the story of John's preaching and baptizing. The heart of John's message is, "Repent, for the kingdom of heaven has come near." John baptized people as a sign of their repentance. John expected that such an action would result in a fruit-bearing life. (The baptism called for by John is a pre-Christian baptism empowered by the will of the repentant one to change his/her life course.) John was calling upon Israel to repent in the advent of the Messiah.

The second story would be the story of the beginning of Jesus' ministry. This ministry begins in Matthew 4:12-23. (This text is appointed for the Third Sunday after the Epiphany.) The key to this brief story telling is to see that the first words of ministry from the mouth of Jesus are identical to the words in the mouth of John:

55

"Repent, for the kingdom of heaven has come near" (4:17). If John's repentance-word was addressed to Israel of old, Jesus' repentance-word is addressed to us.

A third story might be to tell of the relationship between John and Jesus. Jesus himself reflects on this relationship in Matthew 11:7-19. (Only the first four verses of this passage occur in this year's lectionary cycle: Third Sunday in Advent) Tell this story explicating how Jesus sees John as both greatest and least. Reflect then to this week's text where John himself has a vision of this difference: "...one who is more powerful than I is coming after me...." John preached a message of human empowered repentance. Even John seems to know, however, that such repentance is not enough. Repentance needs a more powerful One, a mightier One, a stronger One to turn human striving into divine possibility!

This sermon might well end with an Advent call to repentance in light of the coming celebration of Messiah's birth. Be very clear, however, that this is not a call to a human-powered repentance. This is to be a repentance in which the human self dies to all human will power and turns to a more powerful One, turns to Jesus as the true source of nourishment who can enable the trees of our lives to bear fruit in abundance.

"Repent," Jesus says. "Bring your barren lives to me. Bring your withered limbs to me. I am the more powerful One of whom John spoke. I am the mighty One. I am the strong One. Come to me and I will transform your life from the inside out. I will make the withered tree of your life strong and productive. I will turn your barren lives into fruit-bearing lives." Amen.

If your congregation celebrates Holy Communion on this Sunday the aforesaid words could be transformed into an invitation to the table.

---

1. Robert H. Smith, *Matthew, Augsburg Commentary on the New Testament* (Minneapolis: Augsburg Press, 1989), p. 48.

2. Jack Dean Kingsbury, *Matthew As Story* (Philadelphia: Fortress Press, 1988), p. 49.

3. Smith, *op. cit.*, pp. 46-47.

Chapter 5
Baptism Of The Lord; Epiphany 1

Matthew 3:13-17

This week's assigned Gospel story is a continuation of the story assigned for the Second Sunday in Advent. (See Chapter 4.) A single story has been broken into two parts and divided in our attention by several weeks. One thing our sermon for this week needs to do is to put this story back together again.

Jack Kingsbury speaks of the importance of this passage in the schema of Matthew's story:

> *The crown of the first part of Matthew's story, which treats of Jesus' identity (1:1–4:16), is the baptismal scene. Here God, himself participating as "actor" in the story, empowers Jesus for messianic ministry and solemnly declares "who Jesus is."*[1]

Chapter 3 of Matthew introduces John and his ministry of repentance and baptism. John knows that his baptizing points towards an eschatological event. A mightier One is coming. This coming One will baptize with the Holy Spirit and with fire. Then— that's Matthew's word—Jesus appears at the river Jordan and presents himself for baptism. John protests. "I should be baptized by you," he says to Jesus. Jesus will not be deterred. "Let it be so now; for it is proper for us in this way to fulfill all righteousness." These are the first words spoken by Jesus in Matthew's telling of the story. First words are crucial words. Jesus will fulfill all righteousness!

> *Here at the beginning, in his initial utterance, Jesus points to the very core of all his commands, all his disclosures, all his teachings: righteousness. With a few quick strokes of the pen Matthew has hammered out a solid connection between righteousness and baptism, between being the sons and*

daughters of God and doing the will of God.... Matthew carefully defines baptism as the first step on the way of righteousness.[2]

In his work Robert Smith defines righteousness as making the world "all right." Sinners and the world are made "all right" with God. Joseph Sittler often told the story of a time he was in Jerusalem and his car broke down. He took it to a mechanic to have it fixed. When the mechanic had finished and started up the engine to hear it running perfectly he said, "Zadik." *Zadik* is the Hebrew word translated as righteousness. In this context it means simply: "it works." Sinners and the world are made to "work" in and through the ministry of the One who fulfills all righteousness.

Righteousness is a fundamental theme in Matthew's Gospel. References to this reality are 5:6, 20; 6:1 ("piety" is used here to translate the Greek *dikaosune*), 6:33; 9:10-13; 13:36-43, 47-50; 25:31-46; 27:19, 24. We will suggest below the possibility of putting these passages together in a narrative sermon.

John baptized Jesus. Righteousness was fulfilled. The world was "all right" again. And the Spirit of God descended upon Jesus in the form of a dove. Smith notes that John the Baptist had it wrong about Jesus as the one who "will baptize you with the Holy Spirit and fire" (3:11). There is no mention of fire in Jesus' baptism. Only the Spirit. John didn't get it quite right about the more powerful One who was coming after him. None of the prophets got it just right. We know that because we know the One towards whom they could only point in inspired utterance. Gerhard von Rad once said, "We know the prophets better than the prophets understood themselves."

The Spirit of God does point to Jesus as God's special agent. It was through the Spirit that this One was conceived (1:18). It is through the Spirit that he is now empowered in his messianic ministry. Jesus is the bearer of the Spirit, the very life of God.

The Spirit language strains to say what the next verse (3:17) clearly says: Jesus is the Son of God. "This is my Son, the Beloved, with whom I am well pleased." (Old Testament passages that come to mind with these words of God are Genesis 22:2, Psalm 2:7, and Isaiah 42:1.) God speaks. This passage is clearly determinative for Matthew of Jesus' identity. Jesus is Son of God.

58

God's designation for Jesus ("my Son") both overlaps in meaning the other designations we have encountered thus far ("Messiah" ["Coming One"], "Son of Abraham, "Son of David," and "King of the Jews") and transcends them.... The passage 3:17 is the first place where this truth, uttered by God as "actor," assumes the form of an event that occurs within the story itself... By the same token, God's designation of Jesus as "my Son" also transcends these other designations in meaning. It does so because Matthew imbues it with a quality the others do not possess in like measure. This quality is that it attests to the unique filial relationship that exists between God and Jesus: Jesus is conceived by God's Spirit (1:18, 20) and empowered by God's Spirit (3:16) so that he is Emmanuel, or "God with us" (1:23); as such, he is the one in whom God reveals himself to humankind (11:27) and who is God's supreme agent of salvation.[3]

Kingsbury goes on to say that prior to this time Matthew has made many allusions to the fact that Jesus is the Son of God. See 1:16; 1:18-25 (v. 23); 2:7-23 (Jesus is referred to as "the child" not Mary's child); 2:15, and 3:11, 16. The climax of this series of oblique references to Jesus as Son of God is the voice of God speaking as the actor in the baptismal scene. "This is my Son, the Beloved, with whom I am well pleased."

If Matthew is intent on revealing to us what has been revealed to him, that Jesus is the Son of God, we would expect to find other references to Jesus' filial relationship with God throughout the Gospel story. Some of these references are 8:28-34 (v. 29); 14:28-33; 16:13-20 (Peter's confession); 17:1-8 (Transfiguration); 26:57-68 (v. 63, see also 27:40, trial); 27:45-54 (crucifixion; centurion's confession!); 28:16-20 (Great Commission, baptismal formula).

Homiletical Directions

There are two strong themes from this week's Gospel text that are woven throughout Matthew's work. The first theme we shall look at in preparation for preaching is the theme of *righteousness*.

You may wish to use one of the possibilities suggested above as a down-to-earth translation of the meaning of righteousness: "all right," "it works."

Story One in a sermon dealing with righteousness should begin with the assigned text. Tell the story of Jesus' baptism with the focus on Jesus' claim that he has come to "fulfill all righteousness"; he has come to make everything "all right."

Story Two might be the story of Jesus eating with tax collectors and sinners in 9:10-13. (This text is appointed for the Third Sunday in Pentecost.) This story concludes with Jesus' proclamation that he did not come for the righteous but for sinners. Jesus came, that is, *to make sinners righteous.* Jesus came to make it "all right" between us and God.

Story Three could be the parables of Jesus in Matthew 13 that speak of the final judgment on evildoers and the righteous shining like the sun in God's kingdom. These parables are told in Matthew 13:36-43 and 13:47-50.

Story Four, the final story, ought to be Matthew 25:31-46. This story is appointed for Christ the King Sunday, but it is worth telling on far more than one occasion in the Matthew year! Like the parables in Matthew 13, Matthew 25 is concerned with the last judgment. The righteous receive the kingdom of God prepared for them from the beginning of the world. They receive the kingdom because of their good deeds. They have seen Jesus hungry, thirsty, a stranger, naked, sick and in prison, and they have come to his aid.

The story then takes an incredible turn. The righteous are stunned. They know nothing of their righteousness. "When did we do this for you?" they ask the judging king. A key reality of the righteous is revealed here. *The righteous are totally unaware of their own righteousness.* It is hidden from their own eyes! This is much like the message of Matthew 6:1-6 where we are instructed that our piety (i.e. righteousness) is to be kept in secret. Hidden righteousness. Luther: alien righteousness. That's the righteousness that Christ clothes us with when he makes righteous people out of sinners.

A closing proclamation for this sermon might go like this: "I came to make sinners righteousness. I will judge you one day for

60

your righteousness. But fear not. I am the righteousness of God at work within you. I started this work in your baptism. My work was hidden there. It remains hidden. I am the source of your hidden righteousness which one day will be exposed and shine like the sun." Amen.

The second theme in today's text that presents us with many homiletical possibilities is the theme of Son of God. This theme goes well with a Sunday appointed for The Baptism of Our Lord. If there is time, we might begin a narrative sermon on the Son of God theme by walking through the many allusions to this reality in the Gospel of Matthew leading up to this climaxing revelation in 3:17. These allusions are given in the material above.

Moving forward through Matthew, the story in 8:28-34 might be told. It is not assigned in the lectionary for this year. In this story demoniacs acknowledge Jesus as "Son of God." The powers and principalities of this world are on guard. Jesus comes as Son of God to free us from these powers.

There are at least three more stories that a sermon on "Son of God" ought at least allude to even though they do appear later in the lectionary. They are the story of the disciples' first acknowledgment that Jesus is Son of God (14:28-33); the story of Peter's confession (16:13-20); and the Transfiguration story wherein God speaks a second time that Jesus is God's Son (17:1-8).

Having narrated a number of stories with the "Son of God" theme our sermon can conclude in two quite different directions. It might conclude, firstly, in speaking for God by taking God's word to Jesus and addressing it to the congregation. This is, in effect, what happens in baptism as some of our traditions understand it. In and through baptism God speaks to us saying: "You are my son. You are my daughter. I am pleased with you."

A second possible conclusion would be one that focuses more on the confession of Peter and the disciples. We, too, are called to confess that Jesus is Son of God. Epiphany has taken place. God has been revealed in Jesus. Now we are invited to make confession that Jesus is Son of God. A closing plea to the Spirit might go something like this: "May the Spirit of God prompt you to say this day: I believe in Jesus Christ, the Son of God. I believe your

61

ministry is Spirit-empowered. I believe you have come to fulfill all righteousness. I believe you have come to make sinners, like me, righteous."

---

1. Jack Dean Kingsbury, *Matthew As Story* (Philadelphia: Fortress Press, 1988), p. 51.

2. Robert H. Smith, *Matthew: Augsburg Commentary on the New Testament* (Minneapolis: Augsburg Press, 1989), pp. 55, 57.

3. Kingsbury, *op. cit.*, p. 53.

Matthew 4:1-11

The Gospel text appointed for this week has allusions to many, many stories throughout the Bible. We will not be able to do justice to them all. The Spirit who has just alighted on Jesus in the baptismal scene now leads Jesus into the wilderness to be tempted by the devil for *forty* days and *forty* nights. The wilderness, of course, was the arena of temptation of Israel of old. Even the numbers match up: Israel was in the wilderness for forty years. Moses is also attested to have spent forty days and forty nights being tested by God: Deuteronomy 9:6-12, Exodus 34:27-28. The testing of Moses is a test on Mount Sinai as he receives the Ten Commandments. Elijah, too, spent forty days on a mountain, Mount Horeb, prior to God's revelation to him in a still small voice: 1 Kings 19:9-18.

Jesus' wilderness adventure narrates the first major conflict for Jesus as Matthew tells the story. Conflict will be a major theme of this Gospel. The first conflict is with the devil. The first conflict is with those powers of death that oppose the power of life. Two kingdoms, two spheres of power, engage in cosmic battle. See also 13:36-43.

> *On the one hand, there is the Kingdom of Heaven, which has by God's design become a present, though hidden, reality in Jesus son of God.... On the other hand, there is the kingdom of Satan (12:26). In this sphere of power Satan himself rules, and he has at his command both angels (25:41) and demons (10:8, 12:24), or unclean spirits (10:1). In both Israel and the world, Satan is at work to bring humans under his control (13:24-30, 38-39). The mark of those who serve him is that they are evil (13:49) and lawless (13:41), for they live contrary to the will of God. By withstanding the testing of Satan following his baptism, Jesus Son of God demonstrates that he is stronger than Satan.*[1]

This first conflict, of course, is the granddaddy of all conflict in Matthew's story. Kingsbury goes on to point out that the religious leaders of Jesus' day act very much like the devil acts in this temptation story. The religious leaders also put Jesus to the test. They are portrayed as evil and as the enemies of Jesus bent on destroying him. (See 12:14; 13:25, 39; 16:1; 26:3-4.)

The temptation of the devil centers in that wondrously little and inventive word that the devil just loves: IF. "*If* you are the Son of God, command these stones to become loaves of bread." This temptation is a direct challenge to Jesus' baptism. God had declared to Jesus in the baptismal event, "You are my son." The devil tests Jesus just here. "*If*...you are the son of God." Two of the devil's three temptations come at just this point. IF! The devil challenges Jesus. Does your heart, soul, mind, and strength really belong to God? These are the words of the Shema: Deuteronomy 6:4-9. This is what is at stake in each of the devil's temptations. "Do you love God above and beyond everything else? If so, then I have a little test for you."

Jesus answers each temptation with a Scripture quotation from the verses which follow upon the Shema in the Old Testament book of Deuteronomy: "...one does not live by bread alone, but by every word that comes from the mouth of the Lord" (Deuteronomy 8:3). "Do not put the Lord your God to the test" (Deuteronomy 6:16). "The Lord your God you shall fear; him you shall serve, and by his name alone you shall swear" (Deuteronomy 6:13).

Robert Smith proposes an interesting theory to explain these three temptations. Roman rule, he proposes, was marked by three realities: (1) providing bread and circuses; (2) displaying the power of their *legions*; (3) demanding worship of "Caesar is Lord."[2] The temptation of the devil is that Jesus demonstrate that his "messianic" power equals the power of Rome. He can produce bread. He has legions of angels at his beck and call. He, too, will worship at the world's altar of power. "IF!" says the devil. "NO!" says Jesus. Jesus won't grasp for the glory and power. He won't grasp at being like God as Eve and Adam did in the garden.

The Old Testament reading for this week tells of the devil's "if" word to our first parents. "IF you eat, you will be like God." Our ancestors in life grasped for that. Jesus did not. He "did not regard equality with God as something to be exploited [grasped]" (Philippians 2:6).

This IF word will come Jesus' way again in the Passion story. "IF you are the Son of God, come down from the cross" (Matthew 27:40). Again, Jesus said, "No!" He was obedient unto death, even death on a cross. And so the author of Colossians can proclaim that through the obedience of the Son the powers of evil are finally destroyed. "He [Jesus] disarmed the rulers and authorities and made a public example of them, triumphing over them in it [the cross]" (Colossians 2:15).

This ultimate victory of Jesus over the powers of darkness and death is foreshadowed in the temptation story. Jesus can finally say, "Begone, Satan." Jesus says this same word to Peter when Peter aligns himself with those who could not understand that Jesus must go to Jerusalem and suffer many things from the religious leaders, and be killed and on the third day be raised (Matthew 16:13-28). Peter did not want a Messiah who would die. The devil did not want a Messiah in hiding. "Show your glory, Jesus." They did not understand that the glory of Jesus is the cross!

> *The temptation narrative reveals the inmost workings of the mind of Jesus. Standing as prologue to the entire ministry, this account declares that Jesus will wield speech and silence, power and weakness, action and passion with total disregard for self and in total harmony with the plain will of God.... Jesus, moved by the Holy Spirit and supported by God's holy angels, will press the attack against Satan and his evil empire, sweeping the world clean of demons (12:22-29). In and through Jesus, God touches the universe to cleanse and restore it, to make it "all right," freeing humanity from lawlessness and empowering lives of wholeness and righteousness (1:21).*[3]

Homiletical Directions

There are far more narrative possibilities for a sermon on Matthew 4:1-11 than we have time or space to investigate. We'll put forward two possibilities and mention others. The first possibility is one that makes use of the Old Testament story for this day. Tell first the story of Eve and Adam. Their call to worship God with heart, soul, mind, and strength is what the verses appointed from Genesis 2:15-17 explicate. Satan had other ideas. "Did God say?" the devil gushes as he engages this primeval pair in theological conversation. The temptation, the test, is put simply. IF. "If you eat of it, you will be like God." The Christian community through the ages has referred to this story as a fundamental way of describing the nature of human sin. Sin is pride. Hubris. Wanting to be like God. Egocentricity. Grasping at divinity. It might be well to draw some lines from this story to our own forms of "grasping for divinity" today. Pride and egocentricity always usher in the age of fallen humanity. They are, in fact, key aspects of life in a fallen world.

Story Two will be the story of the text for the day. Tell it in all its power. Jesus, too, faced the question: IF. Jesus said, "No," where humanity says, "Yes." He is the One "who did not regard equality with God as something to be exploited."

A closing proclamation might go something like this: "I faced the temptation to play God also. I faced the same temptation Eve and Adam faced. I faced the same temptation you face each day. I said, 'No.' I did not count equality with God a thing be grasped. I sent the devil and his empty lies packing. I have the power to send the devil packing. I have the power to enable you to send the devil and all his empty promises packing as well. I accept you just as you are. I accept you as humans. There is no need to play God. I have come to make of you the truly human person that God created you to be." Amen.

A second narrative possibility would be to deal primarily with the role of Jesus as the One who conquers the devil, conquers the powers set against life. This would be a traditional theme to engage on the First Sunday in Lent. Some of the material we have discussed above could be included in this sermon. In this proposal we would stick to the narrative at hand. Tell each of the temptations in as much breadth and depth as you can. After each of the stories we might have Jesus proclaim: "I have pushed back the powers of darkness. I have made room for your life to be human again. I have made things 'all right' with the world."

This sermon might well move next to a reference to the book of Hebrews which talks about Jesus as the One who was tested as we are and who can, therefore, be of help to us when we are tested. See Hebrews 2:14-18 and 4:14-16. Closing reference could be made to the reality of the cross as the ultimate test of Jesus. In the dark of the noon-day night Jesus disarmed the principalities and powers of darkness: Colossians 2:15. "I have pushed back the powers of darkness. I have made room for your life to be human again. I have made things 'all right' with the world." Amen.

These narrative possibilities for preaching don't yet touch upon the typology of the wilderness as Israel's world of failure and Jesus' world of conquest. Ezekiel 20 is the clearest Old Testament description of Israel's failure in the wilderness. Jesus, of course, succeeded where Israel failed.

Nor have we touched upon the men and the mountain and the forty days typology. Moses was tested forty days on the mountain. Elijah was tested forty days on the mountain. Now Jesus is tested for forty days and nights.

Still another narrative analogy would take a look at the way the leaders of the people "tested" Jesus just as the devil did. The passages for this series of events are given in the above material.

---

1. Jack Dean Kingsbury, *Matthew As Story* (Philadelphia: Fortress Press, 1988), p. 56.

2. Robert H. Smith, *Matthew: Augsburg Commentary on the New Testament* (Minneapolis: Augsburg Press, 1989), p. 61.

3. *Ibid.*, p. 67.

Matthew 4:12-23

This week's Matthew text takes us from Part I to Part II in the outline of Matthew that we proposed in the Preface based on Jack Dean Kingsbury's work. Part I includes Matthew 1:1—4:16 and is titled "The Presentation of Jesus." Part II includes Matthew 4:17—16:20 and is titled "The Ministry of Jesus to Israel and Israel's Repudiation of Jesus."

This movement in Matthew's story is clearly indicated in the text. John's ministry is over. He has been "delivered up" just as Jesus will be "delivered up," 17:22. John's ministry foreshadows that of his more famous cousin! (See Chapter 4 on the many parallelisms in the ministries of John and Jesus.) We are in transition in the story from the days of John the Baptist to the days and the ministry of Jesus Christ.

There is also movement in the geography of Jesus' ministry. John is "delivered up" and, as if on cue, Jesus moves from Nazareth to Capernaum in the territory of Zebulun and Naphtali. Jesus will begin his ministry in Galilee of the Gentiles!

> Galilee *was no isolated pocket of purely Jewish settlements. It lay astride international trade routes...and had always been open to Damascus and Syria to the north, Egypt to the south, Phoenicia and the Mediterranean to the northwest and west. Jewish and pagan communities dwelled here, side by side, and precisely here in Galilee, not in Jerusalem, Jesus begins his ministry, silently prefiguring the universality he would later openly proclaim (28:19).*[1]

This is all rather astonishing. Shouldn't the Messiah begin and end his work in Jerusalem? Why Capernaum? Why the land of the Gentiles? Matthew seems to know we're going to ask this question, so he gives us a quotation from the prophet Isaiah showing that Jesus goes to "Galilee of the Gentiles" in fulfillment of Scripture. The Scripture he quotes is from Isaiah 9:1-2. (Isaiah 9:1-4 is the Old Testament reading appointed for this week.) This is a people who sat in darkness as the first of those conquered by Tiglath-Pileser III and reorganized as an Assyrian province. Isaiah sees this people *enlightened* on the day when a child is born, a son given who will assume the role of government and be called Wonderful Counselor, Mighty God, Everlasting Father, Prince of Peace (Isaiah 9:6-7). Matthew, in turn, sees Jesus as fulfilling this exalted role. He will be the *light to the Gentiles*. He will be a beacon in the night precisely for the Gentiles. Jesus' ministry, as Matthew sculpts it, has a bias for the Gentiles. That's where Jesus' ministry begins. That's where Jesus' ministry ends: Matthew 20:16-20. This is the language of mission!

Matthew's introduction is now over. Jesus' public ministry is set to begin. We've had a breathtaking introduction to this son born in Bethlehem. As readers we're ready for his ministry to begin; we're now prepared to hear the Sermon on the Mount. "From that time Jesus began to proclaim, 'Repent, for the kingdom of heaven has come near' " (4:17). The message is the same as that of the Baptist in 3:2. Jesus' ministry has begun!

The closing verse of this week's text refers to the "gospel of the kingdom." See 9:35; 13:19, "word"; 24:14. Kingsbury speaks of the content of the gospel of the kingdom as follows:

> *The focus of the term "gospel" in the phrase "the gospel of the Kingdom" is on God. Still, because Jesus is the one in whom God draws near with his end-time Rule, the term "Kingdom" may properly be said to have a double focus... it is the news...that is revealed in and through Jesus Messiah, the Son of God, and is proclaimed first to Israel and then to the Gentiles to the effect that in him God has drawn near with his end-time Rule to humankind, thus inaugurating the age of salvation.*[2]

Robert Smith puts it this way:

Matthew insists that Jesus in the splendid entirety of his being is the approach of God, the epiphany of God. That is a central affirmation of Matthew's Gospel (1:23; 18:20; 28:20). In Jesus something new is already here.[3]

Jesus' ministry begins with the calling of four of his disciples. "Follow me, and I will make you fish for people." Simon, Andrew, James, and John followed!

Fishing for people meant bringing them to justice by dragging them out of their hiding places and setting them before the judge at the end of the world (cf. 13:47).... (Jesus) sets fishing at the head of (his) ministry as a kind of theme. That means that his words and deeds and sufferings have to do with the final judgment or the teaching of ultimate wisdom.[4]

The verb form translated as *make you* fish for people implies that with Jesus' word of call there comes the power to carry out that call. Those who are called are not left up to their own resources to "follow." Jesus energizes and transforms those whom he calls.

This first act of Jesus' ministry, calling disciples (4:18-22), serves as a bookend for the last act of Jesus' ministry, sending disciples to all the nations (28:16-20). Calling and sending are the alpha and omega of Jesus' public ministry.

Homiletical Directions

A first narrative sermon possibility on this text is a sermon rooted in Galilee and focused on mission. Mission is Epiphany's theme after all! Begin this sermon by narrating the setting of Isaiah 9:1-4. We indicated above that this land was the first to fall to Tiglath-Pileser. This took place sometime between 737-732 B.C.E. How dark it must have seemed to these first of the people to experience life in their own place as life in exile! There is little Old Testament material to use for this story. Perhaps we could create a tale of a family and what it was like for them with the coming of the enemy. The transition from light to darkness is a hard transition, indeed.

Isaiah prophesied to these people of Zebulun and Naphtali that the day of their freedom would come. A light will shine in your darkness, Isaiah proclaimed. It would be well to take the Isaiah text on through vv. 6-7 where we hear about the Son who will be born! Isaiah's words mean there is hope for Zebulun and Naphtali; there is hope for the Gentiles.

Our second story can be the story of Matthew's genealogy where he plants four women—*at least three of whom are Gentiles!*—as a foretaste of the universal salvation that will come forth when "God is with us." (See Chapter 1 for a discussion of the women in the genealogy.) The genealogy means that the light of Christ will shine on all peoples including the Gentiles; including those who sit in darkness.

Thirdly, we can narrate today's text vv. 12-15. Jesus is ready to begin his ministry. To put this in story form we will have to back up a bit and highlight some of the events (birth, baptism, temptation) that lead up to this day. The preparation is over. The Gentiles await. God has a bias toward the Gentiles. God has a bias for the people who dwell in darkness.

Finally, narrate the Great Commission in 28:16-20. Note the location. The eleven disciples went to *Galilee.* They are commissioned to take God's light to the nations. And so are we.

A closing proclamation might go like this. "What God in Jesus Christ is saying to us today through these stories is: 'I am the light of the world! I am the light to Gentiles. I am the light to all who sit in darkness and dwell in the shadow of death. I have a bias for the Gentiles. I have a bias for the lost. I have a bias for you. Let my light be the light of your life.' " Amen. A prayer following a proclamation like this would include the hearer as one of those on whom the light has shined and to whom has been given the commission to spread the light to all nations.

A second narrative sermon possibility can be based on Jesus' call to "*follow me*." Tell the textual story first. Emphasize in the telling that Jesus has the power to *make us* fish for people.

Tell next the story of Jesus' conversation with the scribe and others who wished to follow him: 8:18-22. (This text is not included in the Matthew lectionary year.) Jesus' call brooks no excuses!

Thirdly, tell the story that follows the confession of Peter in 16:24-28. To follow Jesus is to lose one's life and to find one's life.

Finally, tell the story of the Rich Young Ruler: 19:16-30. This story is also omitted from the year of Matthew. It is a story, incredibly, that is about *the impossibility of following.* BUT! with God all things are possible. "I will *make you* fish for people." God can do with us what we cannot do of our own power!

A closing proclamation possibility. Jesus is saying to us today: "Follow me. I will make you fish for people. Follow me. Make no excuses. Follow me. Lose your life that you may find it. Follow me. I know that's impossible for you. The good news is: I can make it possible. I make it possible for you, now, in just this moment of time, to follow me." Amen.

---

1. Robert H. Smith, *Matthew: Augsburg Commentary on the New Testament* (Minneapolis: Augsburg Press, 1989), pp. 68-69.

2. Jack Dean Kingsbury, *Matthew As Story* (Philadelphia: Fortress Press, 1988), p. 62.

3. Smith, *op. cit.*, p. 70.

4. *Ibid.*, p. 72.

Matthew 5:1—7:27

Our outline of Matthew's Gospel presented Matthew 1:1—
4:16 as Part One which introduces Jesus of Nazareth. The genealogy tells us who he is; his birth of the Spirit tells us who he is; the
coming of the Wise Ones portends who he is; his baptism tells us
who he is; and his temptation in the wilderness tells us who he is.

Part Two of our outline of Matthew begins in 4:17: "From that
time Jesus began to proclaim, 'Repent, for the kingdom of heaven
has come near.' " This section of Matthew which we entitled "The
Ministry of Jesus to Israel and Israel's Repudiation of Jesus"
(Kingsbury) opens with the ministry of Jesus. In chapters 5-7 we
hear the heart of Jesus' *teaching*. In chapters 8-9 we witness the
many *deeds* of Jesus' ministry. Matthew presents Jesus Christ to us
as the One who brings in the kingdom in his teaching and preaching.
In the latter part of this section of the Gospel Matthew presents
Israel's response to Jesus' words and deeds. Needless to say, Israel
is not presented as a model of reception for the words and deeds of
the Messiah, Son of God!

The first four chapters in Matthew have built to a climax as they
present to us Jesus Christ. We now know who Jesus is. We're ready
to hear what he has to say. We're ready for his ministry to begin.
And begin it does—with the Sermon on the Mount.

*Matthew carefully has been setting the stage for the center-
piece of his presentation of Jesus: the Sermon on the Mount.
The Sermon on the Mount will be Matthew's first detailed
report on Jesus' public ministry. Matthew permits nothing
to overshadow it or even compete with it. The Sermon on the
Mount sets its stamp on the whole of Matthew's Gospel.
Everything so far has been leading up to it. The entire rest
of the Gospel will flow from it, and the resurrected Jesus will*

underscore its centrality, its primacy, its foundational char-
acter, in his solemn charge to his disciples at the end
(28:19).[1]

The Revised Common Lectionary appoints seven of these texts
from the Sermon on the Mount for Sundays in the "Year of
Matthew." Those texts and their appointed days are as follows:

Matthew 5:1-12	Fourth Sunday after the Epiphany
Matthew 5:13-20	Fifth Sunday after the Epiphany
Matthew 5:21-37	Sixth Sunday after the Epiphany
Matthew 5:38-48	Seventh Sunday after the Epiphany
Matthew 6:1-6, 16-21	Ash Wednesday
Matthew 6:24-34	Eighth Sunday after the Epiphany
	Sunday Between May 24 and 28.
	Proper 3
Matthew 7:21-29	Sunday Between May 29 and June
	4. Proper 4

Our approach in this work is on the *narrative* connections in
Matthew's telling of the Jesus story. In the Sermon on the Mount
we encounter Jesus' *teaching*. This is not narrative material! This
is teaching material. Sermons on these texts, therefore, will be
primarily didactic in character. We will, therefore, offer no "Homiletical Directions" for the seven texts from the Sermon on the
Mount. You are advised to consult standard commentaries for
information concerning these texts. Study the teaching of Jesus and
teach it well!

Jesus Interprets the Law

It is important, however, to identify themes from the Sermon on
the Mount which flow through Matthew's narrative. From these
themes you may wish to create narrative flow for some of your
Sermon on the Mount preaching. We will begin this approach to
Matthew by undergirding the theme of Jesus as *Teacher*.

Fundamentally, the teaching of Jesus envisages human
conduct as it comports itself amid life in this sphere [king-
dom]. By citing "teaching" ahead of preaching and healing

*in the summary passages (4:23; 9:35; 11:1), Matthew gives
it the position of stress and invites the reader to attach
special importance to it.... In substance, Jesus' teaching is
the exposition of the will of God in terms of its original
intention (19:4, 8).... Plainly, Jesus advances the claim in his
teaching that he is the supreme arbiter of the will of God...what
he teaches is of permanent validity...when it comes to teaching, Jesus alone is the one who undertakes this. Never is it
even intimated that John or the post-Easter disciples teach,
and when the exalted Jesus commissions the post-Easter
disciples to go to the nations, it is no accident that what they
are given to teach is "all that I have commanded you"
(28:20).[2]*

Jesus is the *only one who teaches* in Matthew's Gospel! It
seems obvious that Matthew presents Jesus as a kind of new Moses.
Jesus teaches on the mountain (4:8; 17:1; 28:16). His teaching is
divided into five great discourses reminiscent of the five books of
Moses. He teaches with authority, an authority that goes beyond
Moses. Time and again in his teaching in the Sermon on the Mount
Jesus cites the law of Moses and adds, *"But* I say to you..." (5:22, 28,
32, 34, 39, 44).

Jesus is the new interpreter of the law. The law stands, but not
as it was. The law stands in a new formulation of its function. The
law is no longer that which the people serve. The people of Israel
had begun to serve the law in the time of the exile. Jesus turns the
law around. Humans are not meant to serve the law. *The law is
meant to serve humans!* The law serves us as we seek to identify
the neighbor and the neighbor's need. The law is not only about us
and our relationship with God. The law is also about us and our
relationship with our neighbor.

The law as interpreted by Jesus puts the spotlight on the
neighbor. People are more important than laws. We should not be
angry with our brother, let alone determine to kill him. We should
be reconciled with others (5:24). We should not think lustful
thoughts, let alone commit adultery (5:27-30). We should love our
enemies (5:43-48). And so on it goes. Jesus puts the spotlight on
the neighbor and rejects those ways in which human beings use the
law as a guide to their own righteousness.

It would appear that Jesus is saying that righteousness is never that which exists purely in our relationship to God. Righteousness has to do with loving God *and* loving neighbor. Love of God and neighbor is the righteousness that exceeds that of the scribes and Pharisees or of self-congratulatory Christians. (See also Matthew 22:34-40.) There is a way in which loving God *and* neighbor is the theme of the entire Sermon on the Mount. Some sections of the sermon put a focus on our relationship to God: 5:1-20; 6:1-34; 7:13-27. Other sections are focused on our relationship with our neighbor: 5:21-48; 7:1-12.

Most interpreters of Matthew see *identity* as a key to understanding the purpose of this Gospel. Whether Matthew writes to a group of Christians that are seeking to understand themselves over and against Jewish communities or charismatic Christian communities the notion of identity—who are we as a people?—is central to Matthew's intent. Part of Matthew's answer to the identity question is that this community is to be the people founded on true and proper teaching. "In the post-70 era the Matthean community understands that in Jesus, not in Moses or in Jewish traditions or in the claims of other revealer figures, is the definitive and authoritative manifestation of God's will."[3] Jesus fulfills the law and the prophets! (5:17)

> *It is not the Mosaic law in and of itself that has normative and abiding character for disciples, but the Mosaic law as it has passed through the crucible of Jesus' teaching.*[4]

> *The exalted Jesus, resurrected from the dead, is the community's one Teacher and one Master, and the centerpiece of his teaching is the Sermon on the Mount.*[5]

Jesus' Word of Blessing

The Sermon on the Mount begins with Jesus' word of blessing upon the disciples. These words are so familiar to us that we can easily miss their power. "Blessed are the poor in spirit, for theirs is the kingdom of heaven." So we begin. The kingdom that Jesus came to bring (4:17) is indeed at hand. Those poor in spirit are pronounced to be members of the kingdom.

The kingdom, we note, begins in the *indicative mood*. "You are!" Not, you might be. Not, you can be a member of the kingdom if you do this or that. Not, you should strive to be. Simply, *you are!* This is a powerful word of gospel proclamation right at the beginning of this sermon. *Imperatives* will follow. But the imperatives must grow out of the indicatives. A sound tree, that is, bears good fruit (7:15-20). Good fruit grows on good trees. Good works are the fruits of the lives of those who are blessed. Hearing turns into doing for those who hear the word of God's blessing (7:24-27). The imperative of neighbor love is carried out by those whom God pronounces blessed (indicative).

Jesus' indicative word of blessing is pronounced over the least likely folk of all. Mourners are blessed. The meek are blessed. Those who hunger for righteousness are blessed, and so forth. To such belong the kingdom of God. To such! To the "little ones" (10:42; 18:6; 10:14); to the "least" (11:11; 25:40, 45). There is a powerful transformation of values taking place here. We don't normally associate the glories and wonders of a kingdom, even the kingdom of God, with the "little ones." This is an affront to every mighty kingdom on earth. Who wants a kingdom made up of such people? Who? God! God in Jesus Christ pronounces blessed, pronounces kingdom place, to the little ones. The beatitudes turn the world upside down. The beatitudes proclaim the graceful nature of God in a most incredible way. God's grace, God's blessing, is the only way to life in the kingdom. First, we must be blessed by God in Jesus Christ. Grace is first. Grace is always first!

The Law and the Prophets

Jesus is the true teacher of the law. In his teaching he attempts to demonstrate for people that his teaching is that which fulfills both the law and the prophets. After pronouncing his blessing on the "little ones" Jesus says clearly: "Do not think that I have come to abolish the law or the prophets; I have come not to abolish but to fulfill" (5:17). What does it mean to fulfill the law and the prophets? Jesus puts the matter clearly in 7:12: "In everything do to others as you would have them do to you; for this is the law and the prophets."

77

Neighbor-love is that which fulfills the law. That's what Jesus appears to be saying in his version of the Golden Rule.

In Matthew 11 Jesus would appear to point to himself as the One in whom the law and the prophets are fulfilled. "For all the prophets and the law prophesied until John came; and if you are willing to accept it, he is Elijah..." (11:13-14). The people of Israel expected Elijah to come to prepare the way for the day of the Lord: Malachi 4:5. Jesus implies here that John the Baptist prepared his way! Jesus stands at the end of the line. He is the fulfillment of the law and the prophets.

Jesus' teaching is the fulfillment of the law and the prophets. One day the Pharisees came to Jesus to ask him about the law. They had many laws, of course. But which was the greatest law? That's what the Pharisees debated. That's what they wanted to find out from Jesus. What did he think? Jesus said:

> *"You shall love the Lord your God with all your heart, and with all your soul, and with all your mind." This is the greatest and first commandment. And a second is like it: "You shall love your neighbor as yourself." On these two commandments hang all the law and the prophets (Matthew 22:38-40).*

Jesus quotes the Hebrew Scriptures in giving forth this answer. He quotes Deuteronomy 6:5 and Leviticus 19:18. Love God and love your neighbor. This is the fulfillment of the law. This is the structure of the Sermon on the Mount, as we have already indicated. Some sections of this sermon deal with our relationship to God. Other sections deal with our relationship with other people.

Kingsbury argues that for Jesus *love* is the fulfillment of the law.

> *Is there a center to Jesus' radical teaching concerning the life of the greater righteousness, the law, and, in general, the will of God? The answer is yes, and this center is "love." ...Jesus advances no less a claim than that keeping the law or doing the will of God is always, in essence, an exercise in love. That "love" is the deepest intention of the will of God*

as taught by Jesus is also apparent from other passages in Matthew's story.[6]

The story of the rich young ruler is a story in which love of God and neighbor are set forth as the good thing one can do to enter eternal life. The rich one who asked about eternal life, however, did not like the answer. He was not prepared to sell all that he had in order truly to love God and *neighbor* (19:16-30).

In his pronouncement of woe upon the Pharisees Jesus finally calls them to stop neglecting the weightier matters of the law which are justice, mercy, and faith. "It is these you ought to have practiced without neglecting the others" (23:23). Matthew 23 stands almost as a parallel story to the story of the blessing theme in Matthew 5. In chapter 23 the word from Jesus' mouth is woe, not blessing. A series of woes. A series of blessings. There is much at stake in the life of the kingdom. Blessing and woe are at stake. Judgment and life are at stake.

Again, Jesus came to fulfill the law and the prophets. We might be able to put some of these stories together in narrative form in order to create this reality in the minds of our people. We dare not stray, however, from the reality that it is the word of blessing from God that will empower our love for our neighbor. Indicative precedes imperative.

The Righteousness of God

Another theme that runs through the Sermon on the Mount is the theme of righteousness. (See the discussion in Chapter 5.) Jesus allowed John to baptize him. "Let it be so now; for it is proper for us in this way to fulfill all righteousness" (3:15). Jesus comes to fulfill all righteousness. Jesus is the righteousness of God. We touched upon this theme in Chapter 5. Hear Robert Smith:

> *The one indispensable fruit of the Spirit desired by Jesus is righteousness. Righteousness may be defined now as hearts set on the will of God, on love toward God and toward the neighbor, and even toward the enemy. But the reality of righteousness surpasses easy definition. Matthew spends 28 chapters describing its contours and singing its praise.*[7]

79

We note that in the Beatitudes Jesus blesses those who hunger and thirst for righteousness (5:6). He blesses as well those who are persecuted for righteousness' sake (5:10). In discussing the fact that he has come to fulfill all righteousness, to fulfill the law and the prophets, Jesus calls his followers to a *righteousness that exceeds* that of the scribes and Pharisees (5:20). The remainder of the Sermon on the Mount may well be a description of this "exceeding" righteousness of which Jesus speaks!

> *One of the biggest problems with the righteousness of Matthew's opponents (whether the opponents be Jewish or Christian) is the matter of* hypocrisy, *6:5. This word in Matthew may mean that one is "under judgment" due to an inconsistency, a double mindedness by which people are convicted by their own standards. "It is this inconsistency, this double mindedness, this hypocrisy, this lack of integrity which Matthew sees as the problematic human condition...."*[8]

David Rhoads proposes four types of hypocrisy in Matthew: (1) inner motives contradict outward actions; (2) inner attitudes are the opposite of the outward appearance of righteousness; (3) people act morally in some situations but not in others; (4) the inconsistency between relating to God one way and treating others another way. These types of hypocrisy are all present in Matthew's narrative.

Etymologically, the Greek word for hypocrisy means actor! Acting is just what Jesus describes in chapter 6. Righteousness is put on public display by those practicing a false righteousness. Matthew holds forth for a kind of *hidden righteousness.* True righteousness is a secret matter between one and God (6:4, 6, 18). The truly righteous one is one whose left hand doesn't know the righteousness being done by one's right hand! (6:3)

Jesus said: "Not everyone who says to me, 'Lord, Lord,' will enter the kingdom of heaven..." (7:21). This is borne out in the parable of the judgment day story in Matthew 25. For the truly righteous ones in that parable, their acceptance into the blessings of the kingdom on the basis of their good deeds comes as a surprise. "Lord, when was it that we saw you hungry and gave you food, or thirsty and gave you something to drink?" (25:37). The issue is clear. Righteous people do not know their own righteousness. Their righteousness is hidden from their eyes. It is a secret. This is the righteousness that exceeds that of the scribes and Pharisees!

Those who are judged in this Matthew 25 parable are those crying out, "Lord, Lord, when did we *not* see you and come to your aid?" They cry out, "Lord, Lord." They are very sure of their deeds. They have counted on their deeds of public righteousness. The judge on the last day does not see this as righteousness at all. Neither did Jesus in his Sermon on the Mount.

Jesus calls upon his hearers to "seek first his kingdom and his righteousness" (6:33). Kingdom and righteousness are inseparable. The One who brings the kingdom has been introduced to us already in Matthew 1 as "God with us" and as the one who will save us from our sin (1:21, 23). Those who receive Jesus receive the kingdom. Those who receive the kingdom receive the power of the kingdom. Those who receive the power of the kingdom are enabled to live lives of righteousness. Those who receive the kingdom are *blessed*. Blessed are you! "As God lays healing hands on the universe and makes it 'all right' again, human beings are freed and made whole to live anew as trusting children in a family of love."[9]

Hearing and Doing God's Word

The Sermon on the Mount closes with a parable about a wise man who builds his house on a rock (7:24-27). Such is the case with those who *hear and do* God's word. Hearing, they do. Hearing, they are blessed. Blessed are you! That's what Jesus says. Jesus' word turns to deed. The hearing is done. The blessing is real. The heart is open. This is life firmly grounded on the rock.

There is another way. There are always two ways. Isn't that what this whole sermon is about? Blessings. Woes. Two ways. Secret righteousness. Public righteousness. Two ways. Hearing and not hearing. Two ways. Hearing and doing, and life is solid. Not hearing and not doing, and life is built on sand.

At the end of this great sermon we hear again of the indicative of grace. God speaks blessings. We hear. The Spirit drives this word deep into our lives. We do what we hear. The imperative of love gushes forth from the indicative of grace.

"Now when Jesus had finished saying these things, the crowds were astounded at his teaching, for he taught them as one having *authority*, and not as their scribes" (7:28-29). (Cf. the endings of the other four blocks of material in Matthew: 11:1; 13:53; 19:1; 26:1.) With these words the sermon ends. Jesus' teaching was teaching with authority. "All authority in heaven and on earth has been given to me" (28:18). His word of blessing has authority! It changes us! It equips us to "Go therefore and make disciples of all nations, baptizing them in the name of the Father and of the Son and of the Holy Spirit, *and teaching them to obey everything I have commanded you.* And remember, I am with you always, to the end of the age" (28:19-20).

In the Gospel of Matthew it is only Jesus who teaches. "But you are not to be called rabbi, for you have one teacher" (Matthew 23:8). As heirs of his teaching we are commanded to become teachers ourselves. We teach what he commanded. We are blessed to be a blessing. We speak his authoritative and creative word in order that people might hear and do the gospel.

---

1. Robert H. Smith, *Matthew: Augsburg Commentary on the New Testament* (Minneapolis: Augsburg Press, 1989), p. 76.

2. Jack Dean Kingsbury, *Matthew As Story* (Philadelphia: Fortress Press, 1988), pp. 62, 63, 64.

3. Warren Carter, *Matthew: Storyteller, Interpreter, Evangelist* (Peabody, MA: Hendrickson Publishers, 1996), p. 87.

4. Kingsbury, *op. cit.*, p. 65.

5. Smith, *op. cit.*, p. 78

6. Kingsbury, *op. cit.*, pp. 66-67.

7. Smith, *op. cit.*, p. 81.

8. David Rhoads, "The Gospel of Matthew. The Two Ways: Hypocrisy or Righteousness," *Currents in Theology and Mission* 19:6 (December 1992), p. 456.

9. Smith, *op. cit.*, p. 119.

Chapter 9
Proper 5

Matthew 9:9-13, 18-26

The Gospel text appointed for this week comes from Matthew 9. This follows a series of texts in recent weeks from the Sermon on the Mount: Matthew 5-7. We notice immediately, therefore, that the material in Matthew 8 has been excluded completely from the Revised Common Lectionary. The rationale behind this omission could be that all the material in Matthew 8 is based on material that is in Mark's Gospel. Some of the stories also appear in Luke's Gospel.

Matthew has arranged his material with precision. As we have noted earlier, the first four chapters in Matthew introduce us to Jesus Christ. These chapters prepare us to listen with care to the teaching of Jesus as it is presented to us in the Sermon on the Mount in Matthew 5-7. Matthew presents Jesus as One who whose *words* have authority. This is complemented in Matthew's structure by chapters 8-9 which present Jesus as One who did great *deeds* of power. *Words and deeds.* That's the wholeness of Jesus' ministry as presented by Matthew. Chapters 5-7: *words.* Chapters 8-9: *deeds.* Through this carefully planned presentation Matthew paints a wonderfully holistic picture of the ministry of Emmanuel, "God with us."

> *The mighty acts of Jesus are not displays of raw energy designed to cow opposition, to gain great throngs of adherents, or to separate the masses from their money.... The power of Jesus enacted in miracle is the power of the speaker of the Sermon on the Mount. His mighty deeds (chaps. 8-9) begin to enact the word of righteousness envisioned in the sermon.*[1]

The lectionary simply fails us at this point! If we follow the lectionary without commentary we will present to our people a Jesus who spoke many words but who did few deeds. The lectionary ordering of texts hears well Matthew's emphasis on Jesus as teacher. It fails us, however, in presenting Jesus' deeds of healing, exorcism, control over nature, and so on. This is a very unfortunate truncating of Matthew's vision of Jesus! In our section on "Homiletical Directions" we will address this matter in terms of our preaching. We might also note here that when Jesus gives an answer to the question of his identity as raised by John the Baptist he says: "Go and tell John what you *hear* and *see*...." What they see are the *deeds* that spring forth from Jesus' word!

The structure of chapters 8-9 is such that it presents us with three miracles of Jesus (8:1-17), followed by a calling story (8:18-22), followed by three more miracle stories (8:23—9:8), followed by a calling story (9:9, this week's text), followed by four miracle stories (9:10-32). In the telling of the final four miracle stories we hear also the first sounds of protest to Jesus' ministry: 9:11, 14. "Why?" questions begin to be heard. These questions will grow in intensity through the course of the Gospel leading finally to accusation, trial, and death.

We might note at this point that there are other clusters of miracle stories in Matthew 12 and in 14-17. As he does with almost every detail of Jesus' ministry, Matthew cites Jesus' healing miracles as fulfillment of Old Testament prophecy: "This was to fulfill what had been spoken through the prophet Isaiah, 'He took our infirmities and bore our diseases' " (Matthew 8:17).

One final word on the structure of this section of Matthew's Gospel. The final paragraph prior to the Sermon on the Mount is nearly identical to the final paragraph that occurs at the end of Matthew 9. See 4:23 and 9:35. The "gospel of the kingdom" clearly includes the miraculous in-breaking of God into the very bodies of people. Emmanuel comes to make things "all right."

As we read through the stories in Matthew 8 and 9 we are struck by the central reality of the *power of Jesus' word.* Time and again Jesus speaks, and it is so! Jesus' word has the power of God's word in creation who also spoke, and it was so: Genesis 1. (Isaiah 55:10-

11 is the classic Old Testament passage on the power of the word that goes forth from God's mouth.) Using the language of John's Gospel, Jesus is very clearly God's *word made flesh* dwelling among us.

The reality of Jesus' authoritative word is put most clearly by the centurion in Capernaum: 8:5-13. He, too, is a man who speaks authoritative words. When he gives orders, men obey. This is how he understands the ministry of Jesus. Jesus blesses him for his faith: 8:10, 13.

The text appointed for this week includes one of the two passages in the material in chapters 8-9 which is centered on Jesus' calling of disciples. Jesus calls. People respond! (9:9) This is a powerful word indeed! The text also includes one of the four miracles which follow this calling story.

The remainder of the text for this week has Jesus once again in the wrong company of people. It's probably not possible for us to get inside the reality of the offense Jesus caused in the way he chose people to eat with! He ate, after all, with tax collectors and sinners. The Pharisees were blown out of the water by this reality. "Why does your teacher eat with tax collectors and sinners?" they asked of the disciples. To the Pharisees' word of doubt Jesus spoke his faith-creating word: "I have come to call not the righteous but sinners." Jesus speaks and sinners become righteous! "I have come as a man of mercy." "I came to announce and to enact a surpassing righteousness (5:20). I came to summon sinners out of their old life into newness of life."[2]

Homiletical Directions

We have two suggestions on incorporating more of Matthew 8 and 9 into our preaching calendar. First, in some years it would be appropriate simply to take some Sundays in the Pentecost season to preach on some of the texts omitted from the lectionary. In those years we might omit some of the texts from the Sermon on the Mount.

Second, briefly tell the stories in Matthew 8 and 9 which lead up to the text for this week. (Chapter 13, on the Third Sunday in Advent, also suggests making use of the miraculous deeds in

Matthew 8-9.) Tell the stories centered around the reality of the *word become deed* which Jesus speaks. In the first story (8:1-4) Jesus says: "'I do choose. Be made clean!' Immediately his leprosy was cleansed." In the second story in Matthew 8, the story of the centurion in Capernaum (8:5-13), the emphasis falls on the clear understanding of the centurion that Jesus' word has creative power. In 8:23-27 Jesus speaks to the wind and the sea and they obey him! In 8:28-34 Jesus simply says, "Go!" and the demons leave the Gadarene demoniacs. To the paralytic (9:1-8) Jesus says two words. He says first, "Take heart, son; your sins are forgiven." To prove to the skeptical scribes that his word had the power to do what it said he also says to the paralytic: "Stand up, take your bed and go to your home." The man stood up and went home! Jesus speaks, and it is so!

This series of stories of the power of Jesus' word leads us finally to this week's assigned text. Jesus ate with the wrong people. The Pharisees didn't like it. But this was the heart of Jesus' ministry. He came to call sinners. He came *to make sinners righteous through the power of his word!* Jesus says to us today: "I have come not only to speak words of power to people in times gone by. I have come to speak words of power to you as well. I see you in all of your sinfulness. I see you in your unrighteousness. I see your sin and I say, Sin, go away. Sin, be forgiven. I see you in your unrighteousness and I say, You are righteous. I have come to make sinners righteous! And so you are. My word has made it so!"

There is an alternative approach to these texts in Matthew 8 and 9. In some years you may choose to accent the nature of *faith* that is present here. You may emphasize the human hearing side of the mighty words of Jesus. References to faith are recorded in 8:10, 13, 26; 9:2, 22, 29. These passages set forth a variety of ways to talk about faith. Most important, however, is to tell these stories in such a way that it is clear to all who hear that *"faith comes from what is heard, and what is heard is the word of Christ"* (Romans 10:17). Faith clings to the word that it hears from the mouth of Jesus. Faith clings to the word that sinners are made righteous, and in the clinging, sinners are made righteous!

1. Robert H. Smith, *Matthew: Augsburg Commentary on the New Testament* (Minneapolis: Augsburg Press, 1989), p. 128.

2. *Ibid.*, p. 140.

Matthew 9:35—10:8 (9-23)

The appointed Gospel reading for this week begins with the words: "Then Jesus went about all the cities and villages, teaching in their synagogues, and proclaiming the good news of the kingdom..." (Matthew 9:35). An almost identical statement concerning Jesus' ministry is found in Matthew 4:23: "Jesus went throughout Galilee, teaching in their synagogues and proclaiming the good news of the kingdom...." This passage introduces us to Jesus' Sermon on the Mount. Matthew 9:35-38 introduces us to Jesus' teaching on discipleship. The *words* (Matthew 5-7) and *deeds* (Matthew 8-9) of Jesus become now the description of the ministry of Jesus' disciples. They, too, will "proclaim" and "cure." They, too, will engage in a ministry of word and deed. See 10:7-8.

Note that Jesus went about teaching in *their* synagogues. (See also 4:23; 10:17; 12:9; 13:54.) "The effect of Matthew's expanded use of 'their synagogue' is to underline the distance of Jesus and his followers from the synagogue."[1]

Matthew 9:36 gives us the first look inside of Jesus' mind. He goes about his ministry of word and deed because he has *compassion.* This is a translation of a Greek work which literally means "bowels." Metaphorically the word refers to that which comes from the very depths of a person. This word for describing Jesus' attitude is used only of Jesus in the New Testament.

Jesus calls the disciples for mission to Israel. That's the heart of this week's text. Let's remind ourselves of the structure of Matthew 8-9. As we pointed out in Chapter 9, the material in these chapters follows this progression: (1) three miracles of Jesus; (2) Jesus' call to follow (9:18-22); (3) three miracles of Jesus; (4) Jesus' call to Matthew to follow (9:9); (5) four miracles of Jesus; (6) this week's appointed text, which sets forth Jesus' call to the disciples to follow him in mission. The appointed text stops this call passage in 10:8. The optional use of 10:9-23 includes the whole of Jesus' call to the disciples at this juncture of his ministry.

In his commentary on Matthew, Robert Smith titles the whole of Matthew 10: "The New Community in Its Mission Encounters Hostility (10:1-42)." He outlines this material as follows:

> *(1) The Twelve (vv. 2-4), nucleus and mirror of the entire new community of all times and places, are (2) equipped with Jesus' own astonishing powers and commissioned (vv. 1, 7-8). (3) They are instructed to travel light, as befits those whose trust is in God (vv. 8-10). (4) Jesus offers no glib promise of easy harvest but instead announces that his agents and envoys may expect the same reception Jesus himself has received, namely, more abuse than welcome (vv. 11-25). (5) Nevertheless, they may live without fear, knowing that they enjoy the Father's watchful care, and with the invincible faith that they will find their own true lives (vv. 26-42).*[2]

In terms of Matthew's structure we ought to note that 11:1 indicates the end of the second discourse in Matthew's shaping of the material: "Now when Jesus had finished instructing his twelve disciples...." The end of the first discourse was in 7:28 at the conclusion of the Sermon on the Mount: "Now when Jesus had finished saying these things...." In this second discourse of Matthew, which includes chapters 8-10, Matthew combines material that impresses us with God's mighty deeds. The deeds of Jesus, however, stand in closest possible connection with his call to follow; his call for mission to Israel. Jesus' saving deeds lead us to thanks, praise, and mission discipleship! So it is with the good news of the kingdom in every generation.

The charge to the disciples is specifically a charge to mission to Israel. They are not to go among the Gentiles or to enter the towns of the Samaritans. Go only to the lost sheep of Israel. God has not given up on Israel! (Cf. 15:24.) We are reminded of Paul's words in Romans: "For I am not ashamed of the gospel; it is the power of

God for salvation to everyone who has faith, *to the Jew first* and also to the Greek" (Romans 1:16).

> *One thing it means is that Israel, contrary to expectation, is a mission field. The tradition viewed Israel in the last times as destined to be a light for the Gentiles, but Jesus is saying that Israel needs enlightening, needs a shepherd (9:36). John preached to Israel (3:2-9). So did Jesus (4:12-16), and so will the disciples (v. 5). Israel will be offered the gospel of the kingdom not once but three times, fully and comprehensively.*[3]

Jesus also gives the disciples instructions as to how they are to go about their mission to Israel. Their message is to be: "The kingdom of heaven has come near" (10:7). This is the same message as that of John the Baptist: "Repent, for the kingdom of heaven has come near" (3:2). It is also the same message that Jesus proclaimed: "Repent, for the kingdom of heaven has come near" (4:17).

The assigned text comes to a close at this point, but the optional reading includes a description of how the disciples are to go about mission to the Israelites. Take no gold or silver. Take no bag. Take one tunic. No sandals. Quite a list. What does it mean? Many commentators indicate that these instructions really say to the disciples that they are to go to Israel in the manner of the people of Israel. Carry out this mission as an Israelite would carry it out. To the Jews be as a Jew. That's not bad missionary advice.

> *To the Jews I became as a Jew, in order to win Jews. To those under the law I became as one under the law...so that I might win those under the law. To the weak I became weak, so that I might win the weak. I have become all things to all people, that I might by all means save some* (1 Corinthians 9:20-22).

But it didn't work! The Israelites rejected the message. They would not repent. We see immediately in the next verses of Matthew (10:16-23) that the ministry of the disciples to Israel is filled with conflict. This presages the rejection of Jesus by the Israelites that begins to fill Matthew's pages once we enter chapter

11. Rejection of Jesus will ultimately lead to his death and a new charge to the disciples to "Go therefore and make disciples of *all nations...*" (28:19).

Homiletical Directions

There is a marvelous possibility with this week's text to set the call of God to mission in the gracious context of the good news of the gospel of the kingdom. We have indicated above that chapters 8-10 of Matthew follow an outline of miracles, call, miracles, call, miracles, call. The call to disciples in every age is a call enmeshed with the incredible grace and enabling power of God.

We suggest that this week's narrative sermon follow this outline of miracles, call, etc. Start in 8:1-17 and tell the miracle stories briefly. Jesus' word has power! In 8:18-27 Jesus issues a call to follow him. The call to follow comes in the context of the powerful words-become-deeds (miracles) in which Jesus brings salvation to God's people (Matthew 1:21) in fulfillment of the words of the prophet Isaiah 53:4.

Move next to the miracle stories told in 8:28—9:8. Obviously we can't tell all these stories in their fullness. Tell them briefly and in such a way that listeners get the point that the Savior is in action in his words-become-deeds. In 9:9 the flow of miracles is interrupted. Jesus calls Matthew: "Follow me." Matthew rises and follows. Jesus' word becomes deed in Matthew's life!

The third section of miracles is in 9:10-34. Again, touch upon the highlights. The point is not so much that people get the details of all these stories as that they follow the flow of Jesus' miraculous activity. The Savior is at work. God's grace is at work.

We come then to the text for this week, 9:35—10:8 (9-23). Once again, in the context of miracles of saving grace, Jesus calls disciples. He sends them to the lost sheep of the house of Israel in imitation of his ministry of preaching and healing.

The goal of this sermon is that our listeners hear the wonders of God's graciousness and in the context of such saving grace hear again, as for the first time perhaps, their call to mission. Stress the need of the world into which they are called. A closing proclamation can use the language of the text. Jesus' word to you today is:

"The harvest is plentiful but the laborers are few. I call you to be my laborers for the harvest. [At this point in the text Jesus named names. You can do that, too: 'I call you, Martha; I call you, Jose...'] Go to your own town. As you go, proclaim the good news: the kingdom of heaven has come near in Jesus Christ. Hear what he has done for you—it will change your life. Amen."

A closing prayer or hymn that asks for God's empowering words to become empowering deeds in our lives would be an appropriate way to bring this sermon to a close.

---

1. Warren Carter, *Matthew: Storyteller, Interpreter, Evangelist* (Peabody, MA: Hendrickson Publishers, Inc., 1996), p. 81.

2. Robert H. Smith, *Matthew: Augsburg Commentary on the New Testament* (Minneapolis: Augsburg Press, 1989), p. 146.

3. *Ibid.*, p. 147.

Matthew 10:24-39

The Gospel assigned for the Fifth Sunday after Pentecost comes out of the heart of Matthew 10. Last week's text brought us through Chapter 10:23. In the optional verses from 10:9-23 we heard Jesus give additional words of instruction for the disciples as they are set to carry out their mission to Israel. In 10:16-23 there begins a section of Jesus' call and commissioning that portends a mission that will be very difficult. The disciples will be delivered up to councils, flogged in synagogues, dragged before ruling authorities, betrayed by members of their own family, and hated by everyone because of the name of Jesus. These verses are of one piece with this week's assigned text: 10:24-33. It would be wise to include these verses from Proper 6 with the assigned verses for Proper 7 in developing this week's sermon.

Matthew 8 and 9 have set before us the reality that Jesus called persons to follow him: 8:18-22; 9:9. In chapter 10 the focus is on Jesus' call to the disciples for a mission to Israel. We have set forth an outline of Matthew's Gospel that sees Matthew 4:17—16:20 as "The Ministry of Jesus to Israel and Israel's Repudiation of Jesus." Matthew 5-7 set forth the *words* of Jesus' ministry. Chapters 8-9 focus on Jesus' *deeds* of ministry. Now the disciples are called to engage in a ministry of *word and deed* to Israel. With this call come the verses for this week which indicate clearly that Israel will repudiate Jesus' ministry. Actual stories of Israel's repudiation fill the pages of the latter part of this section of Matthew's Gospel, chapters 11-16.

> *To conclude, in the first half of the second part of his story (4:17—11:1) Matthew tells of the ministry of Jesus to Israel and, in conjunction with this, of the call of the disciples and of their mission to Israel. In calling disciples, Jesus creates*

a new community described as a brotherhood of the sons of God and of the disciples of Jesus. The purpose of this new community is to engage in missionary activity (4:18-22)...commissioned to preach and to heal in Israel, the disciples receive instructions that portend intense conflict for them and that present this first mission as foreshadowing in numerous particulars the later mission they will undertake to the Gentiles (9:35—10:42).[1]

Elsewhere Jack Kingsbury writes that, though Matthew gives us this story of the call of the disciples and their commission to Israel, he nowhere mentions the departure of the disciples for this mission nor their return.

Accordingly, by stating at the outset of the discourse that Jesus "sent out" the Twelve and yet remaining silent at the conclusion about any actual departure of the disciples, Matthew achieves two objectives: on the one hand, he leads the reader to assume that the disciples did undertake...a ministry to Israel (10:5); and on the other hand, he spares himself the need to take note of any return of the disciples from ministry and hence avoids contradicting the notion that their missionary work in Israel will not have ended until Jesus shall have returned at the Parousia (10:23).[2]

There is a sense of unresolved tension regarding this mission of the disciples to Israel. Kingsbury's suggestion is that this mission is to be continued to the Parousia. This continuation of discipleship would, therefore, land in our lap! The commission is still valid. Disciples are still needed. There are still lost sheep in the house of Israel.

It is certainly clear from the instructions of Jesus in these verses that the church of Matthew's time was a suffering church. Matthew sees the call to discipleship as a call to suffer as the Lord has suffered. There is little glory here! These are hard words for us to hear today. Is suffering always the mark of Christian discipleship? Is that Jesus' message to us in Matthew's story?

The appointed text begins with the notation that the disciple is not above the master. If the master is accused of having a demon

(9:34), the disciples of the master will be likewise maligned. Jesus paints a tough picture of discipleship. But discipleship is not an impossible task. The Spirit of the Father (10:20) will empower the speaking forth of the disciple. This is, by the way, the only reference in Matthew's Gospel to the work of the Holy Spirit in the lives of the disciples.

Jesus' strongest word of assurance to the disciples called to a mission task marked by suffering is "Fear not." Three times Jesus repeats this word of comfort: 10:26, 28, 31. We need not fear the call to make known the word Jesus has revealed to us in the dark. We need not fear those who can only harm our body. They cannot harm our ultimate relationship with God. We need not fear when we know that God even takes care of the cheapest item in the market-place: a sparrow. Furthermore, those who acknowledge God will be acknowledged by God.

Homiletical Directions

The narrative connections for today's text are not strong. Matthew 10 stands somewhat on its own in its presentation of Jesus' call to the disciples and his words of solace concerning their mission. You may, therefore, wish to confine yourself to the text this week and speak of the nature of God's call. There is a strong word here that can ring throughout your sermon as a word of hope. *Fear not!* With Jesus' call to go and to suffer and to be hated, there comes also this repeated word of hope and encouragement.

It is clear that this call of Jesus to discipleship is a call that takes place under the sign of the cross. Disciples will suffer. They will suffer as their master suffered. Three times in Matthew Jesus announces the suffering that will come upon himself: 16:21; 17:22-23; 20:18-19. Chapters 26-27 of Matthew's Gospel are devoted to the story of the final suffering and crucifixion of Jesus. This presents us with a homiletical possibility. Make suffering the theme of the various aspects of this week's Gospel text as you tell it forth. Go on to note that Jesus proclaimed the suffering that was to come his way in a series of passion predictions. Tell a part of the story of Jesus' suffering as presented in Matthew's version of the passion story. Jesus suffered. A disciple is not above his master. We, too, will suffer. We, too, are called to take up the cross in following Jesus (10:38). We are called upon to lose our life in order to find it. See 10:39; 16:24-26. The call to discipleship is a call to suffering.

A word of proclamation for a sermon filled with the story of our suffering in the image of our Savior might go like this: "What Jesus is saying to us through this story today is: 'Go. Bear witness to the words and deeds of my ministry (10:5-8). I send you out as sheep in the midst of wolves (10:16). I send you out to join me in my suffering. Human institutions will malign you. You will be hated for my sake. But, fear not. I *have* walked this path of suffering before you.

'Fear not. I will walk with you as you suffer in the *present* for my name's sake.

'Fear not. I will walk with you in a *future* beyond suffering. When you lose your life for my sake you find that you gain a life that is eternal.

'Fear not.' Amen."

---

1. Jack Dean Kingsbury, *Matthew As Story* (Philadelphia: Fortress Press, 1988), p. 136.

2. *Ibid.*, p. 71.

97

Matthew 10:40-42

We come now to the final passage in the section of Matthew's Gospel which Robert Smith has called: "The New Community in Its Mission Encounters Hostility." (See Chapter 10.) The verses appointed for this Sunday also bring us to the end of a major teaching section in Matthew's structure. We note the familiar words just after the close of this week's text: "Now when Jesus had finished instructing his twelve disciples..." (11:1). The four other instances of a formula closely resembling these verses are in 8:28; 13:53; 19:1; 26:1. Many scholars have pointed out that the verses immediately preceding these formula statements which indicate a new section of Jesus' teaching are passages with a common theme of *judgment*. "I have not come to bring peace, but a sword," Jesus says (10:34).

Those who first heard Jesus speak these words of division and judgment must have been shocked if they had some idea that he was the Messiah. The Messiah promised to Israel surely did not come to earth to bring judgment and war. Isn't the promise that the Messiah will come as Prince of Peace? Then who is this pretender to the promise? Why does he blaspheme the promise? Israel is set to reject this messianic-pretender. Matthew 11 will begin to expose the Jewish repudiation of Jesus.

Jesus says he has come to set family members against one another. Micah 7:5-7 might be an Old Testament background for this saying of Jesus. Jesus seems to be telling his disciples that they are not to love the "old world." There is a "new world" bursting to life. These words of Jesus about division in families need to be set alongside those passages in Matthew where Jesus speaks more positively about family values: 5:27-32; 19:3-12.

In verses 40-42 Jesus shifts his gaze. He has been speaking to his disciples since 10:5. Now he turns his attention to the crowd. He speaks to the matter of *reception*. How will his disciples be reccived? "He who receives you, receives me," Jesus says. Jesus is present in, with, and under the ministry of those who minister in his name. This begins to sound a bit like the judgment passage in Matthew 25:31-46. The Son of Man in the day of judgment will separate the sheep from the goats. The sheep, the "righteous ones," will sit at his right hand because they saw him hungry, thirsty, a stranger, naked, sick, and in prison and ministered to him. (The "righteous" are surprised by their own righteousness! The righteous are always shocked by their own righteousness. That's a hallmark of the righteousness of the Christian. It is a righteousness hidden even from the eyes of the righteous person.) The Son of Man says to the righteous: "Truly I tell you, just as you did it to one of the *least of these* who are members of my family, you did it to me" (Matthew 25:40). Mark Allan Powell comments on this connection:

> *The primary concern in Matthew 25:31-46 is not with acts of mercy performed by church members for needy people of the world but with acts of mercy performed for church members by people among the nations to which they are sent. But the passage develops the latter theme as a corollary to the former, which is established earlier in Matthew. Matthew's Gospel leaves no doubt that followers of Jesus are to meet needs of people outside the community of faith.... Matthew 25:31-46 comes at the very end of Jesus' final great discourse and offers a turnabout that completes the picture. Now the readers are told that the world (the nations) will also be held accountable for its treatment of Jesus' followers... followers of Jesus ought to do unto others as they would have done to them (7:12)...the corollary to this—that others ought to treat the followers of Jesus as they themselves would wish to be treated—is also true....*[1]

To minister to the least is to minister to Jesus. We hear that in both 10:40-42 and 25:31-46. To receive the *little ones* is to receive Jesus. Whoever gives the little ones a cup of water shall have a reward. Most scholars believe that "little ones" is a reference to Jesus' disciples. This term is used a bit differently in Matthew 18. Matthew 18 is a chapter which discusses the fact that Christian life together is to be an ordered community. Jesus says that the greatest one in the kingdom of heaven is *like a child* (18:4). "Whoever welcomes one such child in my name welcomes me" (18:5). These words of Jesus are very similar to vv. 40-42 of this week's text. Receiving the disciples, receiving the little ones, receiving a little child is like receiving Jesus himself: "as you did it to one of the least of these...you did it to me." Matthew 18:10 and 14 make further references to the little ones.

The terms seem to be a bit fluid. On the one hand, the disciples seem to be the "little ones." On the other hand, it seems that Jesus chooses "little ones" to be his disciples. His community is a community of love and acceptance even for the little ones. When people outside of the community of faith welcome these little ones, these tiniest of Christians, they have their reward.

Homiletical Directions

Chapter 10 of Matthew is a chapter filled with the instructions of Jesus to his disciples. The verses appointed for this week are didactic in nature. It will probably be best, therefore, to look at the didactic points one might make in a sermon based on these verses. Our comments will focus primarily on the *little ones.* We propose to begin this sermon with the teaching about the little ones in Matthew 18:1-14. These verses do not occur in the Matthean lectionary year. Our focus in these verses is on the child and the little ones: vv. 4, 6, 10, 14. Verses 10-14 bring to mind Luke's parable of the lost sheep. The concern of God is always a concern with the lost, the least, the little ones. The Christian community is a community of the little ones. God's love for the little ones is the sole basis for life in this community. Saint Paul put it well to the Corinthians: "Consider your own call, brothers and sisters: not many of you were wise by human standards, not many were powerful, not many were of noble birth. But God chose what is foolish in the world to shame the wise; God chose what is weak in the world to shame the strong; God chose what is low and despised in the world, things that are not, to reduce to nothing things that are, so that no one might boast in the presence of God" (1 Corinthians 1:26-29).

A second point to make in a kind of two-point didactic sermon is the reality that the world will be judged on the basis of how it treats the little ones. The little ones are those called as we discussed above. In Matthew's Gospel this may be a reference more particularly to the disciples. To receive the little ones is to receive Jesus.

This same point is made in story form in the judgment parable from Matthew 25:31-46. The nations are judged by the way they treat the little ones. In their attitude to the little ones the nations give expression to their reaction or reception of Jesus himself: "As you did it to one of the least of these who are members of my family, you did it to me" (Matthew 25:40).

---

1. Mark Allan Powell, *God With Us: A Pastoral Theology of Matthew's Gospel* (Minneapolis: Fortress Press, 1995), pp. 146-148.

Chapter 13
Advent 3

Matthew 11:2-11

This week's Gospel text is our first big jump in Matthean order for this church year. We have begun Advent in Matthew 1:18-25 and 3:1-12. Now, suddenly, we are in Matthew 11. We note first the formula in 11:1 that brings to an end the second block of Jesus' teaching in Matthew's Gospel. "Now when Jesus had finished instructing his twelve disciples...." The four other instances of this formula are found in 7:28; 13:53; 19:1; 26:1.

In the outline we proposed for Matthew's Gospel in the Preface we identified this week's assigned verses as the beginning of a section of Matthew's Gospel where *repudiation of Jesus* comes to the fore. People do take offense (11:6) at his words and deeds. We labeled Matthew 4:17—16:20: "The Ministry of Jesus to Israel and Israel's Repudiation of Jesus." 4:17—11:1 revels in the ministry of Jesus in word and deed; 11:2—16:20 focuses on the repudiation of Jesus and his ministry.

Jack Dean Kingsbury summarizes the structural issues in Matthew's narrative as follows:

> *The motif that dominates Matthew's story throughout 4:17 —11:1 is Jesus' ministry to Israel of teaching, preaching, and healing (4:23; 9:35; 11:1). Through this ministry, Jesus summons Israel to repentance and to life in the sphere of God's end-time rule (4:17; 5:45). In 11:2—16:20, which comprises the latter half of the second part of Matthew's story (4:17—16:20), Israel's response to Jesus' ministry becomes the dominant motif. This response is one of repudiation; yet even as Israel repudiates Jesus, it wonders and speculates about his identity. The matter of Jesus' identity, then, surfaces as the second motif of importance in 11:2—16:20.*[1]

102

Kingsbury goes on to point out that two stories in this section of Matthew's Gospel deal with the theme of identity and offense. Our text for this week is the first of these. John the Baptist asks a question about Jesus' *identity*. Jesus answers John's question and warns about possible *offense* at his mission. In 13:53-58 we have a similar story. (This text is not appointed for the Matthean year.) Here it is Jesus' hometown folk who raise questions about Jesus' identity. They could not believe that Joseph's boy could be all that he was cracked up to be. So, they took *offense* at him: 13:57.

Our assigned text announces that John the Baptist is in prison. From prison he sends word to Jesus. He asks the question of the ages in Israel: "Are you the one who is to come, or are we to wait for another?" (We discussed this text in Chapter 4 which deals with the Second Sunday in Advent.) Each generation of Israel wondered if the newly appointed king was the promised Messiah. (The basic messianic promise is in 2 Samuel 7:8-16.) When kings were no more, the people of Israel put such questions to their great religious leaders. John now puts the question to Jesus. The fact that John put the question is a sign, of course, that John couldn't tell from what he had heard and seen if Jesus were the Messiah or not! John is typical here of the people of Israel at the time of Jesus. Jesus did not fit stereotypical messianic expectations.

John asks his question based on the *deeds* of Jesus. Had we been following the flow of Matthew's Gospel this question would make ultimate sense to us. In the outline of Matthew's Gospel chapters 5-7 contain some of the great *words*, great teachings, of Jesus. This is the Sermon on the Mount. Immediately following the Sermon on the Mount, Matthew tells us two chapters' worth of Jesus' *deeds* of ministry: Matthew 8-9. As we point out in our discussion of Matthew 8-9 in Chapter 9, the lectionary omits almost all of the stories of Jesus' deeds. The lectionary, that is, seriously short-circuits Matthew's story which is told in a balance of *words* (5-7) and *deeds* (8-9).

In his reply to John, Jesus makes reference to this word/deed structure: "Go and tell John what you *hear* and *see*" (11:4). Jesus then rattles off a list of his deeds that have been seen. This verse is a kind of summary of Jesus' activity in Matthew 8-9. It sounds, too, like a fulfillment of Isaiah 35:5-7.

In 11:6 Jesus speaks words that raise much puzzlement. "And blessed is anyone who takes no offense at me." Who would be offended at the words and deeds of Jesus? What's going on here? Historically we know that people were indeed offended. We've indicated that this note of offense is a foretaste of the offense to come in the succeeding chapters of Matthew. Offense will be the order of the day. Offense will lead us ultimately to the cross. Offense and repudiation will lead to the death of the man of *word and deed.*

The nature of this offense appears to be related to Matthew's presentation of Jesus as the *righteous One* (3:15, see Chapter 5) who came as *God with us* (1:23) to bring us salvation, even the *forgiveness of our sins* (1:21). This face of the Messiah means that without him we are not righteous. We are living apart from God. We are stuck in our sins. We are called to repentance. Humankind much prefers to think of itself as being like God. That was the sin of our first ancestors in the garden: Genesis 3:1-19. "Who? Me need a Savior? No, thank you. I'm doing quite well on my own." Savior-talk always offends people who are on their own path to self-divinization or self-glorification. Jesus offended lots of people in his day. Jesus offends lots of people in our day. If one hasn't been offended by the gospel that is Jesus we might wonder if that one understands the gospel at all!

Jesus then proceeds to speak of John the Baptist. This section goes on through 11:19. Some comment has been made about these verses in Chapter 4. The death of John the Baptist is told in 14:1-12. These verses do not appear in the lectionary this year either. At some point in this year it might be wise to put these John the Baptist stories together in a narrative sermon.

Robert Smith comments on John as follows:

> *John was great because he had looked at the face of Jesus and knew what he was seeing: the drawing near of the kingdom.... Yet John stood only on the threshold. The kingdom dawns only after John's ministry, with the ministry*

and death and resurrection of Jesus.... John is the great hinge of history, the end of the old, the beginning of the new.... Therefore the only adequate response to John is not admiration but a venture of faith into the kingdom he heralded.[2]

Homiletical Directions

A first sermon possibility for this week would be to deal with the theme of Jesus' identity. That's an important Advent issue. Whose birth are we preparing for, anyway? The assigned text consists of John's question to Jesus about Jesus' identity and Jesus' warning that people are blessed if they find no offense in him. The question of Jesus' identity raises the possibility of offense. Close the telling of this story with Jesus' words: "Blessed is anyone who takes no offense at me."

Secondly, tell the story in Matthew 13:53-58. In this story the people of Jesus' hometown speculate about Jesus' identity. They were plainly offended by the fact that the carpenter's son from their village was spoken of as a prophet, as Messiah. Identity and offense. These are the common themes. Close the telling of this story in the same manner as the first: "Blessed is anyone who takes no offense at me."

Thirdly, tell a story or two of contemporary people who find themselves offended by the identity of the One who whose birth we prepare to celebrate. Use some of the material mentioned above or other material of your own creating to explicate why and how contemporary people are offended by Jesus. Close these stories with Jesus' words: "Blessed is anyone...."

Finally, the question must be put to all those present. What think ye of the Christ?

This sermon should close with the refrain: "Blessed is anyone who takes no offense at me."

A second sermonic possibility would be a sermon which brings to the fore the miracles of Jesus as told in Matthew 8 and 9. We have indicated that these miracles are mostly omitted from the lectionary for the Matthean year. This causes a serious imbalance in the Matthew year. Matthew's Gospel is more didactic in nature than

Mark and Luke to begin with. When the miracles Matthew does tell are omitted, clearly because they are included in the Markan or Lukan year, we wind up with a Matthean Jesus who is much talk and little action.

In this week's story Jesus tells John's disciples to go and tell John what they *see and hear.* Matthew clearly intends to present Jesus to us as a man of action as well as a man of teaching authority. The blind receive their sight (Matthew 9:27-31). The lame walk (9:1-8). Lepers are cleansed (8:1-4). The deaf hear. (There is no corollary story for the healing of the deaf.) The dead are raised up (9:18-26). The poor have good news preached to them.

Begin this sermon with the text's story. Tell the miracle stories in the order of Jesus' mention of the deeds of his ministry. Jesus said that the blind receive their sight. Tell the story from Matthew 9 where the blind receive their sight. Close the telling of each of the miracle stories with words of Jesus. They might go something like this: "Take no offense at me. I have come that the blind might receive their sight." Repeat this refrain adapted to each miracle.

This sermon might close by inserting the minds of contemporary "Advent people" for John the Baptist. In Advent in our time we, too, ask: "Are you the one who is to come, or are we to wait for another?" Get this question planted in the minds of the hearers. Once planted, give them Jesus' answer. Simply recite 11:4-6 from memory. Say, Amen.

---

1. Jack Dean Kingsbury, *Matthew As Story* (Philadelphia: Fortress Press, 1988), p. 72.

2. Robert H. Smith, *Matthew: Augsburg Commentary on the New Testament* (Minneapolis: Augsburg Press, 1989), pp. 155-156.

Matthew 11:16-19, 25-30

The text appointed for this week omits 11:20-24. It may be necessary for us to retrieve these verses in our preaching practices as they help to set the context for the climactic words of Jesus in what follows them. In 11:20-24 Jesus upbraids the cities in which he did mighty deeds to no avail. There was no repentance! For such cities judgment is at hand. "How is the reader to understand that Jesus should meet with such rejection? In private prayer, Jesus explains his rejection by invoking the will of his Father (11:25-26)."[1] In this intimate portrait of Jesus we are given to understand that Jesus' "Father" is in charge of revealing and concealing. "The theme of God's hiding and revealing of mysteries is dealt with also in other passages (10:26-27; 13:1-23, especially vv. 10-17; 13:35, 51-52; 16:17)."[2]

To whom is God's will revealed? To the *babes!* But though God has hidden his revelation from Israel, he has nonetheless also made it known, to "infants," that is to say, to Jesus' disciples (11:25). Within the surrounding context of chapters 11-12, this hiding of divine revelation and making it known corresponds to the fact that whereas all Israel turns away from Jesus (11:16-19; 12:14, 24), the disciples continue to adhere to him (12:49-50). God, then, while hiding his divine revelation from Israel, imparts it to the disciples. But what is the nature and substance of this revelation? As elaborated in the context, it concerns in greatest measure two matters. The one matter is the mysteries of the Kingdom of Heaven (13:11). And the other is insight into Jesus' identity as the Son of God (14:33; 16:16).[3]

Jack Kingsbury identifies the babes as the disciples. In Chapter 12 we discussed Matthew's concept of the "little ones." See 10:42; 18:1-14 (vv. 4, 6, 10, 14) and 25:31-46 (v. 40). These "little ones" are the choice of God's revealing work! The very nature of the gospel is demonstrated here! The babes, the little ones, "get it." John the Baptist did not get it: 11:2-6. "This generation" did not get it: 11:16-19. The mighty cities in which Jesus worked his works didn't get it either: 11:20-24. Neither did the wise and understanding ones get it: 11:25. Only the "little ones" get it. Such is the nature of God's revelation (cf. 1 Corinthians 1:18-31). This story is not at all about some form of predestination. It would appear, rather, that only those who make no claims upon God, only those who stand before God in their need, "get it." These are precisely the people "blessed" by Jesus in the Beatitudes! (Matthew 5:3-11).

There is much of theology in these few verses: "...no one knows the Son except the Father, and no one knows the Father except the Son and anyone to whom the Son chooses to reveal him." Verses such as these are important for trinitarian speculation. The accent here, however, is not on abstract theological speculation but on the reality that Jesus chooses to reveal the Father's kingdom and himself to "babes."

This week's brief pericope closes with other powerful words of Jesus: "Come to me...." Invitation is a hallowed biblical tradition. In the Wisdom tradition it was Wisdom—incarnate as Lady Wisdom—who invited all to her banquet. "*Come*, eat of my bread and drink of the wine I have mixed. Lay aside immaturity, and live, and walk in the way of insight" (Proverbs 9:1-6, *5-6*). The Apocryphal book of Sirach gives the most complete statement of Wisdom's kind invitation:

> *Draw near to me, you who are untaught,*
> *and lodge in my school....*
> *Put your neck under the yoke,*
> *and let your souls receive instruction;*
> *it is to be found close by.*
> *See with your eyes that I have labored little*
> *and found for myself much rest.* — Sirach 51:23, 26-27

We recognize that Jesus' words in our text for today are words that have probably been informed by this Wisdom tradition. The prophet Isaiah also picks up this theme, though he turns it for his own purposes: "Ho, every one who thirsts, *come* to the waters; and you that have no money, *come*, buy and eat! *Come*, buy wine and milk without money and without price.... Incline your ear, and *come to me*; listen, so that you may live" (Isaiah 55:1-3).

In his words from Matthew 11:28-30 it would appear that Jesus has entered this tradition of *invitation*. His words are very similar to those in the Sirach passage. Jesus enters this old tradition but he makes this tradition his own as he reveals God's final invitation to salvation. "Come to me...."

The word *rest* also has an interesting biblical history. In 2 Samuel 7:1 we read that the Lord had given David *rest* from all his enemies. *Rest* is usually identified in the Old Testament as rest from war. In 1 Kings 4:25 we have what some scholars call a definition of *rest*: "During Solomon's lifetime Judah and Israel lived in safety, from Dan even to Beersheba, all of them under their vines and fig trees." *Rest* is associated with God in Psalm 95. There is a lament in this psalm that Israel had turned their hearts against the Lord. The Lord's response was: "Therefore in my anger I swore, 'They shall not enter my *rest*'" (Psalm 95:11).

Hebrews 4:1-13 is a meditation on the concept of *rest*. The promise of entering God's rest still remains. The author now identifies rest with the fact that God *rested* on the Sabbath. "So then, a Sabbath rest still remains for the people of God; for those who enter God's rest also cease from their labors as God did from his. Let us therefore make every effort to enter that rest...." (Hebrews 4:9-11). And how shall we enter such a rest? We enter God's rest through the invitation of Jesus! "Come to me...*I will give you rest.*"

Homiletical Directions

The key to preaching on this week's text is to take up the wonderful proclamation of Jesus that it contains and enable Jesus, through your speaking, to make his proclamation to the people in your pews. One way this can be done in narrative fashion is begin this sermon by telling the stories of rejection as we have them in 11:1-24. John the Baptist (11:1-6) was there from the beginning, and yet he was not sure if Jesus was truly the One he was looking for. He has to ask! He gets an answer. Does he believe the answer? We don't know. We just know that many people seem to be offended by Jesus: 11:6.

This generation also did not get it. See 11:16-19. They reject both John and Jesus.

The cities in which Jesus did his mighty deeds did not get it: 11:20-24. Matthew's Gospel seems to downplay Jesus' miracles. Is that because Matthew's experience was that Jesus' mighty deeds in and of themselves did not call people to faith?

Here we might move from biblical discussion to contemporary discussion. Why is it that people in our day are still offended by Jesus? Why do they not repent? Why do they have ears but they do not hear? And what's wrong with us? Why is it that the words and deeds of Jesus are so slow to take hold of our lives?

What, then, is our hope for "getting it," for coming to faith? Faith comes through the revealing work of Jesus. The babes "get it"! So we encourage our hearers to come as babes to hear the story of Jesus. Come over and over again. Jesus is at work whenever or wherever his story is told inviting people to faith. "Come to me, all you that are weary and are carrying heavy burdens, and I will give you rest." Faith comes through invitation. As preachers we can surely issue the invitation in Jesus' name. We cannot, however, do more than that. Faith-creation is the work of the Holy Spirit. We issue the invitation. We invite the Spirit to drive that invitation deep into every human heart.

Invitation is the very nature of this week's text. A second sermon possibility would be to track the background of this invitation to the Wisdom tradition of the Old Testament and the Apocrypha. Make use of the material from Proverbs 9, Sirach, and Isaiah. Trace the theme of invitation. Jesus enters this tradition and makes the invitation his own. This approach to the text should also conclude in invitation.

A third preaching possibility would make use of the biblical concept of *rest*. 2 Samuel 7:1 and 1 Kings 4:25 speak of rest as real rest from the enemy. Each person is at peace under his or her own vine and fig tree. Psalm 95 indicates, however, that when Israel strays from God it will not find God's rest. The book of Hebrews takes up this theme in 4:13. Rest is reinterpreted as Sabbath rest, and this Sabbath rest is still open to all people.

What kind of rest are people seeking today? What kind of rest are people in your congregation longing for? You might wish to take some time with this theme as you prepare people to hear Jesus' invitation to rest. The biblical tradition of rest comes to its fulfillment in Jesus' words: "Come to me. I will give you rest." This is the word restless people need to hear.

This text includes powerful, proclamatory words of Jesus. However you choose to structure your sermon, do not fail to enable your people to hear Jesus' word of invitation spoken to them.

1. Jack Dean Kingsbury, *Matthew As Story* (Philadelphia: Fortress Press, 1988), pp. 72-73.

2. Robert H. Smith, *Matthew: Augsburg Commentary on the New Testament* (Minneapolis: Augsburg Press, 1989), p. 158.

3. Kingsbury, *op. cit.*, p. 137.

Matthew 13:1-9, 18-23

We come to our text for this week noting that the lectionary has entirely omitted Matthew 12. This is a critical omission because it appears that the material in Matthew 13:1-23, the Parable of the Sower along with its explanations, is Jesus' response to the events that have taken place in chapter 12. We need, therefore, to undertake a summary of the events that lead up to Jesus' Parable of the Sower.

We have given the label to this section of Matthew (4:17—16:20) as follows: "The Ministry of Jesus to Israel and Israel's Repudiation of Jesus." Matthew 12 highlights both of these issues. Jesus' ministry is set forth in this chapter in terms of his healing on the Sabbath (vv. 9-14), his healing ministry in general (vv. 15-21), and his healing of a dumb and blind demoniac (v. 22). Jesus' deeds are front and center.

The repudiation of God's healer by Israel is just as clearly drawn. Matthew 12 is full of terrible conflicts: opposition to Jesus intensifies as Pharisees begin to debate with Jesus directly (12:1-8). Previously, scribes and Pharisees have criticized Jesus among themselves (9:3-4), questioned Jesus' disciples (9:10-11), or rebuked the crowds (9:32-34). Now they speak to Jesus directly and begin to rebuke him for offending their convictions about the will of God, and they depart to plot his death (12:14). By the end of the chapter they are painted as representatives of "this evil generation" (vv. 39, 41, 42, 45).[1]

Jack Kingsbury also notes that "the religious leaders clash with Jesus, and the level of tension in Matthew's story increases perceptibly" in Matthew 12. He cites the "frontal attack against Jesus because of a deed he himself will perform (12:9-13) [as that which] marks the place where the conflict between Jesus and the religious leaders reaches a new level of intensity."[2] For the first time, the religious leaders actually take counsel about how they might destroy Jesus! (12:14) Things are heating up!

Matthew 12 begins with a dispute between Jesus and the Pharisees over the fact that Jesus and his disciples had plucked ears of grain on the Sabbath. Jesus tells the Pharisees in no uncertain terms that he is even greater than the temple in Jerusalem. In this chapter Jesus will also claim to be greater than Jonah (v. 41) and greater than Solomon (v. 42). No wonder the Pharisees were angry. So angry that they lay in waiting for Jesus in their synagogue on the Sabbath to see just what he might do (vv. 9-14). Sure enough, Jesus healed a man with a withered hand right before their eyes. That's when they decided that Jesus had to be destroyed!

There follows next a note about Jesus' healing along with the longest quotation that Matthew ever uses from the Old Testament: 12:15-21. Jesus healed, says Matthew, to fulfill what was spoken by the prophet Isaiah. The reference is to Isaiah 42:1-4. (In a previous section on Jesus' healings Matthew quoted from Isaiah 53:4; see 8:17.) This quotation from Isaiah has wide-ranging implications. There are references in the quotation to Jesus' birth and baptism by the power of the Spirit. This is a reference to the past tense of the Jesus story (v. 18). There is also a reference to the future. In Jesus lies hope for the Gentiles. Isaiah's words help us turn our attention to the future, to the end of the Gospel with its commission to all nations, i.e. to the Gentiles. There is clearly an implication here that *Jesus' ministry to Israel has failed.*

Next Jesus heals a blind and dumb demoniac, which propels the Pharisees to claim that Jesus casts out such spirits by Beelzebul (vv. 22-32). Jesus, that is, is not in league with God. He is in league with the Devil. The Pharisees deny that Jesus' source of power is in God and in God's Spirit. This is the sin against the Holy Spirit as Matthew tells the story.

The Pharisees claim Jesus is in league with Beelzebul. Jesus claims he is in league with the kingdom of God. "But if it is by the Spirit of God that I cast out demons, then the kingdom of God has come to you" (12:28). Jesus is *Emmanuel.* In Jesus, God is with us. In Jesus, the kingdom of God is present—*now.* The Pharisees were scandalized by such talk. Jesus said of the Pharisees that they were bad trees who produced bad fruit. "You brood of vipers! How can you speak good things, when you are *evil*?" (12:34) Jesus repeats his charge that the Pharisees are evil several times: vv. 35, 39, 45. The battle is cosmic: The kingdom of evil vs. the kingdom of God, the kingdom of Beelzebul vs. the kingdom present in Jesus. The stakes are very high.

In 12:38-42 the Pharisees demand a sign from Jesus. Perhaps they are asking him to prove that he is not the evil one. Jesus gives no sign but the sign of Jonah. "The *sign* is either Jesus' passion and weakness, bringing him down to the grave, or perhaps the mute and ambiguous evidence of his empty tomb. In any case, Jesus will not provide the kind of powerful and overwhelming signal which skeptics demand."[3]

In perhaps the strongest language of all, Jesus compares the Pharisees to a house from which an evil spirit has fled. The spirit brings other spirits more evil than itself to enter the house. That's who the Pharisees are! (12:43-45)

The final verses of Matthew 12 deal with Jesus' family. Jesus indicates that his disciples are his true family (12:46-50). The implication is clear. *Only the disciples are left on Jesus' side.* Everyone else has forsaken him. Repudiation is complete. But how can this be? How can God's Son meet such a fate? Why do people not believe? What is going on here? (We ask the same questions today when we encounter unbelief.)

Is there any explanation for the fate we have arrived at by the end of Matthew 12? The answer is: Yes. The explanation begins with simple words: "A Sower went out to sow." "The parable is thus a response to the misunderstanding and plain rejection Jesus has been suffering at the hands of the crowds (11:12, 16-19), Galilean cities (11:20-24), and religious leaders (12:24)."[4]

Homiletical Directions

We begin our homiletical directions without having discussed the text for the week. We felt it was important to get the context straight. The Parable of the Sower is somewhat self-explanatory in

114

its context. Matthew 13:1-23 intends to be Jesus' basic response to the repudiation of his ministry by the people of Israel depicted in Matthew 12. We need to tell this parable *whole* to our hearers!

We propose that the first task of this sermon be to tell the story of the repudiation of Jesus' ministry as we have reviewed it in Matthew 12. You needn't tell all the stories. Tell those that best help you build the case that Jesus has been utterly repudiated—even by his own family. Only the disciples remain.

The hinge of the sermon is the question "Why?" Why has Jesus been repudiated? Why has the kingdom been rejected? Why doesn't Israel repent? You can use language here that bespeaks the questions of why people in our day still repudiate this Son of God. The second task of the sermon, therefore, is simply to raise this "Why?" question.

The third task of our proposed sermon is to tell in our own words or from memory the parable of Jesus and its explanation: 13:1-23. The parable *is* the answer to the "Why?" question. Let it speak for itself! You can include some words of explanation as you tell the story, but *let the story be the frame* of any explanations. This is preferable to sticking the story in a corner and organizing your thoughts around your own way of explaining the parable.

We will make just a few notes here. 13:1-9 simply relates the parable. Then the disciples, the only followers left to Jesus, ask him why he speaks in parables. "To you it is given to know," Jesus says (11:27). To the disciples, secrets are revealed. "And what are the *secrets*? That the kingdom comes with such meekness and weakness, that Jesus who breaks the Law is an agent of God's ruling, that Gentiles and outcasts are included."[5]

Jesus, however, speaks to *them* only in parables. "Them" is probably a reference to Israel. Matthew again uses a quotation from Isaiah to help tell his story: Matthew 13:14 (Isaiah 6:9-10). Israel's eyes are blind. Their ears are heavy of hearing. They do not understand with their hearts. On the other hand, the eyes of the disciples are blessed. Their eyes see and their ears hear because of the One who reveals the secrets to the hearts of humankind. The whole point, of course, is to elucidate the problem with Israel. Hardness of heart also comes in fulfillment of scripture!

The most important part of this lengthy explanation of Israel's hardness of heart is Jesus' explanation of the parable in vv. 18-23. It begins with an admonition: "Hear then the parable of the sower." This word appears to be addressed not only to the disciples but to the reader/hearer of Matthew's Gospel. We have been chosen for this revelation! See 11:25-27; 13:11. We who hear these words are insiders as were the disciples. It is not too late for us.

This section needs to be told forth to our listeners with great care. The very first kind of soil is composed of those who hear but *do not understand*. The *evil One* snatches the word away from them. Remember the many instances in Matthew 12 where Jesus referred to the Pharisees and others as *evil*: 12:34, 35, 39, 45. Others hear and endure only until trials and tribulation come. Still others hear and have the word choked out of them by the cares of the world and the delight in wealth. And still others are the good soil. These are those who hear and *understand.* They bear fruit. (On bearing fruit in Matthew see 3:10-12; 7:15-20; 12:33-34.)

This story of the Sower told in juxtaposition to the repudiation of Jesus in Matthew 12 can end in proclamation. Our hearers need to hear the story of the Sower told over them and their unbelief. They need to hear the story as promise! The final proclamation can go something like this:

"I am the Sower," Jesus is saying to us this day. "I am the Sower and some of the seed I sow falls on ears that fail to understand.

"I am the Sower and some of the seed that I sow falls on ears that understand and endure until trials and tribulation come.

"I am the Sower and some of the seed that I sow falls on ears that hear, but then the cares of the world and the lures of wealth choke it out.

"I am the Sower and some of the seed that I sow falls on good soil and bears fruit in abundance.

"I choose this day to sow my seed upon your heart. I am here to give you to know the secrets of the kingdom of God. I am here because I have chosen you to know my God in heaven. I am here to claim your life for the kingdom of heaven.

"Blessed are your eyes, for they see, and your ears, for they hear."

Amen.

A closing prayer for responsive eyes and ears might be prayed. An appropriate hymn could be sung. We recommend "Lord, Let My Heart Be Good Soil" (*With One Voice* #713).

----

1. Robert H. Smith, *Matthew: Augsburg Commentary on the New Testament* (Minneapolis: Augsburg Press, 1989), p. 160.

2. Jack Dean Kingsbury, *Matthew As Story* (Philadelphia: Fortress Press, 1988), p. 73.

3. Smith, *op. cit.*, p. 167.

4. *Ibid.*, p. 170.

5. *Ibid.*, p. 171.

Chapter 16
Proper 11

Matthew 13:24-30, 36-43

Matthew 13 contains the parabolic ministry of Jesus as Matthew tells the story. The first three of these parables are *seed* parables. Last week's text was the Parable of the Sower who went out to *sow the seed* (Matthew 13:1-9 [10-23]). This week's appointed text is the parable of the one who sowed *good seed* in his field along with Jesus' explanation of the parable of the weeds (vv. 36-43). A few of the omitted verses (vv. 31-33) are appointed for next week.

The parable appointed for this week confirms and adds to part of the reality of the Parable of the Sower. The conflicts raised with Jesus in Matthew 12 (see our Chapter 15) raised the issue of a rationale. Why do people reject Jesus and enter into conflict with him? The answer of the Parable of the Sower is that the seed sown by Jesus falls on different types of soil. The seed sown on the path represents those hear the word of God but do not understand it. The *evil One* comes and snatches away that which had been sown. The answer to the question as to why Jesus is rejected, therefore, is answered by pointing to the enemy.

The second and third types of soil in the Parable of the Sower do not point to evil powers as the problem. The "rocky ground" people receive the seed, the word of God, but have no depth of soil. The "thorny ground" people receive the seed and have it choked out by the cares of the world and the lure of riches. The inevitable question arises as to whether some people are simply predestined to reject the word of God.

This week's parable, however, suggests again and in the strongest terms that this lack of faith is the work of the *enemy*. Good seed is sowed in the field but the enemy comes and sows weeds among the wheat. When the servants of the householder ask why the good

118

seed grows among the weeds the householder replies: "An *enemy* has done this" (13:28). Faith, that is, is in constant jeopardy. "Like a roaring lion your adversary the devil prowls around, looking for someone to devour" (1 Peter 5:8).

The Gospel of Matthew is filled with the reality that Jesus who brings the kingdom is locked in a struggle with the devil. This theme emerges first in Matthew with the temptation story in 4:1-11. (See Chapter 6.) This temptation was the first major conflict of Jesus' ministry.

> *In Matthew's scheme of things, the world is the scene where two kingdoms, or spheres or powers, are locked in cosmic battle (13:36-43). On the one hand, there is the Kingdom of Heaven, which has by God's design become a present, though hidden, reality in Jesus Son of God.... On the other hand, there is the kingdom of Satan (12:26). In this sphere of power Satan himself rules, and he has at his command both angels (25:41) and demons (10:8; 12:24), or unclean spirits (10:1). In both Israel and the world, Satan is at work to bring humans under his control (13:24-30, 38-39). The mark of those who serve him is that they are evil (13:49) and lawless (13:41), for they live contrary to the will of God.[1]*

Kingsbury goes on to point out that when Jesus resists Satan he shows that he is the stronger power! In the parables appointed for this week we discover, however, that Satan continues to wield some power in the world. The cosmic conflict is on!

This teaching is made known by Jesus to his disciples. Kingsbury also mentions that in the latter half of this section of Matthew's Gospel (11:2—16:20) the disciples stand out as recipients of divine revelation. This is clear in 11:25-30 where we hear Jesus say that God has revealed some of his secrets to "babes." We understood that the "babes" are the "little ones," the "least" in Matthew's Gospel. The "babes" are Jesus' disciples to whom revelation is made. This theme is reiterated in 13:10-16, 34-35 where we hear that Jesus spoke to the crowd in parables. The crowd did not understand. The disciples, however, do understand because Jesus reveals the secrets of the parable to them. One of the secrets they come to know is that "...until the consummation of the age, the entire world is the site where people live under the influence of one of two opposing spheres of power: either people live in the sphere of God's end-time Rule under the aegis of the earthly and exalted Jesus, or they live in the sphere of the kingdom of evil under the aegis of Satan (13:24-30, 36-43)."[2] It is no wonder that Jesus taught his disciples to pray, "Deliver us from evil."

Homiletical Directions

Our primary suggestion for preaching on Matthew 13:24-30, 36-43 is to tell forth both of these parables at the outset of the sermon. Tell the stories in such a way that it is clear to all who hear that we live our lives in the midst of the conflict of two great powers: God and Satan. Only at the judgment day will the matter be settled. Set before your people the nature of this conflict. Coming to faith is not an easy matter. There are powers set against us. How shall we stand in the judgment? Do we even have a chance?

The good news, of course, is that Jesus is the Stronger One that John the Baptist prophesied: Matthew 3:11. This Stronger One confronted the evil power in the wilderness: Matthew 4:1-11. This story is familiar by now, but it would be good to recount the basic outlines of this account of Jesus' temptation by the power of evil. In his baptism God announced that this Jesus was his Son: 3:17. The evil one doubted. "If you are the Son of God...." That is the heart of the matter in the temptation of Jesus. But Jesus stands firm. The proclamatory word that comes from Jesus to us through this story is: "I am the Son of God. I am the Stronger One. I have destroyed Satan's final power. I have resisted his every lure. I have turned back his wrath. On the last day I will separate you as wheat from the weeds."

Lead the congregation in the petition of the Lord's Prayer: "Deliver us from evil."

You might next tell the story of Jesus' battle with the powers of darkness and evil on the cross. Use Matthew 27:45-54. There is *darkness* there. There, too, Jesus is tempted to forsake the God whom he believes has forsaken him. He dies believing. And then the whole creation erupts in response. The curtain of the temple is torn in two. The earth shakes. Rocks are split. Tombs are opened. The climax of it all is the word of the centurion. Imagine!—A centurion gets this role at the heart of the story. "Truly this man was God's Son," he confesses (27:54).

The proclamatory word of Jesus coming out of this story might go like this: "The centurion got it right. I am the Son of God. I am the Son of God triumphant over the darkness of that awful day. On that day I disarmed the principalities and powers. On that day I made a public example out of them, triumphing over them through the cross (Colossians 2:15).

"Today I offer my victory to you. Take my hand. I will walk with you through every temptation of the evil one.

"Take my hand. I will gather you one day as wheat in my barn.

"Take my hand. One day you will blossom among the good seed come-to-harvest in my eternal kingdom."

In closing you could lead the congregation again in the response: "Deliver us from evil." Amen.

---

1. Jack Dean Kingsbury, *Matthew As Story* (Philadelphia: Fortress Press, 1988), p. 56.

2. *Ibid.*, p. 137.

Matthew 13:31-33, 44-52

The whole of Jesus' discourse in parables in Matthew 13 demonstrates for us that Jesus did much of his thinking *in stories*. We might more reasonably expect Jesus to teach the nature of the kingdom of heaven through a discourse of ideas. For example, Jesus might have taught that the kingdom of heaven is a secret which is only revealed to disciples. Or that the kingdom of heaven is always in jeopardy because the Devil opposes those who would believe. Such rational discourse would then be taken by us as definitive statements about the meaning of the kingdom of heaven. We would have the whole matter tied up in fine theological fashion.

But, no! Jesus speaks in parables. Jesus thinks in stories. Stories are our entree into the reality of the kingdom of heaven. Stories are always somewhat open-ended. You can't simply extrapolate the points from the stories and think that you have the same thing. "Listen to my points and you will understand the secrets of the kingdom of heaven." Not so. Stories invite our participation. Stories invite us into their reality. With a story there is always room for the Holy Spirit to "apply" the story-reality to our own individual life needs.

Most of the parables in Matthew 13 are parables of the kingdom. See 13:11, 19, 24, 31, 33, 43, 44, 45, 47, 52 for references to the kingdom or the kingdom of heaven in this chapter alone. Other parables of the kingdom are found in 18:23-35 (a king who settled accounts with his servants, Proper 19); 20:1-16 (the householder who pays the same wage to all, Proper 20); 22:1-14 (the king who gave a marriage feast for his son, Proper 23) and 25:1-13 (five wise and five foolish maidens, Proper 27). This reality of the kingdom is front and center in the parables appointed for this week.

We are reminded that John the Baptist's primary message was a message of repentance, "for the kingdom of heaven" is at hand: 3:2. When Jesus announces his own ministry in 4:17 he, too, calls for repentance, for the "kingdom of heaven" is at hand. Likewise, when Jesus sent the disciples on their mission he told them to preach saying, "the kingdom of heaven is at hand," 10:7. The kingdom of heaven is clearly at the heart of Matthew's understanding of Jesus' mission. The parables of the kingdom invite our participation in kingdom reality.

We discussed in our last chapter that the coming of the kingdom of heaven is met with great resistance by the forces of evil. Cosmic forces engage when the kingdom of heaven is at hand. Commenting on the parable of the weeds (13:36-43, omitted from the lectionary) Robert Smith says:

> *What happens in the history of* the world *and in every historical community including the church, all the way up to the* end of the age *is presented as the result of the working both of* the Son of Man *and of* the devil. *Good and evil struggle to gain mastery over people and communities. Good and evil people live cheek by jowl in human communities.*[1]

In Chapter 3 we discussed the fact that Matthew sets before us in his very first characterizations a person who is "righteous"—Joseph—and a person who is "wicked"—Herod. There are ways in which Matthew sees the world always in a basic polarity. Either/or is the order of Matthew's day.

> *The flourishing of evil people in any community is one problem, but another is the arrogance of the pious. Matthew records a number of sayings, noting on the one hand the uneasy coexistence of righteous and evil people, and warning on the other about the inevitable divine discrimination: two kinds of tree (7:17-19), two houses (7:24-27), wheat and weeds (13:24-30), good and bad fish (13:47-50), two sons (21:28-32), wedding guests with and without a proper garment (22:11-14), wise and foolish maidens (25:1-13),*

sheep and goats (25:31-46). The accent in these words falls
at different places, but all urge hearers to examine not others
but themselves.... [2]

This call to self-examination could certainly be a theme in sermons on the parables of Matthew 13.

When we come to the end of the parables we hear Jesus ask the disciples if they *understand.* Understanding is a crucial theme for Matthew. In his telling of the story it is only the disciples who understand. This is due primarily to the reality that God has revealed kingdom secrets to the disciples: 11:25-30; 13:10-17, 34-35. The disciples, however, do not always get it right. We will see this factor at work in the succeeding chapters.

In 13:52 Jesus refers to the disciples as "scribes trained for the kingdom of heaven."

> *Matthew's Gospel seems to some readers to be the product*
> *of Christian scribal activity, and some see a kind of self-*
> *portrait of the evangelist in 13:52. The word translated*
> trained *is* mathteutheis *("discipled" or "apprenticed"). It is*
> *related to* mathete *and to* mathetes = *"disciple," everywhere*
> *in the Gospel. Even Matthew's name* (Matthaios) *is similar*
> *to the Greek word meaning "apprenticed" or "trained."* [3]

Homiletical Directions

All of the parables of the kingdom in Matthew's Gospel stand in narrative analogy with each other. Each one can only be understood in the context of the whole. There would be license here to preach a sermon in which the brief parables appointed for this week are told in narrative analogy with other parables from Matthew 13. One could also make use of the "parables of the kingdom of heaven" found throughout Matthew's Gospel in such a sermon. Such a sermon would major in storytelling with some brief comments to set the context for the stories. Our goal would be to tell Matthew's parables of the kingdom of heaven in such a way that they would invite our hearers into the reality of the kingdom.

In whatever direction our sermon on 13:31-33, 44-52 (and related passages?) takes, the goal must focus on telling the stories.

Jesus told stories. We should not reduce the stories to explanation. That doesn't mean that we cannot help to explain these stories. Include such explanation in the telling of the parables themselves. Let the stories provide the structure of the sermon. Explanations can be woven into the storytelling. This is much to be preferred to reducing the stories to our words of explanation. When we take this path we limit the meaning of these stories to our explanatory expertise. When we focus on the telling of these stories we allow the Holy Spirit to apply them to each individual heart.

Our first homiletical suggestion, therefore, is to use this Sunday as an opportunity to tell the parables of the kingdom of heaven from the Gospel of Matthew. We don't mean to tell them all. Tell the ones you wish to focus on including, of course, the brief parables appointed for this week. Give your telling a structure that helps your hearers follow you from story to story. Then, let the stories and the Holy Spirit work their own way on human hearts.

A second homiletical possibility would be to confine ourselves to the stories appointed for this week in 13:31-33, 44-52. Tell just these stories but tell them in as much amplification as you can. Put some more flesh on the mere bones of these story lines. Do it in your own words. You might wish to set them in a contemporary setting. And that's it. Tell the stories and say Amen. If you choose such an approach you may wish to notify your hearers in advance that your storytelling on this day will be open-ended. Invite them into the stories. What do they hear? Encourage them to share their insights with you and others after the service is over.

A final homiletical possibility would be to create a modern-day story or situation to which the parable is told in response. For example, tell a story you know of the kingdom of God growing to great heights from very insignificant beginnings. When you finish with this story, simply tell the story of the grain of mustard seed: vv. 31-33. Next, tell a story you know about someone who has given up much for the sake of following Jesus. When that story is finished, simply tell the parable in v. 44. Following this you could tell a modern-day story of another person who gave up much followed by a recitation of vv. 45-46. Do likewise with the parable of the kingdom in vv. 47-50. Tell a contemporary story with these verses as response.

However you choose to approach these three little parables of the kingdom of heaven, keep one thing in mind. Let the parables speak for themselves! You may wish to close such a sermon with a prayer that the Spirit might enable us to see ourselves in new ways in the light of Jesus' stories.

---

1. Robert H. Smith, *Matthew: Augsburg Commentary on the New Testament* (Minneapolis: Augsburg Press, 1989), p. 177.

2. *Ibid.*, p. 180.

3. *Ibid.*, p. 182.

Matthew 14:13-21

We move this week from the parables of Jesus (last week's text was Matthew 13:31-33, 44-52) to Jesus' feeding of the multitude in Matthew 14:13-21. The material from 13:53—14:12 is omitted from the lectionary. Some comments on the omitted material are necessary. In the first place, we notice that 13:53 repeats the Matthean formula which comes at the end of the five major teaching blocks in this Gospel: "When Jesus had finished these parables...." (See also 7:28; 11:1; 19:1; 26:1.)

The story in Matthew 13:53-58 is the story of the rejection of Jesus by his own hometown folk. Earlier we have linked this story with that in 11:2-6. In answering John the Baptist's question about his identity Jesus' final word is "...blessed is anyone who takes no *offense* at me." This word of "offense" sets the stage for the material in 11:1—16:20 which has as a major theme the fact that people are offended by Jesus and they repudiate him. In 13:53-58 it is Jesus' own home town people who are *offended* (v. 57). The best they can do in identifying Jesus is to call him "the carpenter's son." This is truly a story of unbelief.

In this story from his hometown Jesus identifies himself as a prophet: 13:57. The identity of Jesus as a prophet is also mentioned in 21:11, 26, 46; 23:37.

As we enter Matthew 14 this theme of identity is still before us. King Herod wonders who this Jesus is. "This is John the Baptist," Herod says to his servants, "he has been raised from the dead..." (14:2). This could sound like a man with a guilty conscience speaking! King Herod feared the people who thought John the Baptist was a prophet. He is a carpenter's son. He is a prophet. He is John the Baptist risen from the dead. These are the identity claims for Jesus in 13:53—14:12. Later in this chapter the disciples will come closer to identifying Jesus. The disciples will confess, "Truly you are the Son of God" (14:33). In Caesarea Philippi Jesus will ask the disciples again about his identity (16:13-20). They give Jesus many proposals before Peter leads the way in confessing: "You are the Messiah, the Son of the living God" (16:16). The identity of Jesus, therefore, is a strong theme throughout these middle chapters of Matthew.

The end of the Herod story in 14:1-12 is also the end of the story for John the Baptist. Herod orders a beheading.

> *So the forerunner completes his work, bearing witness to Jesus not only with his words (3:11-12) but finally also by his execution at the hands of Herod. In his dying, John fore-shadows Jesus' own death and burial.*[1]

When Jesus heard of the death of John he withdrew by boat to a lonely place: 14:13. Jesus' withdrawal in the face of the persecution of the forerunner is hardly surprising.

The story in Matthew 14 moves us from one banquet to another. Herod's bitter banquet and Jesus' joyous feeding of 5,000 stand side by side in awful contrast. Herod kills God's prophet, fearing that he will otherwise lose face or even lose his hold on power. Jesus acts out of deep compassion (9:36; 14:14; 15:32; 20:34) to satisfy the needs of ill and hungry crowds. Together the two meals foreshadow Jesus' last meal and execution. Jesus' path to kingship is not paved with slaughtered corpses but only with his self-offering on behalf of many (20:28).[2]

King Herod presided over a great birthday banquet in the glory and splendor of his palace. His banquet was a feast of *death.* King Jesus presided over a great banquet in the wilderness. His banquet was a feast of *life.* The story of the feeding of the 5,000 is one of two feeding stories told in Matthew's Gospel. The feeding of the 4,000 is told in 15:32-39. This story is not included in the Matthean lectionary year.

Both of Jesus' feeding miracles are modeled closely on the Passover meal which Jesus hosted for the disciples: 26:17-29. (This Passover story is only included in the Matthean lectionary as part of a much longer reading appointed for the Sunday of the Passion: Matthew 26:14—27:66.) The language of the miracle of feeding is liturgical. Jesus took the loaves, looked into heaven, and "*blessed* and *broke* the loaves, and gave them to the disciples, and the disciples gave them to the crowds" (14:19).

Homiletical Directions

We have touched upon two themes that can be put into narrative sermonic form. The first theme is the theme of *identity*. Our first story could be the omitted text from Matthew 13:53-58. Dramatize Jesus' return to his hometown. What will he find? He found people unable to recognize him. The best they could come up with was that he was a carpenter's son. They took *offense* at him. You may wish to make reference to Matthew 11:2-6 on this matter of offense.

Story two could well be the story of Herod's attempt to name and identify Jesus. "This is John the Baptist risen from the dead." This is the attempt to identify Jesus on the part of a guilty man. It is hard to see the reality of Jesus through the lens of our own guilt.

Story three would be the appointed text for this week. Contrast Herod's feast of death with Jesus' feast of life. In this feast we see the identity of Jesus as the One who has compassion on all those in need. Clearly such compassion extends also to us. Here is a man who feeds hungry people. Here is a man who holds a feast of life in the wilderness. Here is a man who offers to stand at our table today and offer us the gift of life as well. Jesus is here today as the Compassionate One, the One who will meet our needs. This is who Jesus is. This is his identity. He is Emmanuel. He is God with us under forms of bread and wine.

If this is a Communion Sunday in your congregation, close this sermon by indicating that this Compassionate One who meets human needs is the host of our table today. He has come to feed us. Take and eat. This is my body. Take and drink. This is my blood.

A second narrative possibility for this week's text is to focus entirely on the *meals*. Tell first the story of Herod's meal in its grand and glorious setting. But this meal is ultimately a feast of death.

Our second story would be the story of Jesus' feeding of the 5,000. This is a feast of life. We would recommend that you note that this is not the only time in Matthew's Gospel that Jesus has compassion on needy people. There is another feeding story in 15:32-39 that is not included in the Matthew lectionary year. Here is another story of a feast of life. Tell it, too.

Finally, tell the story of Jesus' Passover meal with his disciples: 26:17-29. This, too, is a feast of life. The good news, of course, is that this feast of life is set still today in the midst of the wilderness, in the midst of a world filled with death.

These stories should culminate in an invitation to the needy to come to the table of the Compassionate One. Jesus says to us today: "Come to my table. I have seen your need. I have had compassion. I am here to feed you with the bread of life. Come to my feast of life. Eat this bread which will sustain your life. Drink this cup of forgiveness (Matthew 26:27-28). 'I will never again drink of this fruit of the vine until that day when I drink it new with you in my Father's kingdom.'" Amen.

---

1. Robert H. Smith, *Matthew: Augsburg Commentary on the New Testament* (Minneapolis: Augsburg Press, 1989), p. 185.

2. *Ibid.*, p. 186.

Matthew 14:22-33

Jesus is busy and active in this week's appointed text. He made the disciples get into the boat: v. 22. He dismissed the crowds: v. 22. He went alone to pray: v. 23. He came to the disciples walking on the sea in the fourth watch of the night: v. 25. He ordered Peter to "Come," walking on the water: v. 29. He caught Peter's hand lest he sink in the waves of doubt: v. 31.

When Jesus came walking on the sea in the middle of the night the disciples were afraid. "It is a ghost!" they wailed. All the disciples cried out for fear. Jesus spoke simply: "Take heart, it is I; do not be afraid."

> *Jesus' words are more than mere identification. They are really an awesome formula of self-revelation, literally "I AM" (ego eimi). Jesus presents himself to his disciples as the solid and saving presence of the eternal God (1:23; 18:20; 28:20; cf. John 8:58; Exodus 3:14; Isaiah 43:10).*[1]

As we have seen in Matthew's story, it is to the disciples, the "babes," the "little ones," to whom the Father is revealed: 11:25-30; 13:10-17. Now it is revealed to the disciples in a very special way that Jesus is Emmanuel. Jesus can speak the name of the divine as revealed to Moses: Exodus 3:13-15. "I Am Who I Am." "I Will Be What I Will Be." This is the name God revealed to Moses. There was a great desire in the ancient world to know the *name* of God. They thought that if they knew God's name they could control and manipulate God for their own purposes. In the light of this desire, the divine name God revealed to Moses is fascinating. Moses got a name. He did not, however, get the name of a God he could manipulate. "I Am Who I Am." And so it is with Jesus. Emmanuel-Jesus is never a God whom humans can put to work for their own ends. Emmanuel-Jesus ("It is I") works for our ends! Humans never control the God revealed in the Bible.

Peter—who else?—answered Jesus' claim. "If you're really who you say you are, bid me to walk on the water." Peter suddenly takes center stage in this story. In just these few verses we hear of Peter's pride, his fall, his rescue, and his restoration. It is not just in this story that Peter plays a central role. Throughout the central section of Matthew's Gospel Peter plays a vital role.

> *A striking feature of Matthew's Gospel is the prominence accorded to Peter, especially here near the midpoint of the narrative in a series of scenes, most of which find no place in the other Gospels (14:28-33; 15:15; 16:13-20; 17:24-27; 18:21-22).... Readers disagree about the significance of Peter in Matthew's Gospel. Is Peter chief among the Twelve, holding a position of unique leadership among them? Or is Peter typical of the Twelve? The latter seems more likely.*[2]

Peter is pictured in Matthew's Gospel as a man who believes and disbelieves in almost the same moment. In the language of Martin Luther, Peter is *simul justus et peccator*, simultaneously a saint and a sinner. He believes enough to walk on water. When he sees the wind, however, he is afraid. He cries out to be saved: "Lord, save me." We hear this cry to the Lord for help throughout Matthew's Gospel: 15:22, 25 (a Canaanite woman); 17:15 (the father of an epileptic son); 20:31, 33 (two blind men). We take these to be the cries of faith. The person of faith is the one who cries out to Jesus in time of need. That's what Peter did.

Jesus calls Peter's plea "faith." But it is "little faith," v. 31. Jesus often speaks of the disciples as those of "little faith"—6:30; 8:26; 16:8; 17:20. Matthew gives us, therefore, a complex picture of the disciples. They are special. It is to them that God has revealed secrets. (See above.) They understand: 13:51. But at the same time they are those of "little faith." Our rational minds push for one or the other. *Either* the disciples are men of unbelief *or* they are men of great faith. That's logical. Logical, perhaps, but not true to life. We think of our own lives. Sometimes we believe. Sometimes we have "little faith." Matthew paints a true picture. *Simul justus et peccator* is a wise analysis of the Christian person.

At the end of the story the disciples have it right. They all fall down and worship Jesus. (See our Chapter 2 for material on worshiping Jesus in Matthew's Gospel.) "Truly you are the Son of God," they confess. Son of God. This is the identity of Jesus. We have talked in these last few chapters about the question of Jesus' identity that arises in 11:2-6 when John the Baptist sends his disciples to Jesus asking, "Are you the One who is to come or do we look for another?" In Matthew 12 the conflict between Jesus and the Pharisees heightens. The Pharisees do not know who he is. They accuse him of having a demon: 12:24. Jesus' own family has difficulty understanding him: 12:46-50. His hometown folk can only imagine him as a carpenter's son: 13:54-58. They take offense at him. Herod thinks he is John the Baptist risen from the dead: 14:1-12. And now the disciples confess him to be "Son of God." Peter's confession of Jesus as the Messiah, Son of the living God, in Caesarea Philippi is the climax of this series: 16:13-20. With this passage ending in 16:20 we come to the climax of the second part of Matthew's Gospel.

Part Three of Matthew's Gospel begins with Jesus' words to his disciples that as the Son of God he now must go to Jerusalem and suffer many things from the elders and chief priests and scribes and be killed and on the third day arise (Matthew 16:21). In the Preface we named this section of Matthew's Gospel (16:21—28:20): "Journey to Jerusalem." The very first words of this section speak of this reality. In 17:1-11 we have the story of the Transfiguration wherein God confirms from heaven that "This is my Son, the Beloved; with him I am well pleased; listen to him!" (17:5) Identity issues reach a climax in the story of the Transfiguration.

Homiletical Directions

Our first homiletical possibility is to take up the theme we have been discussing: the identity of Jesus. We discussed this as a possibility also in our Chapter 18. If you did not take up that possibility last week you can give it further consideration this week. Such a sermon might walk through the narratives beginning in 11:2-

6 which track this issue of identity. (We have discussed these passages above and in Chapter 18.) Such a sermon might well lead to a question to be put to our modern audience. What think ye of the Christ? Who do you believe that Jesus is?

A sermon that asks the question of Jesus' identity, however, is not sufficient. We have certainly learned from Matthew's Gospel that the reality of Jesus' identity needs to be *revealed.* Humans do not come to faith out of their own insight and inner resources. Remember again 11:25-30 and 13:10-17! The Father reveals these things to babes. To the disciples it has *been given to know* (13:11) the secrets of the kingdom of heaven.

A closing proclamation might announce what it is that God reveals to us in this week's text. (An alternative is to base a closing proclamation on all the identity passages you narrate for this week's sermon.) Jesus says to us today: "It is I. Have no fear. I am Emmanuel come to save you from every wind and wave. I am the Son of God worshiped by the disciples. I invite your worship as well."

Close with a prayer to the Holy Spirit to plant Jesus' word of revelation deep in our hearts.

A second homiletical possibility is to deal with the *simul justus et peccator* theme. Tell first the textual story centered on Peter as one who believes enough to walk on water and disbelieves enough to need to cry out to Jesus in his need. Jesus calls Peter's faith "little faith." Following the story for this week's assigned text tell some of the other "little faith" stories from Matthew's Gospel. There is a very important "little faith" story regarding the disciples told in 16:1-12. (This story is omitted from the lectionary.) The sequence of the stories in 15:32—16:13 follows the Markan order. In 15:32-39 we have the story of the feeding of the 4,000. Immediately following this story the Pharisees ask for a sign from heaven: 16:1. They've just seen a multitude fed and they ask for a sign! Incredible. The disciples are no better, however. They get in the boat with Jesus at the end of a feeding afternoon and they realize they have no bread: 16:5. They, too, have just witnessed the feeding of the thousands and now they are worried about not having enough to eat. Doubly incredible. Jesus calls them men of "little faith" and reminds them of what they have seen. In this bracket of stories the disciples both assist in feeding the multitudes (an act of faith) and appear to be men of "little faith" in almost the same instant.

There is also a "little faith" story in 17:14-20. (This passage is not part of the Matthean lectionary.) The disciples have just come down from the mountain of transfiguration with their faith aglow. Back on the ground they do not have enough faith to heal a boy with a demon. They ask Jesus why they could not cast it out. Jesus answers: "Because of your little faith" (17:20). Once again faith and "little faith" appear to coexist in the disciples simultaneously.

A closing proclamation for this "little faith" theme might report Jesus saying something like this: "I loved Peter. I loved him when his faith was strong. I loved him when his faith was little. Through my love Peter will finally prevail. And so it shall be with you. I love you when your faith is strong. I love you when your faith is little. My love for you will finally prevail. You can trust me on this one. I am, after all, the very Son of God." Amen.

---

1. Robert H. Smith, *Matthew: Augsburg Commentary on the New Testament* (Minneapolis: Augsburg Press, 1989), p. 187.

2. *Ibid.*

Matthew 15: (10-20) 21-28

The assigned Gospel text for this week skips over a couple of sections in Matthew's story. Matthew 14:34-36 cites Jesus' journey to Gennesaret. The crowds of people recognized him immediately and all of the sick came to him for healing. Just a touch of Jesus' garment brought healing to many. The crowd in Gennesaret recognized Jesus. They came to him in their need.

The crowd in Gennesaret presents quite a contrast to the Pharisees and scribes from Jerusalem who encounter Jesus in order to test him with questions: 15:1-20. Jesus tries to get the Pharisees and scribes to *understand* (v. 10) why their traditions about what defiles a person are inside-out and backwards. What comes out of the heart is what defiles a person. That's Jesus' point; "...but to eat with unwashed hands does not defile" (15:20). The disciples, too, lack *understanding* of this matter: v. 16. The issue of understanding is not new to our story. It appeared several times in Matthew 13. See vv. 10-15, 18, 23, 51. Sometimes it seems that the disciples understand, sometimes they do not. They have much yet to learn. Such is the hallmark of a disciple in any age.

Smith comments on the material in Matthew 15 as follows:

> *Chapter 15 is actually a smaller unit set within a number of larger sections. First, it is part of the sequence of material in 15:1—16:12, which in turn is bracketed by two great moments of confession. Disciples hail Jesus as "Son of God" first in the boat on the sea (14:33) and then again at Caesarea Philippi (16:16). The enclosed material (15:1—16:12) begins (15:1-9) and ends (16:1-12) with treatments of the teaching or tradition of the Pharisees. So the twin themes of high confession of Jesus and deep opposition to Jesus, which loom so large in all of 11:1—16:20, are further developed here in chapter 15.*[1]

There is another theme that ties these stories together, and that is the theme of bread. Matthew 14 began with a feast at Herod's palace (14:1-12) which was followed by the story of Jesus' feeding of the 5,000 (14:13-21). The dispute between Jesus and the Pharisees and scribes from Jerusalem is also about eating (15:1-20). The text assigned for this week has Jesus saying to a Gentile woman that he cannot take Israel's *bread* and give it to her. She replies: "Yes, Lord, yet even the dogs eat the crumbs that fall from their masters' table" (v. 27). Matthew 15 closes with the story of Jesus' feeding of the 4,000 (vv. 32-39). Why these stories relate to the theme of bread is another matter. Is this a mnemonic device for storytellers? Is it merely accidental? Were questions of eating crucial questions for the Matthean community? We have no definitive answers to these questions. Robert Smith suggests that bread is a rich symbol for teaching and salvation.

It is this topic of bread and eating that ties together Jesus' discussion with the Pharisees and scribes from Jerusalem with the story of the Canaanite woman from the district of Tyre and Sidon. We're in pagan territory now. Gentile land. Jesus comes face to face here with an *unclean* woman. That has been the topic of conversation between Jesus and the religious authorities. They had all kinds of rules and regulations about what is *clean* and *unclean*. One of the functions of this distinction was to keep the "wrong people," however defined, away from the banquet table. Jesus knows this tradition. He, too, is ready to exclude a woman from the table. "I was sent only to the lost sheep of the house of Israel," Jesus tells his disciples in trying to get rid of this woman. Still she came into his presence. She knelt before him. "Lord, help me," she said. Jesus replied: "It is not fair to take the *children's food* and throw it to the dogs." "Yes, Lord," she retorted, "yet even the dogs eat the *crumbs* that fall from their masters' table."

This is clearly one of the most unbelievable stories in the entire Gospel tradition. What is Jesus doing out there in pagan land, anyway? And why does he try to keep the woman from the table? We wish he had never said these words. But he did. And the unclean Gentile woman responded. She cried out for mercy. Jesus was touched by this cry for mercy. By the *law* the woman should have been excluded from the table. By the *gospel* mercy is be shown. Jesus said: "Woman, *great* is your faith! Let it be done for you as you wish." Her daughter was healed instantly.

The thrust of these stories in 15:1-20 and 21-28 is that the table is thrown open! In the case of the woman the table is thrown open to unclean Gentiles. The story of the Gentile centurion in 8:5-13 is a kind of parallel story to the tale of the unclean woman who helped to remind Jesus of his mission of mercy. The centurion is also commended for his faith: "Truly I tell you, in no one in Israel have I found such faith.... Go; let it be done for you according to your faith" (8:10, 13).

In the case of the Gentile woman we have heard that her faith is *great*. In our previous chapter we discussed the disciples as those who were often characterized as those of "little faith." Here is a woman of "great faith." A Gentile woman. An unclean woman. What is her faith? Her cry for mercy appears to be the mark of her faith. (Other cries for mercy are heard in 17:15 and 20:31, 33.) Such is the true nature of faith. It is a cry for mercy to One who can help. If we wish our faith to be great we need only come to Emmanuel with a cry for help. He could not turn away an unclean Gentile woman. He won't turn us away, either.

The stories told in 15:1-28, a story of the Pharisees and scribes from Jerusalem and a story of a woman from Gentile-land, present us with a grand contrast. The Pharisees dispute and disbelieve. They should know better. The woman disputes and believes. How did she know better? Yet she became Emmanuel's teacher. She reminded him of his mission to the Gentiles. This week's text, therefore, can be treated as a missionary text.

Homiletical Directions

Let's stick first to this mission theme. We have many story telling options here. We can tell the stories of Matthew 15:1-28 contrasting the clean who wished to keep all others clean and the unclean woman who lived in the world of the pagans. Jesus' word to the "clean" opened up the table in a surprising way to the "unclean."

The Canaanite woman is a great teacher of mission! You can have a lot of fun telling these as contrasting stories. The point is clear. Jesus' mission includes the unclean, the Gentiles, you and me!

This reality can be supported by the story of the centurion in 8:5-13, a story not appointed in the Matthean lectionary. Or, we can remind our hearers again of the theme of mission to the Gentiles contained in Matthew 1 (cf. the genealogy, see our Chapter 1) and Matthew 28:16-20, the Great Commission. Such a sermon will underscore both that we as unclean Gentiles are included at God's table and that, as those "made clean" by the blood of the lamb, we have a mission to spread this news to the ends of the earth.

Another option for preaching would be to deal with the theme of faith. Story one would be the textual story told with an emphasis on her cry for mercy and Jesus' final word that her faith is "great." The woman's great faith is clearly evidenced by her mercy cry. Faith is the name for those who come to Jesus with their need.

Story two could be the similar story of the centurion in 8:5-13. This is a wonderful story of one who understands the power of the word. He comes to Jesus in his need, trusting that Jesus' word can heal his paralyzed servant. Jesus names this reliance upon him and his healing word as a faith he has not found even in Israel. Jesus speaks his word to the centurion: "Go; let it be done for you according to your faith."

Other examples of people coming to Jesus with a cry for mercy are the story of the father with an epileptic son (17:14-20, a story not appointed in the Matthew year) and the story of two blind men coming to Jesus for healing (20:29-34, also not appointed in the Matthew year). If you choose to tell these stories as well, focus on their cry for mercy and the reality of Jesus' healing response.

Our congregations are filled with people who are in need, unclean, outsiders. Lead them in a closing litany where you have them say aloud, "Lord, have mercy," as an expression of their need. To each cry of "Lord, have mercy" speak back to them in the name of Jesus with words shaped by the stories you have told. In response to cries of "Lord, have mercy" we can respond, for example, with:

139

"Great is your faith." "I have not found such faith even in Israel." "Your need shall be supplied." "Your eyes shall be opened." Fashion these words of Jesus based in the stories and applicable to the people as you know them.

---

1. Robert H. Smith, *Matthew: Augsburg Commentary on the New Testament* (Minneapolis: Augsburg Press, 1989), p. 189.

Chapter 21
Proper 16

Matthew 16:13-20

With the text appointed for this week we come to the climax of Part Two of Matthew's Gospel. We arrive at this particular point in the lectionary having omitted 15:29-31 (the crowds glorify the God of Israel for Jesus' healing ministry); 15:32-39 (the feeding of the 4,000); and 16:1-12 (the Pharisees seek a sign and the disciples demonstrate their "little faith"). This entire section begins in 4:17 with the words, "*From that time Jesus began* to preach...." The first section of this material, 4:17—11:1, describes the words and deeds of Jesus' ministry to Israel. Chapters 11:2—16:20 deal primarily with questions concerning the identity of Jesus and the repudiation of Jesus by the people of Israel. In 16:21 we hear again Matthew's formulaic words, "*From that time Jesus began* to show his disciples how he must go to Jerusalem and suffer...." These words mark a new stage in Matthew's story.

It is vitally important in our understanding of Matthew's Gospel that we recognize the climactic character of this week's passage which centers in Peter's confession. As we indicated above, the material in 11:2ff. deals with the theme of Jesus' identity over and over again. (See our Chapters 18 and 19 for a discussion of this theme of identity. It might be important to review this material in order to see the big picture of which Peter's confession serves as climax.)

> *The time has come for fresh understandings of Jesus and clarifications of the disciples' role. Jesus begins by asking his disciples,* Who do men say that the Son of man is? *Mark in his Gospel leads readers along until finally they are faced with the solemn declaration that Jesus is the mysterious "Son of man" (8:20) who goes to Jerusalem to suffer. For Matthew that is not the end but the beginning of the matter.*

He takes it for granted that readers know Jesus as Son of man. *That title appears again at the end of this whole section (16:27-28) and so* Son of man *frames all the material between vv. 13 and 28. Matthew has constructed his narrative in such a way as to interpret that somewhat puzzling title by means of the confession of Jesus as* the Christ, the Son of the Living God *(16:16), and by means of the first passion prediction (16:12).*[1]

Jack Kingsbury also discusses the place of this narrative in Matthew's story coming as it does after many conflicting thoughts about Jesus' identity.

Matthew fashions two evaluative points of view which he juxtaposes to each other in the pericope with which he brings the entire second part of his story to its culmination, Peter's confession near Caesarea Philippi (16:13-20). The one evaluative point of view is that of the various segments making up the Jewish public. The disciples, asked by Jesus who people imagine him to be, reply, "Some say John the Baptist, others say Elijah, and others Jeremiah or one of the prophets" (16:13-14). In other words, the evaluative point of view concerning Jesus' identity which the Jewish public takes is that he is a prophet of some stature or other.[2]

Kingsbury goes on to assert that the reader knows that "prophet" is not an adequate title for Jesus for at least three reasons. Firstly, Jesus cannot be John the Baptist because John is the forerunner of Jesus. Secondly, the answer that Jesus is a prophet evokes no blessing from Jesus. Thirdly, this is not the way God "thinks" about Jesus as we know from the story of Jesus' baptism: God calls Jesus, "Son."

So the evaluative point of view of the Jewish public that Jesus is a prophet of some kind is false. According to Kingsbury, there is a second evaluative point of view in this story. This is Peter's point of view. Peter says: "You are the Messiah, the Son of the living God."

This evaluative point of view is correct, for two of the same reasons the other one is false: (a) it elicits from Jesus a "blessing" (16:17); and (b) it tallies with the way God "thinks" about Jesus...although the disciples correctly understand who Jesus is, they do not as yet know that central to Jesus' divine sonship is death on the cross. Hence, they are in no position at this point to go and make disciples of all nations.[3]

Standard commentaries have much to say about this passage. Almost every verse touches upon important realities. We will keep our remarks brief. Peter's confession (v. 16) is the second time that the disciples, here represented by Peter, have confessed Jesus to be Son of God. See also 14:28-*33*. The Son of God theme is, of course, a strong theme in Matthew's Gospel. The first hint of this theme is 1:18 where we hear that Jesus will be fathered by the Holy Spirit. The whole "Emmanuel" story in 1:18-25 underscores Jesus' divine reality. The story of Jesus' birth in Matthew 2 also underscores Jesus' divinity. The climactic "Son of God" passage in the early portion of Matthew's Gospel is, of course, the story of Jesus' baptism: 3:11-17. In 8:28-34 the demoniacs seem to recognize Jesus as Son of God: v. 29. The next reference to Jesus as Son of God comes in 14:28-33. Following 16:13-20 the next important Son of God text is the story of Jesus' transfiguration: 17:1-8. In his baptism and in the transfiguration the reader of Matthew hears how God "thinks" about Jesus. Other important passages with the Son of God theme are: 26:57-68; 27:40, 45-54 (the confession of the centurion!); and the Great Commission passage in 28:16-20.

We have commented earlier on the fact that Peter plays a very strong role in these middle passages of Matthew's Gospel. Commentators tend to see Peter as the spokesman for the disciples. He voices their common convictions. Jesus blesses Peter (i.e. the disciples) for this confession. Jesus speaks forth the truth that the disciples did not come to this confession out of their own power. Flesh and blood, that is, did not enable them to confess Jesus as Christ and Son of God. Their confession is *revealed to them "by my father in heaven."* We have spoken about this in our recent chapters. Again we refer you to 11:25-30 and 13:10-17 as evidence that these disciples, these babes, have been privileged to have made known to them the secrets of the kingdom and the identity of their master, Jesus. A Lutheran author cannot help but be reminded here of Luther's explanation of the work of the Holy Spirit in his Small Catechism:

> *I believe that I cannot by my own understanding or effort believe in Jesus Christ my Lord, or come to him. But the Holy Spirit* has called me through the Gospel....

Faith is always a gift of God!

Peter, or Peter's confession, is the rock on which the church is built. The Greek word for church (*ekklesia*) is used only here and in Matthew 18:17 in all of the Gospels. Commentators have always noted that Matthew has a distinct interest in the church.

> *Jesus looks at Peter, called, instructed, sometimes boldly treading the waters, and sometimes sinking like a rock (14:28-31), full of understanding and often of little faith, but nevertheless at this point knowing and confessing. Peter stands forth among the Twelve as their representative, and on behalf of all he utters the good confession. And in him Jesus sees the whole future community of disciples and confessors. Jesus looks away from the Pharisees and Sadducees and scribes (15:1-20; 16:1-12) and gazing upon Peter and the Twelve, sees the* church...*the new community of the end times.*[4]

The church will be built on the confession of the disciples, and the gates of hell will not prevail against it. We hear once more from Smith where he argues that Matthew understands his Gospel to be the successor of Peter:

> *Matthew's Gospel is all about Jesus and the new community, how Jesus founds it, how its fellowship is entered and its life regulated. It is all about the secrets of life, its standards, values, priorities, and style, what is permitted and what is forbidden, who is included and who excluded.... And how does Jesus instruct the community in the days after Easter?*

Through his words, the fullness of his teaching, deposited in the Gospel of Matthew. The Gospel of Matthew itself, as the treasury of the words of Jesus, addresses the community with authority, teaching how people enter the community (keys) and the standards and criteria for behavior within the community (bind and loose)...Matthew has collected the words and commands of Jesus known from the disciples and Peter, and has recorded them with loving care in his book. This book contains "all that I have commanded" (28:19).... The successor of Peter is the Gospel of Matthew.... Matthew reissued the words of Jesus because of confusion in the church resulting from the energetic and enthusiastic labors of prophets and teachers and leaders. It is Matthew's contention that anyone claiming to speak for the exalted Jesus should be tested by the norm of Jesus' own words, as enshrined in Matthew's Gospel.[5]

Homiletical Directions

Reference to the standard commentaries will present you with any number of ideas that could be the base of didactic sermons on this text. The narrative possibilities are also many. The first we will mention is a narrative sermon built around the theme of *Jesus' identity*. We have discussed this possibility in our Chapters 18 and 19. We refer you to those chapters if you have not chosen to take this narrative path in earlier weeks.

Secondly, the *Son of God* theme can be pursued through a number of passages in Matthew's Gospel. We have listed all these passages in the material above. The point would be to trace the Son of God motif through the eyes of this evangelist. We first raised this possibility in our discussion of Jesus' baptism in our Chapter 5. We refer you to this chapter for more detailed homiletical possibilities.

Thirdly, the theme of *revelation* suggests itself. We have touched upon this theme as well in recent chapters. The three passages that could be narratively tied together under this theme are those mentioned above: 11:25-30; 13:10-17; and this week's passage with a focus on the reality that "flesh and blood" did not reveal to the disciples the true identity of Jesus, Son of God: v. 17. It was *"revealed to them by my father."* Tell these three stories with a focus on this revealing activity of God. This same reality confronts us today. It is still true that "flesh and blood," our mortal powers, cannot lead us to confession. We can't manufacture faith out of the abyss of our sinful condition! Such is the work of the Holy Spirit—to follow Luther's thought. And we know where the Holy Spirit works. The Holy Spirit works wherever and whenever the story of Jesus is told.

We might conclude our sermon with a challenge to our listeners to "tend" the story of Jesus in one of its many forms (cf. Word and Sacraments). There the Spirit will work. There the Spirit will take the story of Jesus on the journey from ear to heart. There the Holy Spirit will work to create faith within you—faith in Jesus, the Son of God. Close your sermon with a prayer that the Holy Spirit might, indeed, make faith happen in our hearts of "flesh and blood."

---

1. Robert H. Smith, *Matthew: Augsburg Commentary on the New Testament* (Minneapolis: Augsburg Press, 1989), pp. 197-198.

2. Jack Dean Kingsbury, *Matthew As Story* (Philadelphia: Fortress Press, 1988), pp. 74-75.

3. *Ibid.*

4. Smith, *op. cit.*, p. 201.

5. *Ibid.*, pp. 202-203.

Matthew 16:21-28

With this week's text we enter Part Three of Matthew's story. In our outline in the Preface we named Part Three: "Journey of Jesus to Jerusalem," Matthew 16:21—28:20. The key words that alert us to a new phase of Matthew's story are, "From that time on..." (see also 4:17). "From that time on, Jesus began to show his disciples that he must undergo great suffering...." The content of this new section of Matthew is not teaching! We enter a journey now, a journey to the cross. The cross of Jesus stands in the near future casting a strong shadow back across the terrain of Jesus' life and ministry.

Jack Kingsbury points out that Part Three of Matthew's Gospel is marked by conflict.

> *Here the conflict between Jesus and Israel (especially the religious leaders), which was foreshadowed in the first part of the story and which, in the second part, burst into the open (chap. 9) and then crystallized into irreconcilable hostility (chap. 12) runs its course to resolution in the passion and resurrection of Jesus (chaps. 26-28). The verse with which this third part begins, 16:21, prepares the reader already for the resolution of Jesus' conflict with Israel in at least two aspects: (a) it underscores the fact that there are three principals involved in Jesus' passion, namely, God (dei: "It is necessary"), Jesus, and the religious leaders. And (b) it reminds the reader that while all three desire the death of Jesus, the objective the leaders pursue is destructive (12:14), whereas that intended by God and Jesus is to save (1:21).*[1]

Kingsbury goes on to point out that the journey motif is the literary device which gives the remaining chapters of Matthew their structure. This was a common literary practice in the ancient world (cf. Luke's Travel Narrative, Luke 9:51—19:27). Jesus has been engaged in travels in the earlier chapters in Matthew, but in these stories Jesus usually withdraws in the face of danger. From 16:21 on Jesus engages in a journey to Jerusalem, a journey into danger that is "necessary." This is God's plan for Jesus.

> *The second literary device Matthew employs to lend cohesion to this third part of his story is the passion-prediction. There are three such predictions (16:21; 17:22-23; 20:17-19), and these in turn are supplemented by a verse in the passion account itself which calls them to mind (26:2). These three passion-predictions are the counterpart to the major summary-passages found in the second part of Matthew's story (4:23; 9:35; 11:1). The function they serve is at least twofold. On the one hand, they invite the reader to view the whole of Jesus' life story following 16:21 from the single, overriding perspective of his passion and resurrection. On the other hand, they also invite the reader to construe the interaction of Jesus with the disciples throughout 16:21—28:20 as controlled by Jesus' concern to inculcate in them his understanding of discipleship as servanthood (16:24-25; 20:25-28).*[2]

Robert Smith refers to the relation of the cross to this passage as a *death shadow* that has hung over Jesus' ministry from the beginning when Herod first sought his life: Matthew 2.

> *Early in his ministry religious leaders charged Jesus with blasphemy (9:3, cf. 9:11) and collusion with Satan (9:34; 10:35; 12:24), and soon they plotted to destroy him (12:14). The execution of John the Baptist (14:1-12), Jesus' forerunner, presages Jesus' own fate. The plot thickened as resistance to Jesus spilled over to include not only local leaders but also Pharisees and scribes who came down from Jerusalem to observe, to debate, to test (15:1-20; 16:1-4).*[3]

The immediate connection with this week's material and that which has gone before is that between 16:20 and 16:21. In 16:20 Jesus charged the disciples to tell no one that he was the Christ. One of the reasons that they were not to tell anyone is that Jesus has not as yet revealed to them the entire reality of his mission. In 16:21 Jesus begins to reveal to the disciples the suffering truth of God's plan (*dei*, "it is necessary") for his life. "I am a Messiah who has come to suffer."

Peter couldn't take this newly revealed reality. "God forbid!" Peter howls. "Let this not happen to you." Peter seems to appeal to the God whom he has just confessed (16:17) to be Jesus' father to rescue Jesus from "the necessity" of the Father's plan. Peter is presumptuous! He is as presumptuous as he was when he asked Jesus to enable him to walk on water (14:28-33). Peter presumptively supposes that his plan can replace God's plan.

Jesus' reply to Peter is that Peter is driven by Satan when he suggests such a plan. (See our Chapter 4 on the work of Satan in Matthew's Gospel.) Just moments before, Peter has been commended by Jesus for his confession. Jesus had told Peter that his confession was revealed to him by his Father in heaven (v. 17). Now it is Satan who drives Peter's action. Peter is caught between cosmic powers! As such he is the representative of humankind. He is the representative of us all. We are all caught in the struggle of cosmic powers. Life is serious business. We are vulnerable. Sometimes we get it right. Sometimes we get it wrong. With Peter we are often caught in the clutches of Satan.

In their encounter Jesus refers to Peter as a stumbling block (Greek: *skandalon*). We have encountered this word also in 11:6 and 13:57 where it refers to people being "scandalized" or offended by Jesus. Now Peter is the offender. He is a stumbling block. In one moment his confession is the *rock* (v. 18) on which the church is built. In the next moment he is a stumbling *block.* A rock and a block. Such is Peter. We are reminded again of Luther's saying that we as people of God are simultaneously saint and sinner (*simul justus et peccator*). This word of Luther is difficult to understand and explain in the abstract. It is true, however, to human life. We see it lived out in the life of Peter, rock and block. We see it lived out in our lives as well.

There are interesting parallels between this story of Peter and words we read in 1 Peter 2:6-8. Here Jesus is referred to as the

149

cornerstone of the Christian community. (Cf. also Isaiah 8:14-15 and 28:16.) Jesus is a *stone,* however, that is often rejected. He is a stone that makes people stumble (*skandalon*) and a stone that makes people fall. Jesus is simultaneously stone and stumbling block. It is almost as if Peter's "offense" is a preview of Jesus as the "offending" one who makes people stumble. Our lives are much like the life of Peter. We, too, stumble and fall. Peter survived his stumbling. So shall we. Our "little faith" upholds us as long as we don't stumble over Jesus!

In vv. 24-28 Jesus applies his language of suffering and the cross to his disciples. For the first time the disciples begin to learn the true meaning of following Jesus. Jesus, by the way, had said to Peter: "Get behind me." The problem with Peter was that he was trying to get *ahead* of Jesus rebuking the very plan of God. Peter's place is not *ahead* of Jesus. Peter's place, our place, is *behind* Jesus. We are called to be *followers.* We are called to take up the cross. We are called to lose our lives in order to find them. We are called to follow in order that one day we might stand before Jesus, the Son of man, and the angels of heaven and receive our reward.

> *Matthew pictures Jesus in scenes of judgment sometimes as judge and sometimes as advocate or prosecutor (7:22-23; 13:14-43; 25:31-46), not because Matthew is harsh, demanding, or brooding and not because he is especially intrigued with the future of the world.... Matthew by all means wishes to drive home the overriding value of very practical deeds of mercy and love. He struggled against trends in his environment, such as the elevation of ritual observance (12:1-14; 15:1-20) or boasting about spiritual endowments (7:15-23) or arrogance on the part of teachers and leaders (23:8-10). These and other currents threatened the vitality and centrality of mercy, and Matthew struggled against them.[4]*

Homiletical Directions

There is much to *teach* from these few verses of Matthew in our sermon for this week. We can teach on topics ranging from the theology of the cross to *simul justus et peccator* to the nature of discipleship and more! These teaching opportunities are difficult to pass by.

There are some narrative possibilities as well. We'll mention two just briefly. We have in the Gospel text the first passion prediction of Jesus' ministry as Matthew tells the story. We've turned a corner in the tale. Jesus' life began under the threat of death by King Herod: Matthew 2. In his ministry the hostility of the religious leaders grew increasingly: 9:10-12, 32-34; 12:9-*14*, 22-24. The story of the murder of John the Baptist is told in 14:1-12. The forerunner dies. The die is cast for Jesus. Jesus' life is in jeopardy, too. With today's text we know where we are headed in this story. In the passion story in Matthew 26-27 we hear the details of Jesus' suffering.

These stories could certainly be woven together as a kind of theology of the cross. Jesus' word out of this bracket of stories would be something like: "I am the Messiah who suffers. I am the Son of God who by God's design *must* be killed and on the third day be raised. I am the Son of God who *must* be betrayed and denied and tried and crucified. I am the Son of God who must suffer for you. I am the suffering Son of God come to join you in your suffering. Your suffering shall never have the last word. I walk with you in your suffering. God raised me from suffering and death. God will also raise you from your hour of death and despair. Do not be offended by my suffering. In, under, and through my suffering I offer you the gift of life eternal."

A second narrative possibility would be to track the story of Peter through these middle chapters of Matthew. (See Chapter 19.) In 14:28-33 Peter as representative of the disciples believes (he walks on water) and disbelieves (he sinks) at the same time. *Simul justus!* In the discussion with the Pharisees in 15:1-20 it is Peter who asks Jesus to explain it all to the disciples, v. 15. This same Peter, the representative of the disciples, our representative!, had just affirmed to Jesus that he did understand: 13:51. Now he does not understand. *Simul!* In 16:13-20 Peter as our human representative confesses Jesus as Son of God. In vv. 22-23 he tries to put himself in the place of God in sculpting the course of Jesus' life. *Simul!* Peter is a rock and a block in almost the same instant.

151

Peter is our representative. If his life is *simul*, our lives will be *simul* as well. And that's OK. We will survive. Peter has pointed us to the rock, the cornerstone of our lives: "You are the Messiah, the Son of the living God." That is our confession. That is the confession of sinful human beings. And it is enough. Jesus, after all, came to save us from our sins: 1:21. Our confession is enough if we do not stumble over the confession itself. It is enough if Jesus does not become for us a rock that makes us stumble and a rock that makes us fall. Jesus' word is simple: "Blessed is anyone who takes no offense at me."

1. Jack Dean Kingsbury, *Matthew As Story* (Philadelphia: Fortress Press, 1988), p. 77.

2. *Ibid.*, p. 78.

3. Robert H. Smith, *Matthew: Augsburg Commentary on the New Testament* (Minneapolis: Augsburg Press, 1989), pp. 203-204.

4. *Ibid.*, p. 207.

Matthew 17:1-9

We need to say at the outset of our comments for this pericope that the transfiguration text contains numerous allusions to Old Testament realities. Standard commentaries will give you the necessary references.

We note first that this week's text is strategically located in Matthew's Gospel. In 16:13-20 Peter confessed Jesus to be the Son of God. This was the climax to Part 2 of Matthew's story. Part 3 begins with the journey to Jerusalem and Jesus' first passion-resurrection prediction: 16:21-23. Jesus, in turn, invites the disciples to join him in his life of suffering: 16:24-28. The disciples, disciples in every age, are to take up their cross and follow Jesus. In the kingdom of God losing is finding. The transfiguration follows which repeats God's word at Jesus' baptism, "This is my Son, the Beloved, with whom I am well pleased" (Matthew 3:13-*17*). In God's speech in the transfiguration God adds to the designation of Jesus as Son of God the admonition: "Listen to him!" (17:5). We have moved, therefore, from Peter's confession, to Jesus' word about the cross and suffering, through transfiguration glory, and then on to another word about suffering: 17:9-13. Jesus informs the disciples that John the Baptist plays the role of Elijah and that he suffers in his role. We have moved quickly back from transfiguration glory to tragic words of suffering on earth. And the disciples *understood* (17:13). Understanding is of utmost importance to Matthew. See 11:20-25; 13:10-17, 51; 16:17.

What we have observed so far in Matthew's narrative is the intertwining of cross and suffering. Which is the reality of the Son of God? Both. And so shall it be with his followers. There is a time to suffer and a time to live in the glory. Jesus' passion-resurrection sayings and the glorious story of his transfiguration indicate, however, that glory will have the last word.

Contextually speaking we are in a segment of Matthew's Gospel which reveals to us very much of the failure of the disciples. See Matthew 14:16-17, 26, 28; 15:16, 23, 33; 16:5-12; 17:4, 10-20. In our text for this week the disciples lack understanding on the mountain. Furthermore, they lack the faith to heal the epileptic lad: 17:14-20. They seem torn between faith and doubt. They are the "little faith" ones: 17:20. (This is the last time in Matthew's Gospel that he refers to the disciples in this way.) The disciples probably are a pretty good mirror of the church that Matthew knew at this point. We note again that Matthew's treatment of the disciples is not uniformly negative as it is in Mark. Matthew paints a fully orbed picture of disciples who at almost the same time understand and do not understand. What they really need to do is *listen!* (17:5). It is this vitally important word that distinguishes God's second public pronouncement of Jesus' identity from the first: 3:13-17.

This text appointed for the Last Sunday after the Epiphany directs us out of Epiphany and on to Lent in a blaze of glory. For the next several weeks our attention will be upon Jesus' journey to the cross. We will need to remember during this journey that we have seen a "foretaste of the feast to come." We know how this journey will end!

The text for the week begins with a temporal notation which is quite unusual for Matthew: "After six days." Moses is present in this transfiguration story, so it may be that Matthew gives this mathematical parallel between the experience of Jesus and the experience of Moses on the mountain as told in Exodus 24:15-18. After Moses had come to Mount Sinai's summit he waited for six days while the cloud covered the mountain. We are faced here, therefore, with two sabbatical revelations.

Jesus leads three disciples up the mountain to an encounter with three of God's special revelatory persons. It is important to note the comments of standard commentaries on the reality of mountains as places of revelation in the Bible. There are stories, for example, of both Moses and Elijah on a mountain. Matthew refers to a mountain in several key passages: 5:1; 14:23; 15:29; 24:3; 26:30; 28:16.

In telling the story of the transfiguration Matthew puts much emphasis on *light*. Jesus' face shone. We know that Moses' face also shone: Exodus 34:29-35. Other Matthean references to the shining light are in 13:43; 28:3.

Jesus is surrounded by Moses and Elijah. What a glorious picture! One at his right hand and one at his left. It won't be many days now until it will be criminals at Jesus' right and left hand: 27:38. See also 20:20-28. Cross and glory mark his days. Jesus really belongs in both places. Jesus belongs in both places in our lives today as well.

The voice that speaks identifies Jesus. "This is my Son, the Beloved; with him I am well pleased; listen to him!"

> *Jesus' sonship is defined by the path he travels. It commenced at baptism-temptation, leads through teaching and miracles, and climaxes in crucifixion-resurrection. This and no other is the way of the Son of God. But it is a path resisted by his closest disciples, and the transfiguration is part of God's own instruction to them and to the readers: "Listen to him!" The cross has cast a harsh shadow on the path of Jesus and clouded the disciples' understanding.... But now in response to their confusion and bleak mood, a great light broke out and shone upon them...they were granted a foretaste of his coming glory.... For one shining moment his present vulnerability was swallowed up by the brilliance of his coming majesty.*[1]

As we have said above, the new word in this text in relation to the voice of God in the baptismal story is God's command to *listen*. Peter has been an example of a disciple who did not listen to God's word. Neither the disciples nor the early Christian community are to follow in Peter's footsteps at this point. We need to listen carefully for God's view of the Jesus story.

> *To what are they to* listen? *Certainly to what Jesus has just said (16:24-28) and to the next words from his mouth (17:11-12) about suffering as the narrow way of sonship and the path of glory. ...in the larger Matthean context disciples are called to listen to all that Jesus has commanded (28:19),*

to bend their necks to his yoke (11:24), to understand that the way of the cross and of servanthood is the way of sonship and discipleship.[2]

Homiletical Directions

The texts for the season of Epiphany begin (First Sunday after the Epiphany, Matthew 3:13-17) and end with God's revelation that Jesus is the Beloved Son of God. We gave some homiletical directions to the "Son of God" theme with the First Sunday after the Epiphany (Chapter 5) and also in Chapter 21. Consult these chapters for homiletical help in developing the "Son of God" theme.

A second sermon possibility for the end of the Epiphany season might be a sermon focused more sharply on the difference between this second time that God speaks in Matthew's Gospel and the first time. The difference, as we have said above, is the words, "Listen to him/Jesus." A didactic possibility would be to gather together in this week's sermon a kind of summary of the Epiphany texts. What have we learned in the Epiphany Season of the mission and message of the Son of God? The Epiphany texts are rich texts to bring back in summary form. They are texts and realities which we ought to *listen to!*

A narrative possibility for this week would be to walk through the successes and failures of the disciples that we have listed above in Matthew 14-17. Even the more immediate context works well to set forth the themes of cross and glory. This more immediate context would begin with 16:13-20 and a summary reminder of Peter's confession. This is a moment of glory for Peter and the disciples. This is followed quickly (as we move into a new section of Matthew's Gospel) by words about suffering, death, and resurrection: 16:21-28. The transfiguration text follows and we are back in glory land again. This is followed by the confusion of the disciples about the role of Elijah and John the Baptist (a role that leads to death) and their faithlessness and "little faith" when confronted by an epileptic son: 17:14-20. These passages may be alluded to this week because the rest of Matthew 17 is omitted from the Matthean pericope selections. The second passion-resurrection prediction

(17:22-23) is also omitted. Note how this second prediction ends with the "distress" of the disciples.

These stories of the disciples could all be briefly told as we lay out this pattern of cross and glory. We can follow up with the reality that our lives follow much the same pattern. Our lives as Christians will have times of suffering and cross. Our lives as Christians will have times of glory and joy. That's the way it is as we follow Christ in this world. It is as if Jesus is saying to us:

"Peter got it right. I am the Christ of the Living God. I am also the Christ who must walk the path of suffering and death. I am the Christ who will be raised in glory.

"I am the Christ who invites you to take up your cross and follow me in my path of suffering service. I am also the Christ who will dazzle you, at times, with my transfigured glory.

"I am the Christ who will be with you when you are faithless and doubting. I am the Christ who will walk with you in your times of doubt and lead you to the land of light.

"I am the Christ of both cross and glory. I will share my cross with you. You will share the glory with me."

This list of "Christ proclamations" can be concluded with a simple word on our part. People have heard Christ's promises. We simply say: "Listen to him!" Amen.

---

1. Robert H. Smith, *Matthew: Augsburg Commentary on the New Testament* (Minneapolis: Augsburg Press, 1989), pp. 208-209.

2. *Ibid.*, p. 210.

157

Matthew 18:15-20

Matthew 18 is of crucial importance to the structure of Matthew's Gospel. As we have said before, biblical scholars indicate that there are Five Discourses of Jesus in Matthew's Gospel. Matthew 5-7 is the first discourse, the Sermon on the Mount. Matthew 10:1—11:1 is the Missionary Discourse. The third discourse is the Parabolic Discourse in 13:1-53. Matthew 18:1—19:1 is the Discourse on the Church. The final discourse is the Discourse on the End Times in Matthew 24:1—26:1.

Narrative preaching needs to pay attention to the entire discourse in Matthew 18. Some scholars refer to this material as a Manual of Church Discipline. It is clearly centered in ordering aspects of the internal life of the early Christian community. The heart of the community is God's presence (Emmanuel): v. 20. God's presence is a presence of love and forgiveness. Love and forgiveness, therefore, are to be the marks of this community. We see this reality throughout the chapter.

Matthew 18:1-14 is omitted from the Matthean lectionary. We discussed this material in Chapter 12. We noted there the theme of the "little ones" who are referred to often in this chapter: vv. 4, 6, 10, 14. Matthew 18:1-14 demonstrates clearly that the God of the kingdom is a God who is concerned with the lost, the least, the little ones. The Christian community is fellowship of the "little ones." That's a wonderful way to image the Christian church!

The verses appointed for this week are 18:15-20. This is a small piece of the whole chapter. We have just said that 18:1-14 is omitted from the Matthean lectionary. Matthew 18:21-35 is appointed for next week. These factors will help us in focusing our preaching for this week.

The appointed text marks a shift in the story from God's concern with one *sheep* who has strayed to one *brother* who has strayed. A process is laid out for a kind of church discipline. Rules for the community were common in Jesus' day. They are common in our day as well. For Matthew, the rules exist as a means toward reconciliation. Matthew embeds the rules within a context of the sheer and utter graciousness of God. The story before this one is about God's care for one straying sheep. The stories that follow are about the importance of forgiveness in the life of the community of God's people. It is God's will that those who stray be won back to the community.

In v. 17 we see that Matthew is, indeed, talking about the church. The story of reconciliation that he tells is to be a model of the life of the church. Scholars have always thought that Matthew had a deeper concern with the church than the other synoptics. It is only in these verses and in 16:18, however, that Matthew specifically mentions the church. In both of these passages the "keys of the kingdom" are mentioned prominently. In the story of Peter's declaration that Jesus is the Messiah, the Son of God, Jesus speaks to Peter saying: "And I tell you, you are Peter, and on this rock I will build my church.... I will give you the keys of the kingdom of heaven, and whatever you bind on earth will be bound in heaven, and whatever you loose on earth will be loosed in heaven" (Matthew 16:18-19). These verses are the equivalent of the words in this week's text concerning that which is bound on earth being bound in heaven and that being loosed on earth being loosed in heaven (16:18). The very heart of the church, that is, is the action of pronouncements of forgiveness and judgment over the lives of people.

The reality of forgiveness in the life of the church is referred to by some traditions as the "Office of the Keys." The keys to heaven and hell are in our hands. We speak them into existence. What we say on earth in Jesus' name is true in heaven. The church has an awesome task! The heart of the task, the heart of the community, is the power to speak forgiveness into the lives of people.

In v. 19 we hear that what we agree upon and speak on earth will be done "by my father in heaven." The work of the "father in heaven" is a theme that runs throughout the Discourse on the Church: vv. 10, 14, 35. We are left in no doubt about what the will of the father in heaven is. The will of the father is that not one of the "little ones" should perish: v. 14. The will of the father in heaven is a word of forgiveness and mercy. The will of the father in heaven is a word of judgment, in turn, upon forgiven people who will not forgive others: v. 35.

Finally, we hear in the text appointed for this week that when two or three are gathered in Jesus' name, Jesus is there in the midst of them. Two or three! The rule among the Jewish people was that at least ten men had to be present in order to invoke the assembly. Among those gathered in Jesus' name it will be different. God is present in Jesus (Emmanuel) when only two or three gather! It is the presence of Jesus that marks the life of the new community of the faithful.

> *Jesus, enthroned on the prayers of the community, is the one leader absolutely necessary for the being and well-being of the church (cf. 23:8-10).... The new community focuses...on God's will as Jesus has revealed and embodied it. And Jesus will be power surging up in the members to ensure that what they ask really is the will of God.... Matthew's Gospel bears witness to the exalted Jesus rather than the torah as the vehicle of the divine presence in the community (1:23; 18:20; 28:20; cf. 11:28-30), as it wrestles in prayer with doing the will of God on earth as it is done in heaven (1 Corinthians 5:4; Luke 24:15; John 14:23).* [1]

Robert Smith reminds us here of the central theme of Matthew's Gospel: the presence of God *with us.* This was the promise in 1:23. A virgin would conceive and bear a son who would be called *Emmanuel.* Emmanuel means "God with us." At the end of Matthew's story we are promised by Jesus that he will be *with us,* he will be Emmanuel, to the close of the age (28:20). The promise to the church is the promise that "where two or three are gathered in my name, I am there among them" (18:20). This is an incredible promise to the people of God. This is an incredible promise to the gathering of Christian people wherever they are. We are promised:

Emmanuel. When God is among us, the "little ones" do not perish. When God is among us, love, forgiveness, and reconciliation reign. When God is among us, what we bind on earth is bound in heaven and what we loose on earth is loosed in heaven.

Homiletical Directions

There are both didactic and narrative possibilities for this week's sermon. The didactic possibilities are crucial ones. We can preach on the manner that conflict is resolved in the Christian community. (This reality can also be communicated through stories.) We could also preach a sermon on the basic nature of the church, gathering such realities from throughout Matthew 18.

The chief narrative possibility we will mention centers in the Office of the Keys. Matthew 18 sets forth the reality of such an office with great clarity. In the exercise of the Office of the Keys we speak new realities into being. We speak words of judgment and our words are bound in heaven. We speak words of forgiveness and our words are bound in heaven. Our speaking becomes a reality because when we gather in Jesus' name God is with us. Emmanuel.

Our sermon with reference to the Office of the Keys and Emmanuel should not be *about* our power to speak new realities into being. We should actually speak them into being over the lives of our parishioners. We might begin such a sermon with the text from Matthew 16:13-20. This was the appointed text that we discussed in Chapter 21. This time tell it primarily to highlight what it says about the foundation of the church. The foundation of the church is the "keys of the kingdom" the power of binding and loosing.

Follow the telling of this story with the story from Matthew 18. The goal of this story, like the story before, is to highlight the power of binding and loosing. It might be helpful to tell the story that precedes this week's text. The story in 18:1-14 makes it very clear that God loves the "little ones." God searches for those who go astray. It is God's will that not one of the "little ones" should perish. This material makes it clear that *God's primary will is forgiveness.* When we come to the binding and loosing material, therefore, we know that God has a preferential option towards forgiveness.

161

The climax of this sermon will be our announcement of judgment and grace our exercise of the Office of the Keys. We will need to make a bridge to our announcement in Jesus' name by reminding all present that we are all sinners. We are the least. We are the little ones whom God does not will to perish. We are called by God to repentance for our sinfulness. You might wish to lead your people in an exercise of repentance at this point.

The climax is our enacting of Jesus' command to bind and loose. We do this in Jesus' name. We do this because Jesus is present with us. We say: What Jesus is saying to us today through these stories is something like this: "I am Emmanuel. I am God present among you. I am God present among you to lift up the little ones. I am God present among you to search out those who have strayed. I am God present among you to loose you from your sins. In the power of my presence: Your sins are forgiven. I am God present among you to speak a word of judgment over your life, to bind you to your sins, when you fail to pass my forgiveness along to others. I am Emmanuel. Receive life in my name." Amen.

Chapter 25
Proper 19

Matthew 18:21-35

In our previous chapter we discussed the importance of Matthew 18 as a whole. It is the fourth of the major discourses of Jesus: the Discourse on the Church. The entire chapter is to be read as a unified treatise on life in the community of believers. Matthew is seeking in this chapter to show that this community is to live as a community of Christ! In the light of Christ, pity, compassion, and forgiveness are to be the hallmarks of the community: 5:21-26; 9:13; 12:7.

There is a second structural comment on the placement of Matthew 18 that needs to be made. In 19:1 we read: "When Jesus finished saying these things...." We recognize this formula as Matthew's way of bringing a section of his Gospel to a close. (See also 7:28; 11:1; 13:53; 26:1.) This fourth discourse of Jesus is the climax to this section of Matthew's Gospel.

The schema of Matthew 18 turns on two questions. The first question (v. 1) asks about who is the greatest in the kingdom of heaven. In 18:2-20 Jesus sets out to answer this question. A second question then arises. Peter, representative of the disciples, asks this question. In Chapter 19 we discussed the pivotal role played by Peter in the central section of our first Gospel. Here he is again. He asks: "Lord, if another member of the church sins against me, how often should I forgive? As many as seven times?" (18:21). (The New Revised Standard Version of the Bible chooses to translate the Greek word for "brother" as "church member" in this passage. Given the ecclesial context of Matthew 18 this may be a wise translation.) Peter has clearly heard Jesus' message that forgiveness is to be at the heart of the life of the Christian community. Now he wants to calculate! How much forgiveness is enough? Seven

163

times? Peter was being generous. The rabbis, after all, taught that it was enough to forgive four times.

Jesus' answer must have shocked Peter. "Not seven times," says Jesus, "but seventy times seven." Commentaries often cite this number as an allusion to Lamech in the Old Testament who wreaked vengeance upon his enemy seventy-seven fold (Genesis 4:23-24). If Jesus has the Lamech story in mind, then it is the case that in Jesus' vision unlimited vengeance is to be replaced with unlimited forgiveness! Unlimited. Incalculable. That is surely what "seventy times seven" means. This is not a new mathematical equation in order to determine how often we should forgive. Jesus simply means that *forgiveness is incalculable.*

Jesus wishes to expand upon the incalculability of forgiveness. He tells a story. Jesus often "thinks in stories." The story is about a king who wishes to settle an account with one of his servants. One servant comes before the king who owes him 10,000 talents.

> Ten thousand *is literally a "myriad," the largest number in the ancient Greek vocabulary, and* talents *were the heaviest weights or largest units of monetary value with one talent the equivalent of 6000 denarii (18:28).* Ten thousand *and* talents *together signify the biggest stack of money imaginable.*[1]

The servant's debt is incalculable. That's Jesus' point. To turn parable into allegory for a moment we might conclude that Jesus is saying here that humanity's debt to God, humanity's sin, is incapable of calculation. The servant cries out for patience. Patience for what? There's no way he can repay such a debt. That's preposterous. Then, surprise! The story takes an incalculable turn. The king has *pity* on the servant and forgives him the entire debt.

This is not the first time we meet the pity of God in Matthew's story. By the way, the Greek word behind the translation "pity" is a difficult word to translate. A literal translation would be: "to be moved in one's bowels." Pity, compassion, mercy are deep inner feelings ascribed to Jesus as he views human need. In a passage that summarizes the deeds of Jesus in Matthew 8-9 we read that Jesus

164

had compassion upon harassed and helpless people, people who were like sheep without a shepherd (9:35-38). In 14:13-14 Jesus is described as having compassion which leads to the healing of the sick. In 15:32-39 (v. 32) it is his compassion that leads him to feed the multitude. In 20:29-34 (v. 34) it is Jesus' compassion that leads him to heal the blind eyes of two men who cry out to him.

"Forgive us our debts, as we also have forgiven our debtors." This is how Jesus taught us to pray in Matthew 6:12. Incalculable forgiveness on the part of God is to lead us to incalculable forgiveness as we relate to each other. The forgiven servant, however, shows no such pity: "...his lord summoned him and said to him, 'You wicked slave! I forgave you all that debt because you pleaded with me. Should you not have had mercy on your fellow slave, as I had mercy on you?' " (18:32-33). The servant was put in jail until his debt be paid. "So my heavenly Father will also do to every one of you, if you do not forgive your brother or sister from your heart" (18:35).

Peter now has the answer to his question. Forgiveness on the part of God and on the part of humans is beyond calculation. Let's not forget the context here. This is how life in the church is to be. The Office of the Keys makes it happen. Sins are loosed and sins are bound (18:18; 16:18-19). The sin of the unforgiving servant is bound on earth and bound in heaven. He is bound in his sins. His debt is incalculable. Our debt is incalculable, too. Fortunately, Jesus has pity upon us. His power to loose us from our sins through words of forgiveness spoken in our churches is also incalculable.

Homiletical Directions

This week's passage does not stand in much narrative connection to other Matthean material. In some ways the passage stands alone as instruction to the church. We mentioned in our last chapter that 18:1-14 was discussed earlier in Chapter 12. If you have not made use of that material as yet, then we might think of a sermon on this text which deals with the entire narrative of Matthew 18. This sermon could begin by narrating the passages we have alluded to concerning the compassion and pity of God. These are found in 9:35-38; 14:13-14; 15:32-39; 20:29-34. These stories could be told briefly as an introduction to the compassion of God which is at the heart of ecclesial matters!

Tell next the story in 18:1-14. Here, too, is a story of God's compassion for the "little ones" who are the "greatest" in the kingdom of heaven. It is an *offense* to God when one of the "little ones" is led astray. The Greek verb in v. 6 is the Greek word *skandalon*. Matthew uses this word many times to describe a false reaction to God's Son, Jesus: 11:2-6 (v. 6); 15:12; 16:21-23 (v. 23); 26:30-35 (v. 31). God is scandalized when we get in the way of God's compassion!

God's compassion for the little ones is next demonstrated in vv. 10-14. God's incalculable compassion leaves the ninety-nine and seeks after the one who is lost. That's the kind of God that the Christian church gathers each week to celebrate.

Compassion is to be our way of settling disputes within the church: 18:15-20. We work to settle such disputes in the presence of our Emmanuel God. Matthew tells us in 1:21 and 1:23 that Jesus is the One who has come to forgive us our sins when he is present among us as Emmanuel. Compassion is the way of God's people with one another. This was last week's text, of course, and can be treated with much brevity in our narrative walk through Matthew 18.

The next story to tell is that of today's assigned text. The very heart of this story is the compassion of the king who acts in this story the way God acts towards us in Jesus Christ. Compassion is to be the way of life for God's people gathered in community. When compassion is missing we are bound in our sins.

In concluding this sermon we can note for our listeners that the church in which we gather each week is, indeed, a house of compassion. The primary activities of the Christian gathering are activities which celebrate the ongoing presence of God's compassion for people whose sins are incalculable.

Here we confess our sins and God says to us through those who exercise the Office of the Keys: "I am a compassionate God. Your sins, though incalculable, are forgiven."

Here we baptize and God says to us: "I am a compassionate God. It is my will that not one 'little one' should perish."

Here we meet at the table and God says to us: "I am a compassionate God. I meet you here in forms of bread and wine that I might be Emmanuel to you. I am present within your very body."

Here we gather around the Word of God through which God speaks to us: "I am a compassionate God. I forgive you your entire debt." Amen.

---

1. Robert H. Smith, *Matthew: Augsburg Commentary on the New Testament* (Minneapolis: Augsburg Press, 1989), p. 224.

Matthew 20:1-16

We come this week to one of the most memorable stories in all of Matthew's Gospel: the parable of the Laborers in the Vineyard. In terms of Matthew's narrative we need to be aware that we come to this wonderful story by omitting Matthew 19 entirely from consideration. The remaining verses of Matthew 20, vv. 17-34, are also omitted from the Matthean lectionary. This means that from chapters 19 and 20 of Matthew only this single story is appointed by the lectionary. As we read through the omitted material we can fairly easily understand the omissions. This material is present in Mark or Luke and is appointed for preaching in the Markan or Lukan year. In a narrative approach, however, this is simply not reason enough to omit these passages from any consideration in the Matthean year. In a narrative interest we need to ask how these stories contribute to Matthew's story. We need to understand specifically how the parable of the Laborers in the Vineyard fits into its narrative niche in Matthew's telling of the Jesus story.

Let us first of all, therefore, do a brief overview of Matthew 19. We noted in Chapter 25 that Matthew 19 begins with the formula for the end of one of Matthew's five sections of material. After that we are immediately informed that Jesus left Galilee. In his first passion-resurrection prediction Jesus told his disciples that he must go up to Jerusalem to suffer many things: 16:21. In 19:1-2 Jesus actually leaves Galilee where he has spent his entire ministry (4:12-16) and begins the dark journey to Jerusalem. In chapters 19 and 20 Jesus begins to address his disciples about the nature of following him and how differently the children of the kingdom live from the normal cultural expectations of the day. These chapters cover such topics as marriage, divorce, celibacy, children, rank, privilege and money! One could certainly consider preaching a sermon on

Matthew 19 and 20, setting forth the nature of the life of Christian discipleship.

The first topic of discussion between Jesus and his disciples is a discussion of marriage, divorce, and celibacy: 19:3-12. Jesus' words on the lasting character of marriage is certainly a word that protects the rights of women. Jesus' words show a concern for these "little ones," these women, who were simply dispensable commodities in the marital practices of his day.

Next comes a word about the children: 19:13-15. Jesus has just said that the greatest in the kingdom of heaven is the one who humbles himself to become like a child (18:1-4). The "little ones" are not to be despised: 18:10-14. It is the Father's will that not one of the "little ones" should perish. Now again in chapter 19 Jesus holds up the child, a "little one," as the model of a member of the kingdom. Chapters 19-20 are filled with people interested in power and position. Jesus has quite a different "take" on such matters. To such as children belongs the kingdom! This is Jesus at his "turn-the-world-upside-down" best!

Matthew 19:16-30 is the well-known story of the one (Matthew calls him neither rich nor young at the outset of the story) who wants to know what *good deed he must do* to complete his holy life of fidelity to the commandments. (Protestant ears pick up quickly at this brazen attempt to do something to earn salvation. There is a problem here!) The man is truly righteous by the standards of his religion. Jesus makes that discovery. Such a man could rank high in the kingdom. Maybe he would be the *first* in line for heaven. The disciples surely think so. They can't figure out who can be saved if this man can't be saved (19:25). Jesus' question cuts to the heart of human vulnerability. He can't give up everything in order to be a servant. That's what Jesus did (Philippians 2:5-8). And so the man goes away sorrowful. *The first becomes last!* (19:30).

The disciples are astonished and wonder who can be saved. That's the matter before us here. Who can be saved? If you can't be saved by being good, then what? Jesus tells the disciples who and how one can be saved. "For mortals it is impossible, but for God all things are possible" (19:26). This pericope closes with a second word of Jesus about who can be saved. He says, "Many who are first will be last, and the last will be first" (19:30). It's the upside-down kingdom all over again! Surely Matthew intends that the story of the man who was first in commandment-keeping and the story of the Laborers in the Vineyard help to interpret each other. The "do-good" man was a first one who became last. The last laborers hired by the householder became first. "So the last will be first, and the first will be last" (20:16). This is the climaxing word of Jesus in relationship to his parable of the Laborers in the Vineyard. Jesus has told a story that shocks us with its news of how one is to be saved. The last will be saved. The least will be saved. The last (laborers in the vineyard) will be first; and the first (the one who kept the commandments) will be last! Amazing grace!

You might note how often the language of first and last is used in the parable of the Laborers in the Vineyard: vv. 8, 10, 12, 16. This theme appears to continue throughout chapter 20. The mother of the sons of Zebedee comes to Jesus asking that her sons might be *first* in the kingdom. "Declare that these two sons of mine will sit, one at your right hand and one at your left, in your kingdom" (20:21). Jesus told the woman: "You're thinking like a Gentile." "...the rulers of the Gentiles lord it over them, and their great ones are tyrants over them. It will not be so among you; but whoever wishes to be great among you must be your servant, and whoever wishes to be *first* among you must be your slave; just as the Son of Man came not to be served but to serve, and to give his life a ransom for many" (20:25-28). The "do-good" man was invited by Jesus to be least of all and servant of all. The sons of Zebedee receive the same invitation. Such is life in the kingdom.

In 20:20-28 two disciples, through their mother no less, want to solidify their "*first* of all" status. In 20:29-33 two men who are blind, two of the "*least* of all," have their eyes opened by Jesus. Jesus came to open our blind eyes that we might see that the kingdom of heaven is offered to the "least of all." Jesus came to open our blind eyes that we might be servants of all. How can we be saved? How can we be fit members of the kingdom of heaven? Only Jesus has the power to make it so.

In commenting on Matthew 19 Robert Smith also underscores the theme of *hardness*.

170

This chapter seems to feature hard or difficult things: hard *for a man to marry and not divorce (vv. 3-9),* hard *not to marry and to become a eunuch for the kingdom (vv. 10-12),* hard *to welcome and value children (vv. 13-15),* hard *to be generous like God who is unstintingly good (vv. 16-23),* hard *to be saved (v. 25).* [1]

We will close our comments with one further word from Smith that summarizes the material we have been looking at.

The parable of the workers in the vineyard (20:1-16) concludes the long section that began with the second passion prediction (17:22-23). All the material in this section comments continuously on the hard and narrow road Jesus is traveling to Jerusalem and death, nudging readers to see the path to the cross as the way of life. So this whole section summons disciples to pay the tax even though they are free and under no obligation (17:24-27), to become like children (18:1-4) and, far from offending any of the little ones, to do everything possible to seek and embrace and joyously include the little ones and the straying (18:5-20), to forgive 70 times 7 (18:23-35), to live with wives as a gift of God or to renounce marriage for the sake of the kingdom, whichever is their gift (19:1-12), to embrace and bless children (19:13-15), to share all they have with the poor (19:16-22), to give up everything and follow Jesus (19:23-29), to abandon calculation and practice wild generosity (20:1-16). [2]

Homiletical Directions

As we hinted at above there is much good didactic material on the nature of life in the kingdom of heaven in chapters 19 and 20 of Matthew. The just quoted summary given by Robert Smith could be a kind of outline for such a sermon.

A narrative sermon on Matthew 19 and 20 could cover almost all the stories told under the theme of the last and the first. You will have to determine how many of these stories you wish to tell as you seek to bring alive the reality of God's love for the least of all. Such storytelling will weave the themes of the least of all, the last and the first, throughout its telling.

171

At a minimum a narrative sermon would tell two stories. These would be the stories of the first becoming last (the "do good" man, 19:16-30) and the story of the last becoming first (the laborers in the vineyard, 20:1-16). These stories should be told to heighten the impact of the last and first language of the text. At the close of the telling of these stories we need to help our parishioners (and ourselves!) understand that sinners such as we certainly qualify for the title: last of all. Confession of sin, which is a standard part of Christian liturgy, is the admission that we are, indeed, last of all. You may wish to include a form of confession at this point in your sermon. Confession is the exercise of the last of all.

An incidental note. The story of Jonah in the Old Testament is also an incredible story of the last (citizens of Nineveh) being first ("should I not pity Nineveh?" Jonah 4:11). Jonah's angry complaint that he did not want to set out on this journey in the first place because he knew (and didn't approve) of God's grace and mercy (Jonah 4:1-5) sounds very much like the complaints of those vineyard laborers who griped about God's grace! The Jonah story could also be told this week in juxtaposition to the parable of the Laborers in the Vineyard. (In what ways do *we* begrudge God's generosity?)

Our stories for this week have much good news for "last-of-all" kinds of people. The master of the vineyard speaks that good news forth in the clearest manner. In this parable Jesus clearly intends that we understand that the master in this story speaks as God would speak to the little ones, the giant sinners. What God speaks to those who were hired at the *last* is what God speaks to us today.

"I have heard your humble cry of confession. I have heard the prayers of my little children, the last of all. I should stand in judgment over you. But I choose to give to the last as I give to the first. Do not begrudge my generosity. I can make the last, first. I can make sinners, saints. With mortals such things are not possible. For me, all things are possible. I call you 'first.' "

The ecclesial material in Matthew 18:23-35 and the story that follows close upon the Laborers in the Vineyard parable (20:20-28) both emphasize that people who encounter God's amazing grace are to become servants who share that grace with others. That's the point of the parable of the servant who was forgiven by the king and would not forgive one who owed him. That's the point of the story of the sons of Zebedee—"whoever wishes to be *first* among you must be your slave; just as the Son of Man came not to be served but to serve, and to give his life a ransom for many" (20:27-28). You may wish to include this reality at the close of your proclamation. "Go now, you whom God has called first. I send you out as a servant of the children. I send you out as a servant of the little ones. I send you out as a servant of the last—wherever you may find them."

---

1. Robert H. Smith, *Matthew: Augsburg Commentary on the New Testament* (Minneapolis: Augsburg Press, 1989), p. 233.

2. *Ibid.*, p. 238.

Matthew 21:1-11;
Matthew 26:14—27:66 or 27:11-54

Matthew's story of the Palm Sunday event is interesting in terms of its narrative connections. On the one hand, this story stands alone in Matthew. It is unique. There is little in Matthew's story that helps us set this passage in a broader narrative context. On the other hand, the Palm Sunday story is shot through with biblical references, most of them from the Old Testament. We will walk through the narrative citing some of the biblical references that help us to grasp the reality of what is going on here. By and large the references are not to stories which can be easily stitched together with the Palm Sunday story into a neatly packaged narrative sermon.

Jesus, at last, draws near to Jerusalem. Jesus' thrice spoken passion-resurrection prophecy now comes true: 16:21; 17:22-23; 20:17-19. It was in 19:1 that Jesus left Galilee and headed south. Robert Smith points out, however, that Jesus' connection to the city runs deeper than just these Matthean references. There are other references as well. "Jerusalem is the holy city (4:5), and Jesus has called it the city of the great King (5:35), and therefore it is his own royal city, for he is Son of David (9:27), Son of God (3:17), king of God's people (2:2)."[1]

We recognize Jesus' entry into Jerusalem as an act of great defiance. This is the city of his destiny. This is the city in which his enemies will rise up and kill him. Still he comes, comes to "give his life a ransom for many" (Matthew 20:28).

Having entered the city, Jesus deliberately moves to make his entry a fulfillment of Old Testament prophecy. He sends his disciples to secure the royal steed(s). The story of the coronation of Solomon in 1 Kings 1:32-40 is clearly the backdrop for Jesus' action. Zechariah has gone to school on 1 Kings and projects a vision of a future when a new king like Solomon will once again mount the royal steed and ride into Jerusalem enthroned on the shouts of the people: " 'Long live King Solomon!' And all the people went up following him, playing on pipes and rejoicing with great joy, so that the earth quaked at their noise" (1 Kings 1:39-40). Zechariah's words are:

Tell the daughter of Zion,
Look, your king is coming to you,
humble and mounted on a donkey.
And on a colt, the foal of a donkey.

Jesus makes it all happen, just as it was written. Jesus enacts a parable for all who have eyes to see. This is a moment of supreme revelation. (On revelation in Matthew see 11:25-30; 13:10-17, 34-35.)

But many could not see through the parable. In spite of the outward appearances of prophecy being fulfilled Jesus was just not the kind of king Israel was looking for: 11:17-21; 20:25-28. This one had his roots as a refugee, not a king: 2:13-23. He was a man who had no place to rest his head: 8:20. Perhaps he was a prophet: v. 11. But not a king.

Matthew has given us a few clues to enable us to grasp that Jesus is king. In 2:2 the Wise Ones from the east come looking for the one who has been born king of the Jews. Later, standing before the governor, Jesus acknowledges that he is king of the Jews: 27:11. The Palm Sunday story is the first place in Matthew's telling of the tale that the title "king" is actually associated with Jesus. Jesus' kingship, however, has been implied throughout the narrative. The One who brought the *kingdom of heaven* in word and deed must surely be the king.

Scholars have had a good laugh at the literalness with which Matthew attends prophetic fulfillment. In Zechariah's poetry both a donkey and a colt are mentioned. Sure enough, as Matthew tells the story, Jesus comes to town riding two animals: v. 7. Smith refutes the humor:

Has Matthew misunderstood poetic parallelism? Hardly.
Playfully, insistently he portrays Jesus as the pluperfect
fulfillment of prophecy. And he pictures Jesus the way
ancient oriental gods and kings are frequently depicted:
enthroned above a pair of animals. He comes meek but royal
nonetheless.[2]

Hosannas ring out to the Son of David. Jesus is called Son of David as well in stories that immediately surround the Palm Sunday story: 20:30-31; 21:15. The promise in 2 Samuel 7 is clear that the Son of David will always reign in Jerusalem. His kingdom will be eternal. Only the Son of David has a right to enact the parable which Jesus enacted that day. Jesus is Son of David. Jesus is the Messianic King. For that we, too, ought to raise shouts of joy that split the earth.

The parable was enacted. Some eyes were opened. Some eyes were closed. "Who is this?" many wondered (v. 10). "This is the *prophet* Jesus from Nazareth in Galilee" (v. 11; see also 21:46). This is the same identity that the crowds were giving to Jesus back when Jesus asked his disciples who the people thought he was: 16:13-20. Acted parable or not, many minds had not changed. Or is there more to it than that? As Jesus proceeds to the temple, he acts there very much like a prophet of old, even quoting Jeremiah as justification for his temple cleansing: 21:12-13.

That bolt of lightning, Son of David, the prophet Jesus from Nazareth of Galilee, *now crackles in Jerusalem. And the city*
— with its lawyers and priests, its aristocrats and bureau-
crats — faces something new in this upstart teacher with his
fresh talk of God and his unbounded care for outcasts. Is he
also more than a prophet? *How much more? In what way*
more? What do prophet *and* Son of David *mean when*
applied to him?[3]

Homiletical Directions
The most important narrative connections for the Palm Sunday text are the Old Testament stories of the promise of everlasting kingship given by God through Nathan the prophet to David the king (2 Samuel 7:8-16) and the story of the coronation of King

176

Solomon which stands as a kind of foretaste or model of the Palm Sunday event (1 Kings 1:32-40). The prophecy of Zechariah quoted in the Matthew text grows out of these texts. These stories could certainly be told as the lead-in to this week's appointed text. We made similar Palm Sunday suggestions in our *Preaching Mark's Gospel* and *Preaching Luke's Gospel.*

We have demonstrated above that the Palm Sunday event can be linked to a variety of passages in Matthew's Gospel. You might find that one or another of these allusions opens up the possibility of biblical storytelling. It may simply be the case that in order to open up the meaning of the Palm Sunday account for our contemporaries we need to tell contemporary stories that could point to Palm Sunday as an event filled with hope for us moderns. There are many aspects of the Palm Sunday event that could open up meaning for us today.

The Revised Common Lectionary joins Palm Sunday and the Sunday of the Passion. As preachers, therefore, we have the opportunity to choose to preach on the standard Palm Sunday texts or of considering in our preaching the greater whole of the Passion story as it is appointed for us. With this second possibility in mind we shall make the same suggestion here as we have made in the works referred to above. Instead of preaching on this entire text, simply *tell the story.* Tell it by memorizing it and sharing it orally with your congregation. One pastor who tried this with the Markan Passion Sunday text wrote to say he did this—and had more requests for the videotape of that service than for any service he had ever had. Why? What happened? The power of the story happened. Never underestimate the power of this Passion story.

Memorizing the whole of the story, of course, is a tall order. An alternative might be to share the memory work with others. Let others join us in orally proclaiming this story. We have also suggested in the works mentioned above the possibility of telling the Passion story in a variety of ways. Some parts could be memorized. Musical selections could cover other parts of the story. Some parts of the story could be enacted or mimed as a reader reads part of the story. Art work could be used. Videos could be played. Tell the story, in other words, in a variety of art forms. Just see to it that the story gets told. The story will take care of itself. Even without all of our wonderful "points" *about* the story the impact of the story itself will create powerful responses in the lives of the hearers.

Matthew's Passion story has its own accent. It is not the same as the story told by Mark or Luke. We will make a few comments here on some of the particularities of Matthew's Passion story. In Matthew 26:1 we read, "When Jesus had finished saying all these things...." We recognize these words as the Matthean formula which brings to an end a particular discourse of Jesus. Jesus' teaching is now completed. *All* these things are completed. The final chapters of Matthew's Gospel focus on Jesus' deeds more so than on his words. Finally Jesus' words (so important to Matthew) and deeds form a single unified ministry.

In 26:2 Jesus tells his disciples that his predictions of the passion are now to come true: 16:21; 17:22-23; 20:18-19. God, Jesus, and the religious authorities are the main actors in this drama.

> *All three principals...desire the death of Jesus, though for different reasons. Through the unfolding of Matthew's story, these reasons have become increasingly clear. God has ordained the death of Jesus because it is to be the crucial event in the whole of the history of salvation. Jesus freely submits to suffering and death because he is, on the one hand, perfect in his devotion to God and, on the other hand, perfect in his service to humankind.... By contrast, the religious leaders desire the death of Jesus because they understood him to be a "deceiver," or false messiah (27:63). They rightly perceive that he stands as a mortal threat to their authority and therefore to the religion and society based on that authority (15:13; 21:43).*[4]

During the Passover meal with his disciples Jesus announces to them that one of them would betray him. Matthew indicates that this event of betrayal takes place in fulfillment of scripture. "The Son of man goes *as it is written of him*..." (26:24). We recall that the opening chapters of Matthew chronicle nearly every step of Jesus' way with the note that scripture is fulfilled. The Passion story is likewise filled with references to the fulfillment of scripture: 26:54, 56; 27:9. What happens to Jesus is not accident. Neither is fate the cause of the Passion. God is in control of these events. God's plan of salvation must be carried out. God is with us in Jesus, and now Emmanuel must die in order that we might be saved, in order that our sins might be forgiven. See Matthew 1:21-23.

Sins are forgiven, as Matthew tells the story, through the blood of Emmanuel. In the words of institution for the Passover meal it is only in Matthew that we read that the cup the disciples are to drink is "...my blood of the covenant, which is poured out for many for the forgiveness of sins" (26:28). Neither Mark nor Luke contain this reference to blood and forgiveness when they cite Jesus' words of institution. The words of institution handed down to Paul do not contain this reference either: 1 Corinthians 11:23-26.

Blood is important to Matthew. An early reference to blood is found in 23:29-36 where Jesus talks about the blood of the prophets that had been killed. Other references to blood in Matthew 27 are vv. 4, 6, 8, 24-25, 49. The end of the story of Judas is particularly intriguing here: 27:3-10. Judas comes to recognize that he has betrayed *innocent blood*. When he returns the thirty pieces of silver to the chief priests they cannot accept this gift to the temple treasury for they are *blood money*. They took the blood money, therefore, and purchased a *Field of Blood*—a place for strangers to be buried.

> *Matthew has pondered the power of the blood of Jesus (26:28; 27:24-25) and sees a strange truth in the use of that blood money. That purchased ground for strangers to the covenant, strangers like Rahab and Ruth (1:5), strangers like the magi (2:1), strangers like the centurion and his squad (27:54), or like the nations (28:19). Strangers (and not they alone) benefit from the dying of Jesus (20:28; 26:26-29).[5]*

In the story of Jesus' trial before Pilate there is much material that is unique to Matthew:

> *...the suicide of Judas, the dream of Pilate's wife, Pilate's hand washing, and several references to the power of Jesus' blood. The material may be divided into three subsections:*

179

Jesus is handed over (vv. 1-2), Judas's end (vv. 3-10), trial before Pilate (vv. 11-26). The first and third sections bracket the second...together the three sections offer a meditation on guilt and innocence and on the power of Jesus' blood. [6]

The triumphant conclusion of Matthew's Passion story is the confession on the part of the Roman centurion that Jesus *was* the *Son of God* (27:54). This confession comes in the midst of all kinds of wondrous events which mark the significance of what has just happened on the cross. The curtain of the temple was rent, the earth shook, rocks split, tombs were opened, and once-dead saints appeared in the city. How's that for an author's way of calling attention to the importance of an event he is narrating! The centurion's confession is paraded on stage with this great pomp and circumstance. The centurion's words are addressed to us. It is left to us to believe or disbelieve such a confession. Matthew finally leaves us at the foot of the cross. We see. We hear. We marvel. Do we believe?

Kingsbury notes that the centurion's confession means at least three things:

First, the acclamation of the Roman soldiers constitutes a vindication of Jesus' claim to be the Son of God (21:37; 26:63-64).... Second, the verb in this acclamation is in the past tense ("was," 27:54). In that the Roman soldiers say that Jesus was the Son of God, their acclamation calls attention to the fact that the cross marks the end of Jesus' earthly ministry.... Third, with this acclamation by the Roman soldiers, Matthew brings the third part of his story (16:21—28:20) to its initial climax. In declaring Jesus to be the Son of God, the Roman soldiers "think" about him as God "thinks" about him. [7]

The centurion's confession is the climax of this part of the story. Here for the first time publicly, humans acknowledge that Jesus is the Son of God. We have heard God acknowledge this on Jesus' behalf in his baptism (3:13-*17*) and in his transfiguration (17:1-8, *5*). Here for the first time it is revealed to babes like the Roman centurion that Jesus' identity is divine.

A Roman soldier makes the confession. From the Gentile women in Matthew's genealogy at the very beginning of the story (1:1-16) to this centurion at the very end of the story, Gentiles play a vital role in God's revelation of salvation in Jesus Christ. We should not be at all surprised, therefore, to find at the end of the story that we who confess Jesus to be Son of God are commissioned to share that confession with *all nations* (28:16-20, *19*).

1. Robert H. Smith, *Matthew: Augsburg Commentary on the New Testament* (Minneapolis: Augsburg Press, 1989), p. 242.

2. *Ibid.*, p. 244.

3. *Ibid.*, p. 245.

4. Jack Dean Kingsbury, *Matthew As Story* (Philadelphia: Fortress Press, 1988), pp. 84-85.

5. Smith, *op. cit.*, p. 318.

6. *Ibid.*, p. 317.

7. Kingsbury, *op. cit.*, pp. 89-90.

Matthew 21:23-32

Jesus enters the temple: Matthew 21:12. It would appear that in this action Jesus fulfills the goal of his pilgrimage to Jerusalem. In cleansing the temple Jesus fulfills scripture: Isaiah 56:7; Jeremiah 7:11. Fulfillment of scripture is a constant theme in Matthew. In fulfilling scripture, in cleansing the temple, Jesus rejects the ritual religious system of his day. This is not renewal. This is rejection. See also Matthew 9:13; 12:6-7. A new religious order is at hand! Those who work in the temple are cast out. The blind, the lame, and the children, on the other hand, are welcomed to the temple: 21:14-17. The first shall be last and the last first! The children proceed to sing praises to Jesus. "Hosanna to the Son of David," they sing out. Again Jesus lifts up the children, the least, the little ones. See also 11:25; 18:2-6; 19:13-15. There is hope here for children of all ages!

> *God's messenger has appeared suddenly in the temple, like a reformer's fire and a fuller's soap (Malachi 3:1-4). The blazing son of righteousness has risen, with healing in its wings (2:2; Malachi 4:1-2; 4:16). For one shining moment he looks exactly like the one prefigured by John, cleaning his threshing floor and gathering his wheat (3:12). But those whom others called "wheat" reject him and those called "chaff" recognize him.* [1]

Matthew 21:18 signals the start of a new day. On this day Jesus encounters a fig tree with no fruit. "May no fruit ever come from you again!" Jesus exclaims. The fig tree withers at once. Jesus' action here may parallel the cleansing of the temple. When proper fruit is not borne, in temple or tree, it needs attention. Jesus is concerned with fruit-bearing. This "fruit" theme will also occur in the succeeding stories in Matthew. It occurs implicitly in the text assigned for this week: Matthew 21:32. John the Baptist called people to repent and *bear fruits* of repentance: Matthew 3:1-10, 8. On Matthew and the fruit theme, see also 7:16-20; 12:33; 13:8, 23; 21:34, 41, 43.

Controversy between Jesus and the religious leaders has been the constant theme of the third section of Matthew's Gospel. Matthew 21:23 inaugurates a series of five controversies between Jesus and the Israelite authorities. The form of these combative controversies is that of question and answer. The authorities question; Jesus answers. All of these controversial dialogues take place in the temple. (The end of the controversies is followed by Jesus' monologue of denunciation of the scribes and Pharisees: Matthew 23.) At the end of the five controversies with the religious leaders they are left speechless: Matthew 22:46. The religious leaders leave Jesus in much the same fashion as Satan left Jesus after unsuccessfully trying to tempt him: 4:11.

Robert Smith reminds us again that we dare not read these controversies as directed at problems in Israel, problems in the past. We ought preach no sermons excoriating Israel and its leaders for the deficiency of their religious life. Smith remains convinced that Matthew tells these stories as an indictment of the church of his day. Our task, therefore, should be to seek to understand how Jesus' words of indictment might also be addressed to us!

> *Through all these old controversies Matthew defines the source and character of Jesus' authority as a model for the community of disciples. It is often said that Matthew's community was locked in mortal combat with synagogue communities and their leaders, and that Matthew applies to them the criticisms which Jesus had in an earlier generation leveled at priests and Sadducees, Pharisees and scribes.... Matthew takes up words spoken by Jesus against past leaders of God's people and applies those words to a new generation of leaders not outside but inside the church.*[2]

The subject of the first controversy is *authority*. The chief priests and elders, the highest authorities in the Israelite community, ask Jesus what the source of his authority is. (Jesus will answer this question definitively only in his Great Commission: "All authority in heaven and on earth has been give to me..." Matthew 28:16. See also 11:25-30, *37*.) The question of the "authorities" is, of course, a trap. Jesus knows it and puts the question back to the questioners. "Did the baptism of John come from heaven, or was it of human origin?" We note how Matthew emphasizes by telling this story that the ministry of the Baptist and the ministry of Jesus closely parallel each other. At any rate, Jesus has reversed the trap. Now the "authorities" were boxed in by any answer they would give. So they said that they didn't know the answer to his question. In the face of their inability to answer Jesus also refuses to answer their question about his authority.

"What do you think?" Jesus continues. (See 17:25; 18:12 for other instances of this question in Jesus' ministry.) Jesus proceeds to tell them a story. Jesus thinks in stories. It's a story of life in the *vineyard*. In Matthew's Gospel there are three vineyard parables. See Matthew 20:1-16 and 21:33-43. One son says he will not work in the vineyard but later *repents* and goes to work. The other son says he will work in the vineyard but he fails to live up to his word. These sons would appear to represent two imperfect sets of Israelites in Jesus' day. Religion, Jesus seems to imply, is about doing, not just talking.

As this story comes to a close we note that the John the Baptist theme ties this story to the controversy that has preceded it. John's ministry centered in his offer of *a baptism of repentance that would lead to fruitful lives* (Matthew 3:1-10). His hearers understood Jesus' parable. They grasped that the son who said he would not go to work in the vineyard but did, was superior to the son who said he would and didn't. "Jesus said to them, 'Truly I tell you, the tax collectors and the prostitutes are going into the kingdom of God ahead of you. For John came to you in the way of righteousness and you did not believe him, but the tax collectors and the prostitutes believed him; and even after you saw it, you did not change your minds and believe him.' " The tax collectors and sinners, of course, are the last of all, the least of all. But they recognized the *authority* of John's baptismal ministry. They *repented*. They bore *fruits* of repentance. The chief priests and elders, however, did not recognize John's authority! They did not believe. They did not repent. They did not bear fruit. Once again in Matthew's story the first are last and the last, first: 19:30, 20:16; 21:16.

A note is in order here about repentance. We remember that John the Baptist opened his ministry with a call to repentance: "Repent, for the kingdom of heaven has come near" (Matthew 3:2). The ministry of Jesus began with this self-same call to repentance: "Repent, for the kingdom of heaven has come near" (Matthew 4:17). It is not surprising, therefore, that Jesus' challenging word to the chief priests and elders is a call to repentance.

Homiletical Directions

It will be important that we set the temple context in our homiletical work with this week's text. We need also constantly to remind ourselves that Matthew may well intend that the words of Jesus in these controversies be addressed to an early Christian community. This means that they may be addressed to us as well. Let us not use the controversy stories of this week and following weeks to give a critique of a religion of old. We need to keep focused on ways these controversy stories are addressed to us.

We have discussed several themes above that can be the center of our preaching. *Fruit bearing* is one. Matthew's repeated theme of the *last, first* and *first, last* is another. We will discuss just one other possibility. Set the stories appointed for this week in their temple context. Tell them in such a way that all who hear will hear for themselves Jesus' invitation to the kingdom. "I invite you tax collectors. I invite you prostitutes. I invite sinners of every stripe to repent and believe. I love sinners. I love you. I invite you to repent." We might make reference here to the centrality of the call to *repentance* in both the preaching of John the Baptist and the preaching of Jesus. The stories of the beginning of the ministry of John and Jesus with their call to repentance can be briefly told as a reminder of the centrality of repentance.

The invitation has been issued. We have heard it with our own ears. We have *seen* it with our own eyes. Note that Jesus' critique of those who did not repent is a critique that they did not *see*: v. 32.

185

Seeing is not yet believing! Seeing is to lead to repentance. We have seen Jesus. We have seen him in the waters of our baptism. We have seen him portrayed to us in the Word of God. We have seen and experienced his presence in the supper.

We have seen. Have we also believed? Have we also repented? Have we also borne in our lives the fruits of repentance? Jesus says to us today through this story: "Truly I say to you, the tax collectors and sinners may well precede you into the kingdom. When these sinners heard the word of the coming kingdom through John's preaching they repented; they believed. They had said *no!* to God in their lives. But they were turned around by the authority and power of John's testimony to the kingdom. Today I call upon you who have seen John's ministry, I call upon you who have seen my ministry, who have heard my invitation, to turn around. I call upon you who have said *no!* to say *yes!* I call on you who have seen me to repent. I call upon you who have seen me to bear the fruits of repentance." Amen.

---

1. Robert H. Smith, *Matthew: Augsburg Commentary on the New Testament* (Minneapolis: Augsburg Press, 1989), p. 247.

2. *Ibid.*, p. 250.

Chapter 29
Proper 22

Matthew 21:33-46

This week's text has important narrative connections in Matthew's story. In the first place, it is the second of three consecutive parables told by Jesus in answer to the question about his authority raised by the elders and chief priests in 21:23. This is indicated in the opening words: "Once more Jesus spoke to them in parables..." (21:33). Once more he spoke to them on the matter of authority. As readers of Matthew's Gospel we know that Jesus possesses all authority in heaven and on earth: Matthew 28:18. The chief priests and elders do not grasp this and they fail to repent: 21:31-32. They reject the ministry of John the Baptist. In this week's parable we hear that the people of Israel rejected the Son himself: vv. 37-39. In the next parable, Matthew 22:1-14, it is the messengers who bear the invitation to the kingdom of heaven that are rejected. Israel's rejection of the kingdom of heaven—its forerunner, its bringer, its messengers—is total! In response to this rejection, "the kingdom of heaven will be taken away from you and given to a people that produces the fruits of the kingdom" (21:43). (We touched upon this fruit theme in Chapter 28. Please refer to that chapter for the Matthean references to fruit.) The kingdom of heaven, therefore, will be given to others! (We'll work with this theme in Chapter 30.)

Jack Kingsbury notes a second strong narrative connection for this text. We quote him at length:

> As Matthew began his rehearsal of Jesus' ministry at 4:17, he depicted Jesus as becoming successively involved with three major groups, each of which functions as a character in his story: the disciples (4:18-22); the crowds, together with the disciples (4:25; 5:1-2); and the religious leaders (9:2-13). As an indication that only the climax of his story

(i.e., the passion of Jesus) still remains to be narrated, Matthew now depicts Jesus' involvement with each of the same three groups as being successively terminated in a reverse order to the initial one, that is to say, in an order that is chiastic in nature. For example, by reducing the religious leaders *in open debate to silence, Jesus forces their withdrawal from the scene (22:46). With the leaders gone, Jesus publicly addresses the* crowds *in the temple, together with the disciples (23:1). And leaving the temple, Jesus delivers his eschatological discourse to the* disciples *alone (24:1-3). Through the use of this chiastic pattern, Matthew signals the reader that the culmination of his story is at hand.* [1]

We pointed out a third narrative connection in the previous chapter. This week's text is set in the midst of five controversy stories located in the temple.

A fourth narrative connection is that this is the third vineyard parable told by Jesus: 20:1-16; 21:20-32; 21:33-44. These narrative connections suggest many possibilities for preaching.

The parable that Jesus tells is really more like an allegory of Israel's history with God. Eduard Schweizer calls it "The Parable of Israel's Rejection of Jesus." The vineyard is a reference to the vineyard spoken of by the prophet Isaiah in 5:1-7. The vineyard, that is, has a history of reference to Israel—the beloved people of God. The householder in the parable/allegory that Jesus tells acts as God acts. God comes to get the *fruit* of the vineyard. There is the fruit theme again. The tenants of the vineyard, however, bring forth no fruit. They reject all the messengers sent to them by the owner of the vineyard. The owner, in desperation, sends his son. In the allegory this is a clear reference to Jesus, Son of God. The tenants kill the son. We get a foretaste of that which lies just ahead of us in this story. The owner of the vineyard pronounces judgment on the tenants/Israel. Their rejection of Jesus is now complete. They took the Son and killed him "outside the vineyard." (Cf. Hebrews 13:12: "Therefore Jesus also suffered outside the city gate....") God's judgment is that the tenants shall be killed and the vineyard given to other tenants who *will produce fruit*: v. 43. (See 21:19, 32, 34.)

This passage is clearly an opening to the ministry to the Gentiles that Matthew affirms in many ways, not the least being the Great Commission with which he climaxes his story. We will pick up this theme for preaching in Chapter 30.

Jesus reveals his identity in this parable in a clear and open way. He is the son of the landowner; he is the Son of God. He is the stone which the builders rejected become the head of the corner: v. 42; Matthew 16:18; Psalm 118:22-23; Acts 4:11; Romans 9:23; 1 Peter 2:6-7. The response to this revelation of Jesus' identity is rejection, not repentance. The chief priests and Pharisees perceived that he was speaking about them. In their rejection they sought to arrest him immediately but they feared the multitudes who believed Jesus to be a prophet. See 21:11. Their final solution would await another day. Death to the heir is their final goal.

Robert Smith reminds us again that we must not read this parable as a parable addressed to someone else. It is addressed to us.

> *Matthew is really addressing not Jews but Christians, especially Christian leaders. They feel secure as members of the new community which has inherited the kingdom (v. 43) and they pride themselves on being teachers and guides (23:8-10) in that community. Matthew thinks they need stern warning. It is not sufficient to hold membership in the correct people or community. Nor does it suffice to be counted as a leader or teacher. The Lord in fact scrutinizes leaders with particular care, seeking more than labels or slogans. The Lord desires* fruits in their seasons *(see 21:19 and 7:16-23).... Matthew uses the narratives about Jesus' past conflicts with Jewish religious authorities to press contemporary Christian leaders to critical reflection and self-examination. That is even clearer in the opening parable of chap. 22 (vv. 1-14).*[2]

Homiletical Directions

We have mentioned above a number of narrative connections in which this week's text can be placed as stories to tell for preaching. We will comment here on just two of these possibilities. Jack Kingsbury suggests that this week's passage fits into a much larger pattern in Matthew's Gospel. As Matthew tells the story, Jesus came to minister to the disciples first, then the crowds, and then the religious leaders. (See the text citations in the above quotation from Kingsbury's *Matthew As Story*.) According to Kingsbury, each of these groups, in reverse order, rejects the ministry of Jesus. (Again, the texts are given above.) The big picture of Matthew is ministry to disciples, crowds, and leaders followed by rejection by leaders, crowds, and disciples. This week's text focuses on the rejection by leaders. In our sermon we could paint this chiasm in broad strokes. Tell briefly of Jesus' ministry to disciples, crowds, and leaders. Then tell briefly of Jesus' rejection by leaders, crowds, and disciples. This is the big picture! The big picture is about a Savior who comes to die for our sins. See Matthew 1:21! Today's passage specifically points to the response of the leaders as a response intended to kill the Son of God: vv. 38-39.

A closing proclamation might go like this: Matthew's story presents for us a Savior who must die; a Savior who says to us: "I came to minister to the disciples, to the crowds, to the leaders of Israel. I came and was rejected by the leaders, the crowds, and the disciples. As a rejected stone I have become the cornerstone of meaning for your life. I came as the Son of God to die for you. I came as the Son of God that I might forgive you all your sin. I came as the Son of God to die that you might receive from me a new life that bears the fruits of repentance." Amen.

A second possibility is to tell the three vineyard parables. The first two would be told as reminders and review of what has transpired in the vineyard. From Matthew 20:1-16 we can remind our listeners of the laborers in the vineyard. We can briefly summarize the grace of God at work in this story. In the power of the grace of God the first become last and the last first.

The second vineyard parable is told in 21:28-32. We've dealt with this text in Chapter 28. In the vineyard part of the story we hear about two sons. One son says Yes and means No; the other says No and does Yes. The one who says No and does Yes is like the tax collectors and prostitutes who go into the kingdom before the authorities of Israel because they repented and believed. Here, too, the last become first.

190

This week's text is the third vineyard parable and it has a similar theme. The chosen people kill the chosen son. So, the kingdom of heaven is taken away from the first, the chosen, and given to Gentiles who may produce the fruits of repentance. Once again the world is turned upside down. The first become last, the last first.

A closing proclamation might go something like this: "What Jesus is saying to us through the vineyard parables is: 'I told you a story about laborers in the vineyard in which favor was expressed to the last and the least of the laborers. I announced to the chief priests and elders that tax collectors and sinners would go into the kingdom before them because they did not repent and bear fruits befitting repentance. I told a parable about a vineyard that did not bear fruit for its owner and was given to others in order that they might bear the fruits of repentance. So I choose for you. I love you the last and the least. I love tax collectors and sinners. I give my vineyard to you who are outsiders to Israel. The vineyard is mine. The kingdom of heaven is mine. I give it to you. I give it to the last people on earth who might expect such mercy.' " Amen.

A proclamation of this nature might well be followed with a prayer of repentance—a prayer that the vineyard owner might empower us with the fruits of repentance.

---

1. Jack Dean Kingsbury, *Matthew As Story* (Philadelphia: Fortress Press, 1988), p. 84.

2. Robert H. Smith, *Matthew: Augsburg Commentary on the New Testament* (Minneapolis: Augsburg Press, 1989) p. 255.

Chapter 30
Proper 23

Matthew 22:1-14

"Once more Jesus spoke to them in parables...." That's how this week's appointed text begins. Once more. Jesus has already told two stories in answer to the question of the chief priests and elders about the source of his authority. Jesus' first story was about two sons. One son said Yes and meant No. The other said No and did Yes. This son represents tax collectors and prostitutes who go into the kingdom ahead of the chief priests and elders because when they were confronted by the ministry of John the Baptist they repented, believed, and, so it is implied, bore fruits of repentance (Matthew 21:23-32).

Jesus' second story was about a householder who planted a vineyard (read: Israel) but could not get the tenants to produce for him the fruit of the land. In desperation the householder sent his son (read: Jesus) but they killed the son. So the householder took the vineyard away from the initial tenants and gave it to other tenants (read: Gentiles) who might bear fruit (Matthew 21:33-46).

These stories have much in common. Those who by logic and by call ought to bear fruit do not bear fruit. People are called and fail to respond. They reject the ministry of John the Baptist. They reject the ministry of the Son of God. So, others are chosen. "For many are called, but few are chosen" (Matthew 22:14). Tax collectors and prostitutes are chosen. Another nation that will produce fruits is chosen.

This week's text follows the same plot line. Many are called. They are invited to the marriage feast that the king will host for his son. But they will not come. They reject the message of the king's messengers. (John's ministry was rejected. They killed the Son. The messengers of the kingdom of heaven fare no better!) The king, however, will have a feast. He sends out his servants again noting

192

that those who had been invited were not worthy. (They bore no fruit?) The king says: "Go therefore into the main streets, and invite everyone you find to the wedding banquet" (22:9). And they came. The bad and the good. The wedding feast was ready to go. Many are called; few are chosen.

Robert Smith notes the similarities among these three consecutive parables of Jesus. He also notes a progression of thought.

All three paint vivid pictures of sharply contrasting responses to plain obligations, and in doing so they condemn disobedience or fruitlessness and summon readers to unflinching self-examination. They have much in common, and yet they have been so arranged as to lead readers forward step by hard step. The first (21:28-32) yields the lesson that prostitutes and tax collectors (little ones) come more quickly to fruits and obedience than the leading lights in the religious community. The second (21:33-44) pronounces a verdict: unresponsiveness and disobedience deserve punishment (vv. 41, 43). The third (22:1-10) describes the execution of terrible punishment upon nay-sayers (v. 7). The appendix (22:11-14) to that third parable applies the lessons of the parable neither to ordinary members nor to leaders of the Jewish community but to the new Christian community and its leaders. In fact that surprising appendix (vv. 11-14) encourages reading all three parables as arrows fired at deficiencies inside the new community.[1]

The wedding feast was filled with the bad and the good. On the one hand this is a signal of God's grace. In each of these parables the kingdom reaches out to claim the outsiders for life. Still, these outsiders are expected to bear the fruits of repentance. That may well be the point of the wedding garment segment of the text: vv. 11-14. Having no wedding garment, that is, may be a sign of a lack of bearing fruit. Robert Smith calls this a sharp warning to the new community. "It is not sufficient to hold membership, to sit at table as invited guest, to have said yes instead of no. What is being promoted here is doing the Father's will, bearing fruit, being properly garbed."[2]

193

Smith also notes that Matthew is quite consistent in portraying the new community as a mixed body of good and bad. The parable of the wheat and the tares (13:24-30), the good fish and bad (13:48), obedient and disobedient sons (21:28-32), and sheep and goats (25:31-46) make the same point.

> *Matthew pondered the strange make-up of the new community, he saw the grace of God in its odd assortment of people.... Matthew loves to celebrate the surpassing depth and splendor of that grace. At the same time Matthew was painfully aware of sad tendencies among the good and the bad: (1) "Good" people in the community are tempted to embark on programs of purification, to weed out the tares or to cast out the erring. (2) And the "bad" are tempted to count on God's foolishness and to misconstrue grace as divine indifference to morality or behavior. So Matthew is tireless in warning that judging others is no business of the community, and equally ardent and insistent that history will end with God's judgment.*[3]

Matthew, therefore, is always goading the new community toward self-examination.

Homiletical Directions

There are a number of ways that we can move narratively with this week's text. We can put it together with the two parables that precede it. The earlier parables have been the texts for the last two weeks, so they can be briefly retold. One goal of putting these texts together would be to fashion a sermon which calls for repentance and self-examination with an eye toward fruit bearing. A second homiletical goal of putting these three stories together might be to accent the closing line of this week's text: "For many are called, but few are chosen."

We will explore in more depth a third possibility. This possibility will focus on the graciousness of God's inviting. This graciousness is clearly seen in all three of these parables. Tax collectors and prostitutes go into the kingdom before the chief priests and elders because they witnessed the ministry of John the

Baptist and believed. Other nations (Gentiles) are offered the kingdom of heaven because the tenants of the vineyard (Israel) killed the son. People in the thoroughfares of the city are invited into the kingdom feast because those who were first invited were not worthy. The first task of this sermon, therefore, would be to tell this week's text in light of the previous week's text as a text offering God's gracious inviting.

This gracious inviting into the kingdom of heaven offered to the unworthy is the alpha and omega of Matthew's Gospel. In the alpha chapter, Matthew 1:1-16, there is a genealogy which contains some amazing surprises. We have discussed the women that appear in this genealogy in Chapters 1 and 7. We even suggested that a sermon on the women in Matthew 1 would make a wonderful Advent series. If you have not as yet told the stories of the women in Matthew's genealogy, here is another opportunity to do so.

First comes Tamar, the "righteous prostitute." Her story is told in Genesis 38. Righteousness is a key theme in Matthew's Gospel, so it is not surprising that Tamar is the first women mentioned in the genealogy. Next comes Rahab. Her story is told in Joshua 2 and 6. Rahab is a non-Israelite woman who helps to save Israel at the time of the conquest of the land. Then comes Ruth, a Moabitess, the great-grandmother of David. Once again a non-Israelite woman plays a role in the birth of David of whom Jesus is Son. Finally, there is Bathsheba. She is a Hittite who gives birth to Solomon. Here, too, a non-Israelite woman plays a key role in God's saving plan.

These women—three of them Gentiles!—are an early clue to Matthew's message. The kingdom of heaven proclaimed by Jesus is not just a kingdom for Jewish men. In Judaism it was primarily the men who carried out the worship life. It will not be so in the kingdom of heaven, the kingdom brought by Jesus. Women are included from the very beginning of the story as mothers of the faith. And they are not just Jewish women. There are Gentile women as well. The fact that the first chapter of Matthew includes these Gentile women is a sign of the missionary character of this book. The alpha word of Matthew's Gospel is that the kingdom of heaven is open to the little ones, the unworthy, the bad and the good, the Gentiles.

Story two of this sermon, therefore, would be the story of these women as the story of God's gracious invitation to the whole world.

The omega word of Matthew's Gospel is also a missionary word. "Go therefore and make disciples of *all nations...*" (Matthew 28:16-20, *19*). We recognize this as the Great Commission. The word that the message is to go to "all nations" reminds us directly of Matthew 21:43: "...the kingdom of God will be taken away from you and given to a people/nation that produces the fruits of the kingdom."

Story three, therefore, would focus briefly on the Great Commission. We are charged by God to be agents of God's gracious invitation to all the world.

These three stories portray a God of gracious inviting. A closing proclamation might go like this: "I am the God of gracious invitation. I invite tax collectors and prostitutes into my kingdom. I invite the bad and the good. I invite people from the highways and byways. I invite Tamar and Rahab and Ruth and Bathsheba into my kingdom. I will to invite all nations into my kingdom. Most important of all, I will to invite you into my kingdom. Get your garment ready. We're going to have a great kingdom party." Amen.

----

1. Robert H. Smith, *Matthew: Augsburg Commentary on the New Testament* (Minneapolis: Augsburg Press, 1989), pp. 256-257.

2. *Ibid.*, p. 259.

3. *Ibid.*, p. 256.

Matthew 22:15-22

The opening words of this week's text indicate a change of venue and actor. "Then the Pharisees went and plotted to entrap him in what he said" (Matthew 22:15). The venue has changed. Matthew is no longer reporting stories of Jesus in answer to the question of the chief priests and elders concerning his authority: 21:23-27. For the past three weeks we have been dealing with Jesus' stories in response to this challenge. Now it is the Pharisees' turn to speak. The counter-attack is on. They hope to entangle Jesus in his own words. They hope to force Jesus to discredit himself publicly. Entrapment is the name of the game.

We begin in Matthew 22:15 a series of four dialogues in which entrapment is the paramount issue. In the minds of the opponents of Jesus, entrapment will hopefully come about through a series of questions that will be addressed to Jesus. The Pharisees ask if it is right to pay taxes to Caesar (this week's text). The Sadducees ask if there is such a thing as resurrection (Matthew 22:23-33). A lawyer of the Pharisees asks about the great commandment in the law (Matthew 22:34-40). Jesus counter-attacks the counter-attack by asking the Pharisees if the Messiah is the Son of David (Matthew 22:41-45).

Robert Smith asserts that the theme of these passages is Jesus' own radical love for God. "His oneness with God constitutes his authority, and his obedient and trusting love is a glorious example of the fruit God seeks."[1]

Of these four dialogues only this week's text and 22:32-40 (the question of the greatest commandment) are included in the Matthean lectionary. The question of the Sadducees concerning the resurrection is included in the lectionary for the Lukan year. Jesus' own

197

question about the sonship of the Messiah is included in each of the synoptic gospels but is never appointed as a lectionary text.

Smith makes the following observation on these dialogues:

> *The words of Jesus throughout all these debates are certainly full of wit and intelligence, but intelligence and wit are at the service of holiness. Jesus is not just flexing his intellectual muscles. Burning in his words is the hard gemlike flame of his own love for God and for the will of God, and precisely that connection is the source of his authority.*[2]

Homiletical Directions

This week's text is clearly a teaching opportunity for Jesus and for us. There are few if any stories in Matthew's Gospel which undergird this teaching of Jesus on rendering to Caesar and God. There are no Matthew stories to tell along with the textual story. So we teach. The standard commentaries will be helpful to us in properly understanding this word of Jesus. We will also want to refresh our memory on what it is that our particular denomination teaches on the subject of God and Caesar. The topic is important in an age when the relationship between state and church is debated from every side.

While there are probably no Matthean stories to tell with this text, we can tell stories from other sources which would help us to make Jesus' point. May whichever way you choose to work with this short story of Jesus help to equip your people to better understand their relationship to God and Caesar.

---

1. Robert H. Smith, *Matthew: Augsburg Commentary on the New Testament* (Minneapolis: Augsburg Press, 1989), p. 260.

2. *Ibid.*, p. 262.

Matthew 22:34-36

This week's text includes the third and fourth controversies between Jesus and the religious leaders. This series of controversies began in 22:15. This time it is a lawyer of the Pharisees who rises to test Jesus. The test is a simple one. "Which commandment in the law is the greatest?" According to some biblical scholars there were as many as 613 commandments in the ancient scribal tradition. Rabbis traditionally argued amongst themselves about which of these laws was the greatest. What is the hub of all this teaching? This appears to be the test question of the lawyer. What is the basic principle at work here? What unites our many laws and gives them cohesion? Jewish teachers, of course, have given their own answers to this question. That's the trap. No matter how Jesus answers he will offend some school of Jewish teaching.

Jesus' reply to the lawyer's question is that love of God and love of neighbor is the fulfillment of the law. Jesus quotes the Old Testament as the source of his answer. "You shall love the Lord your God with all your heart, and with all your soul, and with all your mind" (Deuteronomy 6:4-9, 4). This passage from Deuteronomy is the Shema, the fundamental confession of Israelite faith. "You shall love your neighbor as yourself," (Leviticus 19:18). Love of God and neighbor fulfills not only the law but also the prophets.

We have commented on the matter of love of God and love of neighbor in Chapter 8 in our discussion of the Sermon on the Mount. (A re-reading of portions of that chapter might be helpful.) We said there that the Sermon on the Mount can be summarized as teaching love of God and love of neighbor. In the Sermon on the Mount, the material in 5:1-20; 6:1-34; 7:13-27 focuses on love of God. The material in 5:21-48; 7:1-12 puts its focus on love of neighbor. "In everything do to others as you would have them do to you; for this is the law and the prophets" (Matthew 7:12). Jesus has come to fulfill the law, not abolish it: Matthew 5:17.

In Chapter 8 we also spoke of Jesus' new interpretation of the law. The way that the law was used in the post-exilic community in particular was that *Israel served the law*. Jesus turned that around. He argued that *the law served Israel*. The law served Israel in that it pointed the way to the needs of others as the means of fulfilling the law. In Jesus' teaching the law puts the spotlight on the neighbor and in this way serves humans. People, says Jesus, are more important than the laws. Love of God and neighbor is the righteousness that exceeds that of the scribes and the Pharisees (Matthew 5:20). Again in Chapter 8, we quoted Jack Kingsbury as saying that there is a center to Jesus' radical teaching concerning the will of God. The center is "Love." "Jesus advances no less a claim than that keeping the law or doing the will of God is always, in essence, an exercise in love." Kingsbury points to other passages in Matthew that bear this same reality. He refers to the rich young ruler (Matthew 19:16-30); Jesus' designation of *mercy* as one of the weightier matters of the law in his denunciation of the Pharisees (Matthew 23:23); and Jesus' suppression of the sabbath law in favor of love (Matthew 12:1-8, 7). In Matthew 9:10-13 Jesus has table fellowship with tax collectors and sinners in his desire to have mercy on sinners.[1]

Robert Smith comments on the absolute necessity of holding love of God and love of neighbor together.

> *These two commandments stand or fall together, and together they have absolute priority, in the sense that every other law, ordinance, or regulation is a refraction of the hard and bold light shining from this pair. Jesus resisted every effort to drive a wedge between love for God and love for neighbor (15:1-9), insisting graphically and forcefully on their inner connectedness (cf. 25:31-46).*[2]

Smith's reference to 25:31-46 is important. This judgment day parable is crucial to Matthew's understanding of many aspects of Jesus' ministry. In this parable the righteous live at God's right hand because of their deeds of love. They gave food to their hungry master, drink for his thirst, welcomed him as stranger, clothed him in his nakedness, and visited him when he was sick and imprisoned. They are righteous because of their deeds. But they are not aware of their deeds. They are not aware of their righteousness. "When did we see you in such state and minister to you?" they queried Jesus. Jesus replied: "Truly I tell you, just as you did it to one of the least of these who are members of my family, you did it to me" (Matthew 25:40). When you loved your neighbor you loved me! That's what hidden righteousness knows! The left hand knows not what the right hand does: Matthew 6:3.

The early church certainly understood that love of God and love of neighbor were the heart of the matter: Romans 13:9-10; Galatians 5:14, 6:2; James 2:8. The reality that emerges from all of this evidence is that the only way one can love God is by loving one's neighbor. Would you love God? Love your neighbor! Love the least of these! This reality stands at the heart of biblical spirituality.

A final word from Smith on this section of this week's text:

> It is vital to note that these words are uttered in Jerusalem during Jesus' final days as he draws near to the cross. There he will quite literally yield up heart and soul and mind in loving obedience to God (26:39, 42), and there he will complete his loving service to the neighbor (26:26-28, cf. John 13:1). Thus these words stand not only as ethical instruction for the Christian community. They are that. But even more fundamentally these words are Jesus' own commentary on the narrow path he was treading toward Golgotha.[3]

In vv. 41-45 of our text Jesus takes the offensive in the question-asking department. He asks the Pharisees who they think the Messiah is. "Whose son is he?" They answer: "David." One thousand years of tradition since Nathan gave the messianic promise to David (2 Samuel 7:8-16) had well familiarized the people of Israel with this answer. "Son of David. Son of David. Son of David." The words literally rolled off their lips. They knew everything about the Messiah to come. It was all familiar to them. "Son of David."

Jesus queries on. He quotes from Psalm 110:1, the most quoted verse from the Old Testament in the New Testament. Jesus' question is simple. If the Messiah is Son of David, how is it that David calls him Lord? If the Messiah is David's Lord, how can he be David's son? Jesus had them. No one could answer. "No one was able to give him an answer, nor from that day did anyone dare to ask him any more questions." The controversies between the religious leaders and Jesus comes to an end in this silence. We are reminded of the way Matthew closes his story of another controversy. When Satan tested Jesus (Matthew 4:1-11) he, too, was sent away silent. *"Then the devil left him*, and suddenly angels came and waited on him" (4:11).

Jesus seems intent here on demonstrating to the Pharisees that they don't know as much about the Messiah as they think they do. If they did, of course, they would recognize Jesus! But no. Jesus did not fit their well-crafted image of Messiah. He was something *other* then they expected. He was something *more* than the temple, *more* than Jonah or even Solomon: Matthew 12:6, 38-42.

The religious leaders of days past and days present miss the *otherness* of Jesus. The clearest signature of this otherness is the cross. The cross is a scandal, as Paul writes: 1 Corinthians 1:18-25, *23*). Matthew quite often refers to the scandal surrounding Jesus: 11:1-*6*; 13:53-58, *57*. The cross is a scandal, to be sure. There was silence in the noonday darkness as the Messiah died forsaken by God. So were the Pharisees silenced (22:46). So was the devil silenced (4:11). The silence may descend upon us as well. There is something *more* here than we imagined. There is something *other* in our midst. Who, indeed, understands? But it has been revealed to us as babes (11:25-30). It is given to us to know the secrets of the kingdom of heaven (13:10-17). Thanks be to God!

Homiletical Directions

We have put forward a number of points for a didactic sermon. You can arrange the "ideas" above in many different forms in a teaching sermon.

One narrative possibility would be to tell first the textual story in 22:34-40. We can put a lot of the background material, including the Old Testament sources of Jesus' words, into the story. Stretch the story out in your imagination. What it comes down to, of course, is Jesus' word that we are to love God and neighbor. To love God is to love our neighbor as our selves.

There are other Matthean stories that can be told along with the textual story. Matthew 9:10-13 is the first possibility, though this text was appointed for Proper 5. (See Chapter 10.) In this story Jesus is seen to live out his teaching as expressed in love—*mercy*—to sinful neighbors.

A second Matthew story, one not used in this lectionary year, is Matthew 12:1-8. This is the story of a Sabbath day when Jesus and his disciples were hungry and Jesus broke the Sabbath law in order to see that all were fed. The law is broken but the neighbor is served. So, God desires mercy, not sacrifice. Love of neighbor, even if it breaks the law, is love of God. The Son of Man is lord of the Sabbath!

A third Matthean story that could be told under this theme is 19:16-30, the story of a rich man who asked Jesus how he might enter eternal life. (This story is not included in the Matthean year.) This story points precisely to love of God and love of neighbor as the path to eternal life. This is a helpful story because its message is that with human beings such behavior is impossible. "Who then can be saved?" the disciples ask of Jesus. Jesus answers: "For mortals it is impossible, but for God all things are possible" (19:26). This story will help us avoid a sermon that simply sets forth love of God and love of neighbor as a human possibility. Such love is precisely what we fail to produce as sinful human beings. We are sinners. But with God even sinners can be made righteous (Matthew 9:13).

This story in turn points us to the cross. We heard from Robert Smith that it was on the cross that Jesus gave his heart, mind, and soul for us. It is precisely the love of God for sinners that we see on the cross that saves us, makes us whole, and empowers us to neighbor love. Matthew 25:31-46 can also be used to talk about the hidden or alien nature of our righteousness that serves Jesus in his need. However, this text will be coming up in the near future.

We will suggest a proclamation that can conclude the stories we have proposed for the telling. Through these stories Jesus is saying to us today:

"I will tell you the greatest commandment of them all. I will tell you how to live in the image of God. Simply love God and love your neighbor. Do this and you will have eternal life. To love God and neighbor fully, of course, is not possible for mortals. I am something more than a mortal. I am more than the temple. I am other than the Messiah you expected. I have come as Messiah to save you from your impossibilities. I have come to make the impossible, possible. I have come to die on a cross that you might be empowered to live a new kind of life. I have come to enable you to be loved by God. I have come to enable you to love God by loving your neighbor." Amen.

---

1. Jack Dean Kingsbury, *Matthew As Story* (Philadelphia: Fortress Press, 1988), pp. 66-67.

2. Robert H. Smith, *Matthew: Augsburg Commentary on the New Testament* (Minneapolis: Augsburg Press, 1989), p. 265.

3. *Ibid.*, p. 266.

Chapter 33
Proper 26

Matthew 23:1-12

There is much material that is unique to Matthew in the final chapters of his Gospel. Not all of this material is incorporated into the Matthean lectionary. Matthew 23 and 24 are primary examples of this reality. Matthew 23 is composed of Jesus' teaching to the crowds and disciples on the nature of the religion of the Pharisees. This week's text includes the first twelve verses of Jesus' discourse. Matthew 23:13-39 is omitted from the lectionary completely. So are the first 35 verses of Matthew 24. We touch upon the material in Matthew 24:1-35 in Chapter 34 in our discussion of the text appointed for the First Sunday in Advent. We will include some comments in this chapter on the omitted portion of Matthew 23.

The teaching material in Matthew 23 that closes Jesus' public ministry does not stand in narrative analogy to very much other material in Matthew. It is didactic material that stands on its own. The goal of our comments, therefore, will not be directed towards discovering narrative analogies for preaching but in giving some shape for a teaching sermon on Matthew 23.

We need first of all be clear on the addressee of this material. Jesus is not addressing the Pharisees! He is addressing the crowds and the disciples with the intention of calling them to repentance. Robert Smith, of course, reminds us of his thesis that this type of material in Matthew is addressed to the church leaders of Matthew's and perhaps of our day.

> *The key to this interpretation is the sudden switch in 23:8-12 from "they" (talking about scribes and Pharisees) to "you" (obviously addressed to Christians). In these verses Matthew tips his hand concerning his real interest. He is not reporting Jesus' opposition to Pharisees for the sake of the*

historical record. No. He recalls Jesus' sharp criticism of scribes and Pharisees in order to criticize the same or parallel faults in his own contemporaries.[1]

The worst thing we can do with this material, therefore, would be to spend our time critiquing the religion of the Pharisees who seem by their religion to call attention to themselves rather than to God. Here, rather, is teaching material for the leaders of our congregations, beginning with ourselves!

Many biblical scholars note that this chapter filled with *woes* is a kind of darker image of the chapter filled with *blessings*, i.e. the Sermon on the Mount, Matthew 5-7. Many themes are treated in both sections of Matthew's Gospel. The teaching in Matthew 23 begins with a warning about preaching and not practicing in vv. 1-12, this week's appointed text. In vv. 13-36 there follows a list of seven woes. This is the most sustained material of denunciation in the entire New Testament! Finally, in vv. 37-39, there is a closing lament with an implicit call to repentance unto blessing.

Smith summarizes that which is condemned and that which is valued in Jesus' address to crowds and disciples.

Condemned: preaching without practicing (v. 3), aggression towards pupils (v. 4), love of flattery and prestige (vv. 5-12), blocking and judging (vv. 13-15), evasive word games (vv. 15-22), superficial spirituality (vv. 23-24), posturing (vv. 25-28), resistance to the divine word (vv. 29-31). Valued: deeds in harmony with teaching (v. 3), enabling toward righteousness (v. 4), humility and a spirit of service (vv. 5-12), desire to enter God's kingdom and to open the way to others (vv. 13-15), simplicity and sincerity (vv. 16-22), justice and mercy and loyalty (vv. 23-24), generosity (vv. 25-26), integrity (vv. 27-28), attentiveness to the voice of God (vv. 29-32).[2]

In the verses appointed for this week there are a couple of connecting comments that need to be made. The problem with Pharisees who preach and do not practice, says Jesus, is that they lay hard burdens on those who would follow. This stands in marked contrast with Jesus who has said to his followers that his yoke is easy and his burden, light (Matthew 11:28-30).

As we heard from Smith above, Jesus' teaching in v. 8ff. is addressed to "you." It is addressed to Christian leaders who are to learn from the Pharisees and practice a new form of egalitarian leadership in which no one is called rabbi. There is just one rabbi, one teacher, one Father and one Christ. Jesus is the heart and center of the new community. Is Matthew here already leveling a critique of hierarchies that had developed in the early church? What do Jesus' words mean for our church structures today? Is ours an egalitarian community where even the "little ones" have their place?

It is not easy to preach on these matters. If there is an indictment present in these verses it would appear to be leveled precisely at us who are today's rabbis and teachers. It would certainly not hurt matters for us in our preaching and teaching on this text to raise questions publicly about ecclesial authority (most especially ours!) in our present context.

Matthew 23:11-12 continues on the theme of the nature of leadership in the community. The greatest is to be the servant. The exalted one shall be humbled and the humble one exalted. Matthew touches these themes elsewhere: 18:1-4 and 20:20-28. Neither of these stories is appointed in the Matthean lectionary and could certainly be told alongside this week's text. This narrative possibility, at least, does exist for this week.

It is probably not surprising that the lectionary omits the remaining verses of this chapter. We and our people are spared the *woes!* But the word of woe cannot always simply be omitted. In some years, on some occasions, we ought to include them in our teaching/preaching on Matthew 23. We will need to contemporize them, of course, so that we see the parallel religious behavior patterns in our day as well. Tell them. Contemporize them. Let them stand as an invitation to repentance. There are many religious practices alive among us today for which we most certainly ought to repent!

The final woe (vv. 29-36) and the closing lament (vv. 37-39) turn our attention to the inability of humans to recognize the prophets among us. The history of the human race from A to Z (Abel to Zechariah, v. 35) is a history of killing the prophets. The *blood* of the prophets has been shed continually according to this "miniature history of the world" that Jesus unfolds for us in vv. 29-36. (Cf. Other "histories in miniature" in Matthew 1:1-17; 21:33-43; 22:1-14.) Jesus laments over this reality. He laments over Jerusalem, the city of David and the city of God, which epitomizes this blood-shedding aspect of human life.

> *And that scriptural story is not a closed book. For Jesus suddenly announces, All this will come upon this generation. This sad story will reach its climax in this generation. These verses prepare the way for Matthew's unique report about the spilling of Jesus' righteous blood and the defiling of the temple by Judas's return of the blood money (27:3-10). That report connects the murder of Jesus to the whole long history of disobedience to God's agents.*[3]

Jesus' blood will be shed. Another prophet will be killed by those whose religion blinds them to the presence of God's prophets among them. Jesus laments. "Jerusalem, Jerusalem!" Jerusalem has been reduced to this! Think of her glorious history. Glory now turns to ashes. The City of God will become the city that kills God. And we are Jerusalem! Jesus' word is addressed to us. We are convicted for our blindness. But we are also invited to repent. Perhaps we murderous Jerusalemites will sing aloud the next time a prophet rides into Jerusalem: "Blessed is the one who comes in the name of the Lord."

---

1. Robert H. Smith, *Matthew: Augsburg Commentary on the New Testament* (Minneapolis: Augsburg Press, 1989), p. 268.

2. *Ibid.*, pp. 269-270.

3. *Ibid.*, p. 279.

Matthew 24:36-44

As we indicated in the Preface we have chosen to arrange the chapters of this work in their Matthean order. This means that for most readers your first reading from this publication is Chapter 34; First Sunday in Advent. We are confronted immediately, therefore, with the difficulty that the lectionary system can pose to understanding the Gospel of Matthew as story. One would certainly not begin to read a novel in Chapter 24. It is likewise very difficult to begin reading Matthew in his chapter 24! The verses for this week's assigned text from Matthew 24, therefore, come to us totally out of context. In a traditional reading of the text for preaching we would study these eight verses and produce an Advent sermon. To follow this approach, however, distorts Matthew's narrative. We might get ourselves a sermon from such an approach, but it will likely have little to do with the reason that Matthew tells this story at this precise point in his gospel tale.

Chapter 1 of this work treats the text for the Fourth Sunday in Advent: Matthew 1:18-25. We would advise you to read this chapter now in conjunction with your preparation. There are suggestions made in that chapter, comments on the beginning of Matthew's story, for Advent preaching. We particularly recommend that some years during the Advent season we preach a series of sermons on the women in Matthew's opening genealogy: Tamar, Rahab, Ruth, Bathsheba and Mary. What stories these are to tell! Matthew's genealogy is found in 1:1-16. (Chapter 30 also touches on the use of these women for preaching.)

Genealogy. That's how Matthew begins his story. He begins his story in a very surprising way by including women in his genealogy. Women don't belong in Jewish genealogies! Most certainly *Gentile* women don't belong in Jewish genealogies. What are these women doing in the opening verses of Matthew's story? Clearly they are a sign that the central figure of Matthew's story, Jesus of Nazareth, brings salvation (1:21-23) to all the peoples of the earth.

According to the outline we proposed for Matthew's Gospel, this week's text comes from the Fifth Discourse of Jesus: Discourse on the End of Time, 24:1—26:1. Verses 1-35 of this chapter are omitted from the Matthean lectionary. These verses are important to us in setting this week's text in its narrative frame. As Matthew tells the story, Jesus makes his Palm Sunday entrance into Jerusalem in 21:1-11. Following this event Jesus immediately enters and cleanses the temple: 21:12-13. Except for the story of the cursing of the fig tree (21:18-22) Jesus is in the temple continuously until the opening of Matthew 24 where we read that Jesus *left* the temple. On leaving the temple the disciples point out to Jesus the glory of the temple buildings (24:1). (Was there another building like it anywhere in their experience?) Jesus' reply to his disciples is that the temple will be destroyed (24:2). Jesus' comment would appear to be related to his lament over Jerusalem in 23:37-39.

Following Jesus' harsh and surprising words about the temple the disciples ask him two questions. "Tell us, *when* will this be, and *what will be the sign* of your coming and of the end of the age?" (24:3). These two questions govern all the material in this Fifth Discourse. The material in 24:3-35 answers the question about the sign. As we noted above, none of this material is included in the Matthean lectionary. The material itself is strongly apocalyptic in character. According to Robert Smith, however, its content is compassion.

> *Jesus uses apocalyptic but teaches compassion. The discourse opens with the disciples talking about the splendor of sacred buildings (24:1-2) and closes with Jesus speaking of the unsurpassable splendor and holiness of compassion toward the little ones (25:31-46). Between that beginning and that end Jesus focuses on the transitoriness of all things. What endures?...We are finally confronted (25:31-46) with a new version of the old commandment of love. Compassion or care for the needy is the most splendid and only really*

durable work of the human community. ...traditionally apoca-
lyptic rhetoric is stretched to its limits and made to carry the
message of the everlastingness of love.[1]

The material in Matthew 24:1-35, that which precedes our assigned text in this chapter, is basically given to Jesus' answer of the second question asked by the disciples: what will be the *sign* of the coming age? 24:4-14 gives Jesus' first answer. He urges his disciples not to be led astray by those who come in his name with all kinds of prognostications. The most important sign that we are to cling to in the midst of the rage of those who wish to lead us astray is the sign of the preaching of the gospel throughout the whole world. This is a hopeful sign indeed, for this is where we live. We live in the time of the preaching of the gospel. We, ourselves, are preachers of that gospel. We participate in this sign of the coming age. God is at work in such preaching. Preaching itself is a sign that God is moving history towards its fulfillment.

In 24:15-28 Jesus offers a second word concerning the sign of the end. His word here is that his coming will not be done in a corner. It is not some esoteric occurrence that only few can know. The world always seems to abound with people who claim to have the "inner secret," the biblical code, to decipher the time of Christ's coming. Don't believe them. Jesus' coming is an *exoteric* occurrence. It will be plain for all to see. It will be as plain as lightning in the skies. The sign of the Son of man will appear in heaven and all the earth's people will witness his coming.

In 24:32-35 Jesus offers a fig tree as a sign. Just as we know when a fig tree is ripe with fruits, so shall we clearly see when the time is fruitful for Christ's coming. One final word of comfort for all concerned with signs: "Heaven and earth will pass away, but my words will not pass away" (24:35).

> *His words are the great treasure of Matthew's Gospel, the reason this book has been prized through successive genera-tions. They have endured and have enabled readers to endure, by placing them squarely within a structure of love: loved by God in the mercy of Christ and summoned to yield an answering love toward every neighbor and toward God,*

no matter how evil waxes and no matter how foolish compassion appears to be.[2]

The appointed text for the First Sunday in Advent occurs next in this Matthean context. The context is basically set by the two questions asked by the disciples in 24:3. Jesus has dealt with the question of the *sign* of his coming. The text now turns to the second question: *When* will this be? The remainder of the material in the Fifth Discourse is an answer to this question. Jesus thinks in stories. He tells five consecutive stories to answer the *when* question. Jesus' first answer is the story he tells in our "First Sunday in Advent" text.

The second story-answer is given in 24:45-51. This story makes it clear that the Master comes in an hour we do not expect. We are called, therefore, to be watchful and faithful to our humble earthly calling. This answer of Jesus is omitted from the lectionary.

Jesus' third story-answer to the *when* question is Matthew 25:1-13, the story of the wise and foolish maidens. This text is appointed for Proper 27 of the Matthean year.

His fourth story-answer is Matthew 25:14-30, the parable of the talents. This text is appointed for Proper 28 of the Matthew cycle of text.

His fifth and final story-answer to the *when* question is the story which brings Matthew's presentation of the ministry of Jesus to a close: 25:31-46. This is the great judgment parable which is appointed for Christ the King Sunday. We deal with ways in which these several stories can be put together in a single sermon in our Chapter 35.

We come then to the verses appointed for the First Sunday in Advent: 24:36-44. As we indicated above this material picks up the second of the disciples' questions: "*When* will this be?" Jesus' first answer to this question is that no one knows the day or the hour. No one knows *when*. Only the Father knows. This is a vitally important answer. In it lies the very possibility of our salvation. If we knew the hour, we would think to prepare ourselves in some perfect manner for its coming. We would bend every effort of mind and will to be ready. And we would be surprised. We would be surprised when the Son of Man sits on his glorious throne and selects us, with

212

the goats, to be at his left hand. Judgment shall be ours! (25:31-34). The goats have one thing in common. They are quite sure they are properly prepared. They are quite ready to defend their own righteousness. "Lord, when was it that we saw you hungry or thirsty or a stranger or naked or sick or in prison, and did not take care of you?" (25:44). The goats are always confident in their own righteousness. But salvation does not come to humans as a reward for their own righteousness. Salvation comes to humans as a gift of God's grace. We don't know *when*. So we cannot get our righteousness in order. We must rely on God's grace alone in the day of judgment.

Matthew 24:40-41 are the biblical verses on which much of the "rapture" theory is based.

> *But these stories have nothing to do with the rapture. They have everything to do with vigilance in the time before the sudden advent of the Son of man.... These biographies of Noah's generation and of peasants and housewives are intended to do nothing more complicated than make the case for unrelenting watchfulness, as the conclusion (v. 42) plainly shows.*[3]

The plain ending, v. 44, is that preparation for the Day of the Lord is watchfulness. We watch because we do not know the day nor the hour. We have defined the nature of this watchfulness. Watching for the end is a matter of trust in the grace of God to take away our sins (Matthew 1:21) and clothe us with divine righteousness (Matthew 3:13-17, *15*).

Homiletical Directions

The assigned text for the First Sunday in Advent is plucked out of its context in Matthew's tale telling. Advent, of course, means simply "to come." Advent texts have historically centered on God's coming, whether that coming be in the birth of Jesus Christ (in preparation for Christmas) or in the coming of the Son of man at the end of the age. It is the coming at the end of the age that is accented in the text appointed for Advent I.

In some years' preaching on this text we ought to deal seriously with its framework in the Gospel of Matthew. This can be done most simply by beginning our sermon with the questions of the disciples in 24:3. The disciples want to know *when*; they want to know the *sign.* Verses 4-35 deal with the matter of a sign. These verses are nowhere appointed for preaching. We have commented on the content of these verses in the above material. Our sermon certainly could begin with the sign question and the stories Jesus tells about a sign. Jesus gives us some very helpful teaching in these verses.

In Matthew 24:36 and following, the conversation turns to the second question the disciples asked of Jesus: *when* will this be? Jesus proceeds to tell five stories in order to answer this question. This week's appointed text is the first of these stories. Jesus' first answer to the *when* question is about being ready for the day of which we know neither day nor hour. The most vital element of this story is this reality of our lack of knowledge of the coming of the Day of the Lord. As we indicated above, it is precisely this lack of knowledge which opens for us the possibility for salvation. The call to "be ready" must not be interpreted as a call to get our own righteousness in order. The call to "be ready" is a call to put our lives in the hands of the One Who Knows: our gracious God. Our first day with God, our baptismal day, was a day full of grace. Our last day with God will be gracious as well. We trust in that graciousness. We believe that righteousness is a gift from God. Trusting, believing, we shall certainly be prepared for the coming of the Son of man.

If we choose to work only with the appointed text for this Sunday we will have a fairly simple teaching sermon which makes clear the reality of v. 44! Such a sermon could certainly make use of contemporary stories we tell which would demonstrate proper and improper ways of preparing for the Son. Probably the most important kind of story we could tell would be of a person who gave every ounce of one's life in order to create one's own righteousness and thus be prepared for Christ's coming. Such a person will receive a shock in that great day. The righteousness that carries us through the Day of the Lord is the righteousness offered to us as a gift by God through the Son, and not the righteousness of our own doing.

We will have more to say about this *alien righteousness* in our discussion of Matthew 25:31-46. In this parable the righteous are surprised by their righteousness. "Then the righteous will answer him, 'Lord, when was it that we saw you hungry and gave you food, or thirsty and gave you something to drink...?' " (Matthew 25:37)

---

1. Robert H. Smith, *Matthew: Augsburg Commentary on the New Testament* (Minneapolis: Augsburg Press, 1989), pp. 280-281.

2. *Ibid.*, p. 290.

3. *Ibid.*, p. 291.

Matthew 25:1-13; Matthew 25:14-30

We have chosen to discuss two texts together in one chapter. We set the context for the relationship of these texts to each other in Chapter 34. In Matthew 24:3 the disciples asked Jesus about the *signs* and the *when* of his coming at the end of the age. The material in 24:4-35 is primarily directed to the question of the *sign*. Jesus begins to answer the *when* question in 24:36. As we noted in the previous chapter, Jesus proceeds to tell five stories in answer to the question: *when?* We discussed Jesus' first story in Chapter 34. Jesus' second story-answer is located in 24:45-51, a text which is omitted from the Matthean lectionary. Jesus' third and fourth story-answers to the *when* question are the texts we are considering together in this chapter. Jesus' final story-answer is his parable of the judgment of the nations in Matthew 25:31-46. This text is appointed for Christ The King Sunday and will be discussed in Chapter 36.

Our proposal is that on one of the two Sundays for which these texts are appointed we tell three of Jesus' story-answers as our sermon. The three stories for our telling would be 24:45-51 and the stories under consideration in this chapter.

> *All three stories have similar casts of characters: a master or lord and one or more servants or attendants. And the plots are also similar: the lord assigns tasks (or tasks are clearly defined by tradition); the master or lord leaves for an indefinite period of time; the servants or attendants perform their tasks well or badly; suddenly the lord returns, and the servants are called to account; some are praised and others are blamed.*[1]

When we look at these stories in the larger framework of Matthew's Gospel it is quite clear that they *mean what they say*. Here are stories told to answer a question. (Once again we catch Jesus thinking in stories.) The lectionary, however, calls upon us to take up two of these three stories as isolated texts in their own right. We are called upon to mine them for deeper meanings for our sermon. We agree with Smith when he cautions us about the allegorizing that will inevitably result when we treat these stories/parables as texts to be examined in isolation from their context. We can certainly press the details of these stories and discover hidden meanings. We can let the stories stand for our doctrines of the end times. We can find an idea hidden here and there that might be worth a point in our sermon. Such approaches to these texts, however, might violate their basic nature. We end up forcing *stories* to yield *ideas*. It is hard to believe that this is what Jesus had in mind when he told these fairly simple and straightforward stories to answer the disciples' question: *When?*

It is interesting to note that in each of the three stories that we would recommend for telling, the subject is engaged in quite ordinary tasks of life. A servant is put in charge of his master's possessions. Ten maidens prepare for a wedding. Three servants are entrusted with talents which they are to steward until the journeying one returns. Jesus does not imagine our human waiting for the end of the age to be some kind of spiritual exercise quite separate from daily life. There is no advice about going into seclusion or retreat. Rather, we are called to fidelity in the vocations of life. It would be good to underscore this reality in the telling of these stories.

Homiletical Directions

Our homiletical directions have already been given. On one of these Sundays in November tell three of the stories that Jesus told (Matthew 24:45—25:30) in answer to the disciples' *when* question. The disciples' *when* question, of course, is our question as well. Our introduction should make that clear. Once the question is established as *our* when question—simply tell the stories. The stories say

217

what Jesus means. We will not need any explanations. No points need to be made. Let the stories do their work! Trust them. Trust the Spirit to work with them. If this open-endedness is too risky for you or your people it might be well to close with a prayer that helps people gather up the stories for their own lives. A carefully chosen sermon hymn will also be important.

1. Robert H. Smith, *Matthew: Augsburg Commentary on the New Testament* (Minneapolis: Augsburg Press, 1989), p. 292.

Chapter 36
Christ The King; Proper 29

Matthew 25:31-46

We come to the end of the Church Year. We come also to the climax and capstone of Jesus' teaching ministry in Matthew's Gospel. Jesus tells a story, an eschatological vision, which serves as the climax of his five discourses recorded for us by the Gospel writer Matthew. What a spectacular teaching it is! Jesus' vision of the final judgment is unique to Matthew and unique in the ways it reveals certain aspects of the gospel.

In the two preceding chapters we have spoken of the context for this week's text. The disciples asked Jesus for a *sign* of the end. They asked *when* the time would come (Matthew 24:3). In the material from 24:45—25:46 Matthew arranges five stories of Jesus that give an answer to the question: "*When* will this be?" In the story appointed for this week Jesus goes beyond the other stories he has told and actually sketches what "*when*" will look like. "*When* the Son of Man comes in his glory, and all the angels with him, he will sit on the throne of his glory" (Matthew 25:31).

> Like the farewell discourse of John 13:31—16:33, it sums up the life of Jesus, comments on his death, and addressed the church quite directly about its own life situated between his lowly ministry and his glorious epiphany.... The questions When? and What sign? have entirely faded from sight, and every phase is concentrated on describing as literally and nonparabolically as possible the meaning of preparedness and watchfulness. Or, the question of When? is given a different and surprising answer: The Son of man is coming now, in the lowly. And what is the sign of his coming? The poor and needy are themselves odd and often unwelcome signs of his presence.[1]

219

In his vision Jesus portrays the world on trial before himself. The One who had no place to lay his head, the One who will shortly be condemned to death on religious grounds, this One will judge the world. This is a breathtaking vision. The Lowly One reigns! Truly such realities need to be revealed: 11:25-30; 13:10-17. All the nations stand before the Sovereign. (Cf. the "all nations" in Matthew 28:19.) The day of reckoning has come. Peoples and nations are separated. The sheep live at the right hand of the Ruler of all Nations. The right hand, of course, was the traditional place of honor. The goats, on the other hand, live in infamy at the left hand. And the Sovereign speaks *blessing* to those on his right hand. "Come, you that are blessed by my Father, inherit the kingdom prepared for you..." (25:34). The blessing of the Sovereign One reminds us of the Beatitudes. Jesus reveals to us a God who speaks words of blessing on the little ones!

Righteousness has been a constant theme of Matthew's Gospel. The very first story is about a righteous man by the name of Joseph: Matthew 1:19. (In Chapters 1 and 3 we spoke of the contrast between the righteous Joseph and the unrighteous Herod. The theme of righteousness was also treated in Chapter 5.) Matthew's alpha story is about righteousness. His omega story, the last word he reports from King Jesus, is also about righteousness. In his vision, Jesus gives us an in depth picture of righteousness. The sheep, those on the right hand, are righteous. And we know why they are righteous. They are righteous because of their deeds. They have cared for the Ruler. They saw him hungry and gave him food, they saw him thirsty and gave him a drink, they saw him a stranger and invited him home, they saw him naked and clothed him, they saw him sick and imprisoned and they visited him.

Now for the stunner. The righteous are surprised. They don't know their deeds. They haven't kept score. Their left hand doesn't seem to know what their right hand is doing (Matthew 6:3). "Then the righteous will answer him, *when* was it that we saw you hungry and gave you food, or thirsty and gave you drink?" They protest each act of kindness for the King that Jesus has ascribed to them. Jesus gives them an answer: "...as you did it to one of the least of these who are members of my family, you did it to me."

The righteous were righteous because of their deeds and they didn't know it. They didn't know their own righteousness. We have spoken earlier in this work of Luther's concept of alien righteousness. The righteousness of the sheep was precisely an alien righteousness. They didn't even know they possessed it! How can this be? Theologically it can be because the blessed are those in whose lives Jesus has taken up residence. Saint Paul could write: "I have been crucified with Christ; and it is no longer I who live, but it is Christ who lives in me" (Galatians 2:19-20). Or, this from Colossians: "...for you have died, and your life is hidden with Christ in God" (Colossians 3:3). The Sovereign's people are people in whom the Sovereign lives. Righteous people are the people in whom the Righteous One dwells. Just so it can be true for us that our left hand does not know what our right hand is doing. Just so it can be true for us that we are righteous on account of our deeds and yet not know what our deeds are. To be righteous is to be clothed in the righteousness of Christ. Such righteousness is based on faith! (See also Romans 3:23-25; 2 Corinthians 5:21; Galatians 3:6; Philippians 3:9.)

Note that in the story the opposite is also true. The unrighteous ones *know* their deeds. They have kept score. This is true of "Pharisees" of every age and religion. "Then they also will answer, 'Lord, when was it that we saw you hungry or thirsty or a stranger or naked or sick or in prison, and did not take care of you?' " The unrighteous are quite confident about their righteousness. It is always so with humanly crafted righteousness. Those who measure their righteousness on human scales are in for a shock at the day of judgment. "Not everyone who says to me, 'Lord, Lord,' will enter the kingdom of heaven..." (Matthew 7:21).

There are other themes in this story which occur throughout the Gospel of Matthew. The Emmanuel theme is here. (See Matthew 1:23; 18:20 and 28:20 for instances of the Emmanuel—God with us—theme. This theme was discussed in our Chapter 1.) It is in this eschatological vision of Jesus that we have our eyes opened to the presence of Jesus among us in the needs of common humanity. Again, "...just as you did it to one of the least of these who are members of my family, you did it to me." We have adopted language in which we describe our faith as receiving Jesus into our heart. In Jesus' eschatological vision we discover that when Jesus does come into our heart, he brings all of needy humanity along with him!

This reality alerts us to another Matthean theme: love of God and love of neighbor (Matthew 22:34-40). This theme is developed in our Chapter 32. There we asserted that for Matthew love of neighbor is our way of loving God. This reality is underscored mightily with Jesus' words that love of the least of these, love of the little ones, is love expressed to Jesus. What will be the *sign* of Jesus' coming? Jesus is here, now. He is present in the least of these. They are the sign. Matthew would appear to be encouraging his community to care for the little ones. His words give direction to our lives as well.

Jesus' vision makes it clear. The life of the Christian is a life given in love to the least of these. But that's good works, isn't it? Won't such good works for our neighbor destroy the "faith alone" foundation of our faith? (We Lutherans actually worry about this at times.) The answer to our question is "No." Our good works will not destroy our "faith alone" posture. We can do all the loving of the least and little ones we can possibly imagine and not be liable to belief in works-righteousness. We are called to do lots of good works. We are also called not to keep score. When we keep score of our deeds we want to credit our love of neighbor to our heavenly bank account. Loving our neighbor is not the problem. Keeping score of our good deeds of neighbor-love is the problem. The truly righteous don't keep score. Their left hand doesn't know what their right hand is doing. Such as these will stand before the Sovereign one day clothed in Christ's righteousness alone.

These words of Jesus, identifying with the world's outcasts, stand immediately before the narrative of his own betrayal, arrest, torture, and execution. As the vision ends, everything is ready for the Passion Narrative to begin.

> *Indeed that great and final vision (25:31-46) prepares readers for the Passion Narrative (chaps. 26-27). In his vision Jesus speaks about being identified with the world's*

outcasts, and in his passion he actively and actually identi-
fies with them. The Son of God (27:40, 43) stands deliber-
ately and voluntarily in the shoes of the powerless, the weak,
the defenseless, the hated, the tortured. He began as a
refugee and he ends as a condemned criminal. He gave his
blood for them and for many (20:28; 26:27).[2]

Homiletical Directions

This text is simply too rich to be confined to one Sunday of our preaching. Hopefully you have alluded to it in earlier sermons during the Matthew year. There are many possibilities of narrative analogy. The themes of righteousness, Emmanuel, and love of neighbor relate to many other stories in Matthew's Gospel as we have indicated above. Our sermon could certainly link this week's textual story with one of these themes in Matthew.

Jesus' eschatological vision is appointed for Christ the King Sunday. This is a fitting text for such a Sunday in that it speaks quite directly to Jesus' reign. It also speaks clearly of the final day of judgment which is the liturgical emphasis for Christ the King Sunday. *How shall we stand* before Jesus on the day of judgment? Maybe we don't talk about this topic much anymore. But here it is, and it is a topic which is well worth our preaching time.

Our suggestion is that we deal with the theme of our own standing before judgment as we preach on this glorious text. Rather than finding narrative analogies in other stories from Matthew to tell in our sermon it might be best to *tell just this story well.* Set the context. Tell the story. As you tell the story, make what points you wish to make as you go. Let the story itself supply the structure of the sermon. Alternate between story and application of story as you walk through these powerful verses.

There is certainly a textual proclamation that can be put to service for the conclusion of our sermon. That proclamation is: "Come, you that are blessed by my Father, inherit the kingdom prepared for you from the foundation of the world..." (25:34). When we stand before the Sovereign on the final day we believe the Sovereign will speak this blessing over our lives.

All who put their faith in the righteousness of Christ as their basis for standing before the Ruler will surely hear the Ruler say on that final day: "Come, you that are blessed by my Father, inherit the kingdom prepared for you from the foundation of the world...."

All who have eaten at the Ruler's table where Jesus comes to live within us through forms of bread and wine will surely hear the Ruler say: "Come, you that are blessed...."

All whose left hand does not know what their right hand is doing in serving the neighbor will surely hear the Ruler say: "Come, you that are blessed...." Amen.

---

1. Robert H. Smith, *Matthew: Augsburg Commentary on the New Testament* (Minneapolis: Augsburg Press, 1989), p. 296.

2. *Ibid.*, p. 299.

Chapter 37
Resurrection Of The Lord:
Vigil Of Easter; Easter Day

Matthew 28:1-10

Resurrection is the heart and climax of Matthew's story. There are three scenes in this climactic event. 28:1-10 constitutes the first scene: the reality of an empty tomb. Verses 11-15 make up the second scene. Jewish religious leaders will not give up their opposition to Jesus. They spread rumors that the disciples have stolen the body. The final scene, vv. 16-20, brings Jesus and his disciples together again on a mountain in Galilee. There he utters his commission to take his message to all nations. "I am with you always." This reminiscence of the Emmanuel theme (1:23) indicates to us that Jesus is truly Emmanuel, God with us, a presence to us even beyond his grave.

> *By his death and resurrection Jesus fulfills the promise of his name (1:21) and begins to bring life and freedom to God's beleaguered people. By resurrection he is manifested as Emmanuel (1:23), the presence of God shining in the midst of the new community. He is there in the midst, as Savior and as Teacher of God's people (23:10), with creative power and with his words, establishing the community in the way of righteousness. The death and resurrection of Jesus are not only the climax of Matthew's narrative. In Matthew's mind they are the turning point of world history and are revealed as such by the quaking of the earth (27:51; 28:2).[1]*

Mary Magdalene and the other Mary went to see the tomb. The presence of these women provides continuity with the crucifixion scene where there were many women looking on from afar (27:55-56). Matthew fills the opening page (genealogy: 1:1-16) and this closing page of his story with women! Matthew appears to have a

225

glimpse of a new kind of community in which male and female live in equality. (Cf. Galatians 3:28.) All are one in Jesus Christ.

And then an earthquake, an angel, and a rolled-back stone. Astonishing. The guards are filled with fear. Fear and admonitions to "fear not" dominate this story: vv. 4, 5, 8, 10. We have probably lost the sense of this emotion. Over time the story has become domesticated and tamed in our experience. In the midst of the fear stands the central proclamation of the story: "Do not be afraid; I know that you are looking for Jesus who was crucified. He is not here; for he has been raised...."

> *In raising Jesus from the dead, God certifies the truth of Jesus' words and the efficacy of his trust, which is to say that God vindicates Jesus: God resolves Jesus' conflict with Israel by showing that Jesus is in the right.*[2]

The message of the angel turns from resurrection proclamation to words of comfort to the disciples. The disciples have had a complex relationship with Jesus. Sometimes they seem to believe and understand. Other times they are clearly "little faith" disciples. During the last days of Jesus' journey the disciples' faithlessness is on full display. Jesus senses their faith condition. He tells them the time is coming very soon when they will all fall away from him (Matthew 26:31-32). Jesus quotes the prophet Zechariah: "I will strike the shepherd and the sheep of the flock will be scattered." Jesus does not leave the matter there. "Scattered" will not be the end of the disciples. He will gather them again in Galilee: "...after I am raised up, I will go ahead of you to Galilee" (26:32).

Jesus then asks his disciples to accompany him to the Mount of Olives and watch with him in prayer. Promptly, they *fall asleep.* Three times they fall asleep (Matthew 26:36-46). It is right after this sleeping-event that Judas appears on the scene. He *betrays* Jesus. One of the disciples draws a sword to protect Jesus from the mob with Judas. Jesus puts a stop to the violence. Scripture must be fulfilled! (26:47-54). This seems to be the end of the line for the disciples. They flee. They *desert* their Shepherd. They are like scattered sheep (26:56). That's the last word we hear about the disciples prior to the Easter story. But Peter has not deserted. He has followed at a distance as Jesus is brought to the high priest's house. Good for Peter. But when a maid recognizes Peter as one who had been with Jesus, Peter *denies* the whole thing (26:57-58, 69-75). Bad for Peter. Three times he denies. Three times before the cock crows, just as Jesus had said.

Truly the sheep have been scattered. They fall asleep, betray, desert, and deny. We don't hear any more about the disciples until the Easter account. How comforting, indeed, are the angel's words: "Tell the disciples that he will meet them in Galilee as he promised" (26:32). And the angel is not the only one who makes this speech. Jesus appears to the women. He authorizes them to give the same message to the disciples. "Do not be afraid," he says to the women; "go and tell my brothers to go to Galilee; there they will see me" (28:10). And so he did. The scattered sheep, the faithless disciples did meet Jesus on a mountaintop in Galilee (28:16).

Galilee becomes the name, the place metaphor, of the world in which Jesus fulfills the promise of Matthew 1:21, 23. Here he will save people from their sins. Here he will be Emmanuel/present for them. This is an incredibly good news story. We've just reviewed the story. At the end the disciples sleep, betray, desert, and deny. Sounds every bit like disciples today. And what shall happen to such disciples? The resurrected Jesus will meet them in Galilee. The resurrected Jesus will meet us in our Galilee—in the places where he has promised to meet us in Word and Sacrament. What a gospel story this is for sinners! We are saved. God is Emmanuel for us. We need not be afraid.

Homiletical Directions

The resurrection story is the climax to Matthew's Gospel. This event is the fulfillment of Jesus' entire ministry. Many Matthew stories could be told again on their way to fulfillment in the Risen One. It is clear, however, that it is the stories of Jesus' disciples that come most obviously to a climax in the story of Easter. We rehearsed above the "little faith" character of the disciples in the last days with Jesus. That is one narrative approach to this great tale. Our people know these stories of the disciples in a general way, but

227

they are not appointed for specific consideration in the Matthew year. Tell them now. That's the first thing one can do with this sermon. Paint a full picture of the disciples as disclosed in the Passion material. They sleep. They fall away. They desert and deny. They betray. Theirs is a road to death. Tell their stories. Make the point.

Secondly, in your own way connect the lives of today's disciples to the disciples of old. We, too, sleep, fall away, desert, deny, betray, and are destined for death. Their story is our story.

Thirdly, tell the Easter story with the focus on the word of comfort to disciples of every generation. This word is given twice (v. 7, 10). The fact that we hear this word repeated indicates that it is clearly a vital word in Matthew's telling of the story.

We alluded to Galilee as a metaphor for the places God has promised to be present for us. God has promised to be Emmanuel whenever we tell the story of Jesus. The story of Jesus is our Galilee. We tell Jesus' story and he is present for us through scripture, sermon, and sacrament. "You will meet me in Galilee," Jesus said. We take this to mean that Jesus is present whenever his story is told.

A closing proclamation might go something like this. Jesus is the speaker: "You have all fallen away. You are scattered in your sins. But fear not! I have come to save you from your sins. I have come to gather all who are scattered into my new community.

"You have deserted and denied me. Betrayal is the name of your sinful life. For this you deserve judgment. But fear not! I have come to reconcile you unto myself. Meet me on the mountain and we'll be friends again.

"As sinful humans your sin brings death upon you. But fear not! I have faced death and God has raised me to new life. I have overcome death. I have overcome your death. Put your trust in me and Easter shall be the foundational reality of your life eternal." Amen.

---

1. Robert H. Smith, *Matthew: Augsburg Commentary on the New Testament* (Minneapolis: Augsburg Press, 1989), p. 331.

2. Jack Dean Kingsbury, *Matthew As Story* (Philadelphia: Fortress Press, 1988), pp. 90-91.

Matthew 28:16-20

The closing verses of Matthew's Gospel include the Trinitarian formula in the call to go to all the nations. For this reason these verses are appointed for the Sunday of the Holy Trinity. (See the Preface for a brief comment on the place of the Holy Spirit in the Gospel of Matthew.) There is little in the text to help us grasp what "Trinity" might mean. We will have to import that from our theological traditions. It is often said that this Sunday is the only day in the church's year devoted to a doctrine. There is a call here to teach the meaning of this complex Christian doctrine. The text is filled with many other motifs fit for teaching as well.

The narrative itself is the third scene in Matthew's post-resurrection account. In scene 1 (vv. 1-10) the women discover an empty tomb and the disciples are told to go to Galilee to meet the crucified and risen Jesus. In scene 2 (vv. 11-15) we hear the last words about Israel's religious leaders in their dogged rejection of their Messiah.

> *Once again the enemies of Jesus hatch a plot (26:3) and pay out money to ensure cooperation (26:14-15). Once they sought out false testimony (26:59-60), and now they pay a sum of money (26:15) to suppress the truth and spread a lie.*[1]

The soldiers were *taught* by their leaders and they did what they were taught. The Greek verb translated by the RSV as "directed" is a form of the Greek word for teaching. It is the same root word as that used by Jesus when he commands his disciples to go, baptize, and *teach*. The disciples, like the soldiers, go and do as they were taught! Two kinds of teaching are present here. Matthew gives the reader a choice. Whose teaching shall we listen to?

Scene 3 of Matthew 28 is our appointed text. The eleven disciples meet Jesus on a mountain in Galilee. Our Chapter 37 discusses this incredible gathering of the disciples by their Risen Lord. The disciples have just fallen asleep on Jesus, they have betrayed him, deserted him, and denied him. (See Chapter 37 for scripture references.) They have all fallen away just as Jesus, their Shepherd, had foretold: Matthew 26:31. Jesus had also foretold that he would meet the disciples in Galilee after his death (Matthew 26:32). And so he does. Jesus gathers the scattered flock.

> ...the resurrected Jesus meets the disciples as the one who reconciles them to himself. True, some of the disciples worship him while others of them doubt (28:17). Nonetheless, doubt is "little faith," or weak faith, but is not "unfaith" (14:32), so that the assertion stands: the resurrected Jesus gathers the scattered disciples and reconciles them to himself.[2]

This is the Christian Church in nuce. Sinners gather around the graceful presence of Jesus/Emmanuel.

It is not surprising that Jesus meets the disciples again in Galilee. Galilee is where his ministry began: Matthew 4:12-16. His ministry took place primarily in Galilee. The report of his leaving Galilee comes in 19:1.

Nor is it surprising that Jesus meets them on a mountain in Galilee. Jesus' ministry began with his temptation on a mountain: 4:1-11, 8. On a mountain Jesus gave his great sermon: 5:1. Jesus often withdrew from his ministry in order to pray in the mountains: 14:23. Crowds came to Jesus for healing on a mountain: 15:29-31. It was on a mountain that he was transfigured: 17:1-9. In the end, therefore, it is fitting that it is on a mountain that Jesus teaches the disciples their task of obedience and discipleship. Mountaintops were also of importance in the Old Testament as places of the revelation of God. Mountains and revelation go together in biblical thinking. Now, on this mountain, Jesus will reveal to his disciples their mission.

When the disciples encountered Jesus they worshiped him. We were told in 28:9 that the first response of the women to the presence of the resurrected Jesus is also that of worship. When we encounter the Risen Jesus, worship is to be our basic human response. It's easy to lose sight of this. Perhaps we have spent so much time in the presence of the Risen One that we have lost sight of the awe that his presence among us should inspire.

They worshiped him *but some doubted.* Those words jump right off the page. We are prepared for the disciples to worship their Risen Lord. We are not prepared for them to doubt. Smith comments:

> *To the close of the age, the church is a mixed body consisting of good and evil (22:10), wheat and tares (13:24-30, 36-43), sheep and goats (25:32-33), and even "the good" are sometimes people of "little faith" (6:30; 8:26; 14:31; 16:8).*[3]

Matthew's picture of the Christian community is very realistic. We don't want it to be that way. Still, there is some perverse comfort to be taken from the fact that on the mountain in Galilee where the disciples first encountered Jesus as the Risen One—some doubted! It's always been this way. This side of the kingdom of heaven it probably always will be this way. It's healthy to accept this reality. We are challenged to realize, however, that mission starts at home!

> *Jesus issues orders, and they may be translated: "Be busy constantly making disciples of all nations." Discipleship is the heart of the matter. And the charge to* make disciples *is aimed at telling the church not only what to do about people outside but especially what to do with the people inside the new community. This is a command about the integrity of the church.*[4]

Jesus speaks to the disciples as the One to whom *all authority* has been given. In Matthew 21:23ff. Jesus is challenged about the nature of his authority. Matthew reports three vineyard stories told by Jesus in answer to the authority question. We discussed this matter thoroughly in our Chapters 28 and 29. If you did not deal with the earlier material in narrative form you could certainly consider telling the vineyard stories at this juncture in your preaching.

We might just note the recurring theme of *all* in these brief verses. It is *all* authority, *all* nations, *all* I have commanded you, and I will be with you *all*-ways.

> *All that teachers and scribes saw in Torah or Wisdom—existing before the foundation of the world, seated on the lap of the heavenly King, the principle by which the world hangs together and makes sense, guide and light for the life of God's people—Matthew sees in Jesus (5:21-48; 11:28-30; 16:12; 18:20; 23:1-36). And all that priests saw in the temple—the great ancient focal point and public symbol of God's presence and provision and of Israel's devotion and identity—Matthew likewise locates in Jesus (12:6; 21:12, 23-27).*[5]

The Authoritative One commissions the disciples in the name of the Triune God to make disciples of all nations. The disciples have gotten the point at last. Jesus is the crucified and risen savior.

> *...the disciples are not again commanded by Jesus, as previously, to silence concerning him (16:20; 17:9), but are instead commissioned to go and make all nations his disciples (28:19). In reconciling the disciples to himself and in giving them this commission, Jesus resolves the conflict he has had with them. With this conflict so resolved, the disciples move from Easter into the world Jesus predicted for them in his eschatological discourse (chaps. 24-25).*[6]

Baptism was the first public act of Jesus' ministry. He was baptized by John in the river Jordan: 3:11-17. So shall his disciples begin their ministry. They will go to all the nations—baptizing! They shall wash people in the cleansing waters of Christ's righteousness. Mission begins with proclamation and washing. Jesus shall be announced. People will be washed in his name, in the name of the Triune God. All people are to be washed. Gentiles are on the horizon here at the end of Matthew. That is no surprise. Gentiles in the persons of Rahab, Ruth, and Bathsheba were there at the beginning of the story: 1:1-16.

And teaching. Just what we might expect at the end of this Gospel. "Teaching all that I have commanded you." Jesus has taught a righteousness that exceeds that of the scribes and Pharisees: 5:20. His teaching has been summarized in the Sermon on the Mount and the two great commandments of the law. Jesus has fulfilled the law and the prophets. Matthew certainly sees his Gospel as the sum and substance of what is to be taught. Matthew has, as well, pointed towards Jesus as that which is to be taught. Matthew calls us to obedient discipleship and mission in the name and authority of the Risen One. In Jesus' name, in the name of the Triune God, a church is to be born. Matthew's Gospel reaches its fulfillment in the life of the church.

Finally, the Emmanuel theme is present in Matthew one last time. "I am with you always." We met Emmanuel first in 1:23. Emmanuel is the name of the God who is near us to save us from our sins. In 18:15-20 we heard that whenever two or three gather in Jesus' name, whenever the church assembles, "there am I in their midst." The reality of the church is Emmanuel. And, whenever the church carries out its basic mission of baptism, teaching and making disciples, "I am with you always." (We have discussed the Emmanuel theme for preaching in our Chapter 1.)

Homiletical Directions

This text for Trinity Sunday presents us with an embarrassment of riches for preaching. Local need will determine for you whether this week's sermon calls for preaching on the nature of the Trinity or baptism or mission or discipleship or Emmanuel. The list could go on. In our Chapter 37 we presented the possibility of an Easter sermon which would rehearse the story of the disciples which culminates most stunningly in their being gathered, graced, and commissioned by the Lord. If you did not follow this suggestion for Easter Sunday, such a sermon could certainly be preached on this week's text.

A second narrative possibility would be a sermon on the mixed nature of the church. We commented on this earlier when we talked about the doubting of disciples. Matthew tells several parables that underscore this reality. We could tell the story of the wheat and the tares as our first story: 13:24-30. Our second story could be that of the work of the evil one who plants his evil seed in the midst of the good seed. Story three could be the parable of the king who gave a marriage feast for his son: 22:1-10. The servants are to go out into the highways and hedges and bring in both bad and good. Finally, tell the story of this week's text with the focus on the "some" who doubted. Jesus is present for us, Emmanuel, just as we are. "I am with you always." This word of Jesus could be our word of proclamation particularly to those inside the church who have their doubts and other foibles. Emmanuel will not give up on any of us!

A sermon on mission to the whole world is, of course, an obvious possibility. Mission to all nations. All nations come into view. Gentiles come into view. Connect this last word of Matthew with his first word that includes those wonderful Gentile women. (Please refer to our Chapter 7 for suggestions for a sermon on mission to the Gentiles.)

---

1. Robert H. Smith, *Matthew: Augsburg Commentary on the New Testament* (Minneapolis: Augsburg Press, 1989), p. 334.

2. Jack Dean Kingsbury, *Matthew As Story* (Philadelphia: Fortress Press, 1988), p. 91.

3. Smith, *op. cit.*, p. 336.

4. *Ibid.*, p. 338.

5. *Ibid.*, p. 337.

6. Kingsbury, *op. cit.*, p. 92.